Feminist Visions

Feminist Visions

Toward a Transformation of the Liberal Arts Curriculum

edited by
Diane L. Fowlkes
and
Charlotte S. McClure

The University of Alabama Press

Permission to quote material or to use illustrations is gratefully acknowledged as follows:

Lines from the poem "Planetarium" from *Poems Selected and New, 1950–1974,*
by Adrienne Rich. Copyright © 1975 by W. W. Norton and Company, Inc. Reprinted by
permission of the publisher.

Photographs by Geoffrey Clements of oils on canvas, *Philip Golub Reclining* and *Paul Rosano
Reclining,* by Sylvia Sleigh. Photographs reprinted by permission of Sylvia Sleigh.

Excerpt from *The Dinner Party* by Judy Chicago. Copyright © 1979 by Judy Chicago. Reprinted
by permission of Doubleday & Company, Inc.

Passages from Mary Boykin Chesnut's original Civil War journals, 1861–1884, South Caroliniana
Library, Columbia. Reprinted by permission of the University of South Carolina.

Table "Sex Differences in Cognition" from *Sex-Related Differences in Cognitive Functioning:
Developmental Issues,* ed. M.A. Wittig and A. C. Petersen. Copyright © 1979 by Academic
Press.

Passages from "Sexual Matters: On Conceptualizing Sexuality in History" by Robert A. Padgug,
Radical History Review 20 (Spring–Summer 1979). Copyright © by Radical History Review.

Library of Congress Cataloging in Publication Data

Main entry under title:

Feminist visions

   Selected papers from a conference, "A fabric of our own making": Southern scholars on
women, held Mar. 4–7, 1981, at Georgia State University, Atlanta.
   Bibliography: p.
   Includes index.
   1. Feminism—Southern States—Congresses. I. Fowlkes,
Diane L., 1939–   II. McClure, Charlotte S., 1921–
HQ1438.A13F45 1984   305.4'2'0975   83-6539
ISBN 0-8173-0172-0

Contents

List of Figures

Preface

The contents of this book were selected from a conference, "A Fabric of Our Own Making": Southern Scholars on Women, held March 4–7, 1981, at Georgia State University, Atlanta, Georgia. The conference was part of a larger project entitled "A Model for Gender-Balancing the General Curriculum in Higher Education" and supported by a grant to Georgia State University from the Women's Educational Equity Act Program of the U.S. Department Of Education (USDHEW Grant No. G007901140).

The purpose of this book, as was that of the conference, is to contribute to the self-education of scholars/teachers in the disciplines who are striving to bring gender-based equity to the liberal arts curriculum in their colleges and universities. This collection of essays represents scholarship from women's studies as well as from disciplines in the liberal arts and is for use primarily by scholars/teachers in their own disciplines. Although some of the essays are applicable in beginning women's studies courses, the collection is designed primarily to provide substantive research for those scholars/teachers who are beginning or are continuing in their own disciplines to integrate the new scholarship on women into their courses and curricula.

This book can be read and used on two levels: (1) by the general reader reflecting on new ideas regarding women's lives and knowledge, and (2) by the scholar/teacher looking for new gender-related ideas for transforming courses and curricula. Some essays provide first levels of awareness, gatherings of information, and analysis. Examples of essays at this level include the review of scholarship on women's communication by Wood, McMahan, and Stacks; Locke's analysis of the origins of sexual-racial obstacles to South African women's development; and Muhlenfeld's revelation of the paradoxical Southern lady, Mary Boykin Chesnut, who was a feminist and abolitionist in a hostile aristocratic environment. Other essays provide more complex theoretical interpretations. Rosser's and Hogsett's interdisciplinary approach to Darwin's theory of sexual selection and the usefulness of the approach in understanding women's reality results in a new awareness of how social and cultural beliefs can prejudice a scientific investigation. In questioning the reasons for women's historical secondary role in polytheistic cultures in the early Western tradition, historian Ochshorn draws on opposing factors verifiable from other sources and formulates an alternative hypothesis that an androgynous world view coexisted with the traditionally recognized patriarchal world view. A reader or teacher new to feminist interpretations of knowledge might at first find the former kind of essay more useful when beginning to transform activities and the latter kind more useful as development proceeds.

Transforming the curriculum begins with understanding the cultural, social, economic, political, and psychological experiences of women and proceeds to asking questions, doing research, and changing courses and curricula. The experience with Catharine Stimpson's piece at the conference was that it promoted a collective understanding of a whole new realm of scholarship on women replete with references that suggest a breadth and depth of new knowledge, inviting incorporation into new perspectives. For the purpose of transforming the liberal arts curriculum through integrating new knowledge of women into ongoing courses, these essays do not lead immediately to comprehensive change in the curriculum, but they do describe some small but significant beginnings for scholars/teachers in the new approaches the writers take and in the new questions they are asking in their disciplines. These approaches and questions serve as models that can be used by scholars/teachers in other disciplines as they reassess their own topics.

The Southeastern Women's Studies Association held its annual meeting in conjunction and coordinated its program with the conference. We appreciate the Association's contribution to and support of our common efforts to further women's educational equity, especially in the South. We also wish to thank the Georgia State University Women's Studies Group, the University Women's Committee, the Student Government Association Women's Life and Development Committee, and the following faculty for their key contributions: Linda Bell, philosophy, Georgia State University; Pauline Clance, psychology, Georgia State University; Kathleen Crouch, vice president for academic services, Georgia State University; Etta Falconer, mathematics and natural sciences, Spelman College; Valerie Fennell, anthropology, Georgia State University; Kathie Gilbert, economics, Mississippi State University; Phyllis Johnson, nursing, Georgia State University; Shelby Lewis, political science, Atlanta University; Thomas McHaney, English, Georgia State University; Elizabeth Meese, women's studies, The University of Alabama; Linda Papageorge, history, Kennesaw College; Zenaide Reiss, art, Georgia State University; Juanita Sanford, women's studies, Henderson State University; Christine Sizemore, English, Spelman College; Janice Snook, women's studies, University of South Florida; Ina Jane Wundram, anthropology, Georgia State University.

Finally, we thank Mary Elizabeth Schwantz, Jacquelyn Ward, and Lucy Hayes for their essential clerical and organizational support. Karen Maschke was invaluable as a research assistant and public information specialist. David Karan distinguished himself as a research assistant and person who gave beyond the call of duty in bringing the project, conference, and book to successful completions. Malcolm MacDonald, of The University of Alabama Press, and manuscript editor Beverly Denbow gave us superb guidance and support throughout the editorial process. As coeditors, we take equal responsibility for any errors and omissions that remain in the work.

Diane L. Fowlkes   Charlotte S. McClure

Atlanta, Georgia
December 1, 1981

Part I
Introduction

Chapter 1

The Genesis of Feminist Visions

for Transforming

the Liberal Arts Curriculum

DIANE L. FOWLKES and CHARLOTTE S. McCLURE

First Person Plural: From the Case of Integrative Women's Studies at Georgia State University to a Southern Regional Model for "Gender Balancing" the Liberal Arts Curriculum

The spring of 1976 found a group of predominately white female faculty, staff, and students at Georgia State University meeting for the first time to discuss a common interest in research on women. As individuals in departments we experienced a lack of intellectual responsiveness to our scholarly pursuits. Meeting together for discussions, we found the intellectual ferment and stimulation we were seeking. We decided as an informal group to call ourselves the Georgia State University Women's Studies Group, thus acknowledging our membership in the academic arm of the resurgent women's movement.[1]

We began by assigning ourselves two tasks. One task force reviewed the literature on black studies, which was expected to provide insights on how a relatively analogous type of educational program was developing. The other task force conducted a survey of a random sample of undergraduate students to determine the amount of interest on campus in taking courses on women.

The task force findings helped us to plan our next strategic steps. The student survey, completed in January 1977, revealed substantial interest in courses about women among female and male students. The literature on black studies revealed that a possible danger for such programs would be cuts in budget and staff. Our experience in our particular institution, a relatively young urban university that began as an evening business college, suggested that the university administration would not support setting up special programs for minority groups, including women, as such. Thus, we decided that the best strategy to follow at Georgia State University was not to propose a women's studies program with its own budget and staff. Rather we decided to continue working informally, to use our powers as faculty members to enhance our own existing courses, to design new courses on women in our respective disciplines, and to introduce the courses to the curriculum through the normal procedures for curriculum change. From what Donna Jean Wood reports, our experience and strategy were not unique, just late, as was the southern region in general.[2] In effect, we decided to integrate women's studies into the curriculum proper.

In order to integrate the curriculum with knowledge of and about women, one must have more than a passing acquaintance with some of the new scholarship on women. One must know the theoretical issues in the new interdisciplinary field and the ways in which women's studies require changes in the theoretical approaches and the content of one's own traditional discipline. Aware that generally we were unprepared through our graduate training to develop courses on women, we knew that we needed self-education in the new field. Aware that we were predominately white and middle class, we knew that we needed to reach out to other scholars and to community people who could bring diverse perspectives to this work. Finally, aware through professional associational ties that our colleagues on other southern campuses, black and white, were experiencing similar needs, we reasoned that a conference could draw together the diversity of people and knowledge needed to accomplish the larger goal of curricular change throughout the region. Thus, we decided to mount a conference that would bring together community activists and scholars from many disciplines to present their research on women and gender-related issues.

Such a conference needed large-scale funding. Through information shared at a meeting of the newly formed Southeastern Women's Studies Association we learned that the Women's Educational Equity Act Program (of the then Office of Education of the U.S. Department of Health, Education, and Welfare) had funds that might be granted for such a project, should the project be eligible under the program guidelines. By proposing that our strategy at Georgia State University become a southern regional model for what we called "gender balancing" the curriculum, we eventually were granted funding for a thirty-month project that began in the fall of 1979.

The model involves several types of activity that together initiate and become part of an institutional change process. These types of activity have been carried out in a variety of institutional settings, as we now can see in the issue of the *Forum for Liberal Education* that is devoted to "The Study of Women in the Liberal Arts Curriculum."[3] Thus, Georgia State University's gender-balancing project is simply one of many that have been developing simultaneously as logical extensions of the women's studies movement.[4]

While the types of activity can be described generally, the forms the activities take on particular campuses are very much affected by three variables: (1) Who are the protagonists? (2) What are the institutional goals, structures, and resources? and (3) What is the climate for change?[5] The types of activity include:

1. formation of groups of interested faculty, administrators, and students — These groups develop ideas, assemble resources, and provide supportive networks.
2. assessment of interest and resources — Curricular change usually is justified in part on the basis of student interest and need, scholarship, and instructional resources; more often than not outside funding has provided necessary monetary support, and women's studies scholars from programs on or off campus have provided theoretical direction.
3. awareness of community and tradition — The communities and traditions within which most educational institutions exist contain sources and resources that can be tapped for support.
4. assessment of institutional power structure — Change agents must understand their own power, leadership styles within the institution, and sources of support and opposition for new directions in curriculum.
5. choice of strategies — Curriculum may involve comprehensive program development or incremental course-by-course development.
6. provision for faculty development — Curriculum development usually is preceded or accompanied by some form of faculty development; that is, faculty must come into contact with and assimilate the new scholarship through hearing and talking with leading scholars in the field and through bibliographic work.

This book grows out of the Georgia State University project[6] and out of what we have learned as a result of subsequent relationships with similar projects. Our purpose is to contribute to the self-education of others in the disciplines who are striving to bring gender-based equity to the liberal arts curriculum in their respective colleges and universities. In the remainder of this chapter we present the rationale for gender balancing the liberal arts curriculum and discuss the longer-range goal of a feminist transformation of that curriculum. As a benchmark for comparison with other regions, we emphasize the knowledge of and about women developed under the influence of southern regional forces.

From Gender Balancing to Feminist Transformations of the Liberal Arts Curriculum

The experiences of women's studies scholars/teachers in transforming human knowledge provide insight into the process that scholars/teachers concerned with women's educational equity undergo in their faculty and curriculum development. The process involves three stages: critique of the present body of knowledge, enrichment of the present body of knowledge with the new scholarship on women, and transformation of the theoretical underpinnings of the present body of knowledge. The process is not necessarily linear, but these three dimensions of scholarly and teaching activity are involved in transforming the curriculum.

Why transform the liberal arts curriculum? The argument begins with a general critique. Students in higher education, female and male, of different racial, ethnic, economic, and age groups, are exposed to the liberal arts curriculum in varying extents in their different degree programs. Ideally the liberal arts curriculum should speak to the needs of individuals to learn, regardless of their sex classifications that are complicated by race, status, and age distinctions. But in actuality the liberal arts curriculum is discriminatory in that, for the most part, it presents, as general or universal knowledge, knowledge developed mainly from the perspective of white masculine middle-class experience and values. A philosophical assumption underlies this proposition. White masculine culture is not coterminus with the white male population. Some white males are not so acculturated, and men other than white men as well as women of diverse racial and class origins may accept or aspire to white middle-class masculine culture as their own. The realities of the lives of individuals and groups who do not or cannot partake of the white masculine middle-class experience and values are not reflected, interpreted, or explained by supposed universals. The extent to which the liberal arts curriculum distorts our knowledge of human diversity and potential is detailed in the critiques of various bodies of knowledge included or cited in review essays published in almost every issue of *Signs: Journal of Women in Culture and Society* since its inception in 1975 at the University of Chicago Press.

The argument continues with a rationale for enriching, or what the Georgia State University model called "gender balancing," the curriculum. The new scholarship on women provides a wealth of knowledge about the realities of women's lives that have gone undiscovered or unrecognized through the centuries. Students are receiving a distorted or incomplete education to the extent that this new knowledge of and about women is not brought into the curriculum as a balance to what has come to be recognized as white masculine knowledge. If they are exposed to a gender-balanced or integrated curriculum, female and male students of various races, statuses, and ages will have better opportunities to recognize the diversity of values that women as well as men bring to society. As a result students should be better prepared to transcend traditional gender roles and race roles and behave as individuals in community.

The process of gender balancing the curriculum takes two forms. On the one hand, new disciplinary or interdisciplinary courses on women are developed, introduced, and accepted into the curriculum. These types of courses may or may not be organized into women's studies programs. On the other hand, courses already in the curriculum are enriched by the addition of materials on women. Some of this material may still provide distorted perspectives on women; some of it will come from the new scholarship on women. In either case this process has been occurring on increasing numbers of campuses as either direct or indirect consequence of the women's studies movement. The process has been called mainstreaming, integrating, or gender balancing.[7]

The argument ends with the rationale for a feminist transformation of the curriculum.[8] Once the critiques of the disciplines have revealed omissions and distortions of the realities of women's lives, once the infusions of new knowledge have filled the gaps to some extent, the true scholar/teacher — curious, skeptical — recognizes the need to go further. It is not enough to "balance" sexist and racist content and perspectives with nonsexist and nonracist content and perspectives. Reconstructions of the theories that direct knowledge development and knowledge transmission plus new methodologies for research and pedagogy are necessary to pursue answers to the questions that the new scholarship on women raises.[9]

Feminists are among those who are conscious of asymmetrical power relationships in society and the uses of knowledge for reinforcing asymmetry or informing change toward symmetry. Inside the academy feminists operate on the assumption that knowledge developed from the perspectives of powerlessness in asymmetrical terms can be turned into power in symmetrical terms. Such knowledge can contribute to students' transcendence of those asymmetrical structures in their own lives and in the life of the community. Feminist transformations of the curriculum then are part of a larger continuing human endeavor to transform society.

The New Scholarship on Women in the South: "A Fabric of Our Own Making"

Human beings imagine their world; they produce images and figments of all sorts that serve as symbols for ideas about themselves and their world. In this process of imagining, as philosopher Suzanne K. Langer reminds us, we live in a "web of ideas, a fabric of our own making."[10] Human beings "grow" knowledge by exploration, adding new facts, correcting old beliefs, yet in our culture consistently assuming that the masculine is the measure of all things. Traditionally they transmit their expanding knowledge to present and future generations in the curriculum of schools and colleges. Although in Langer's process the nervous system is the "growing center" of each human being, women appear to have not participated as actively in nor added to the "fabric" and expansion of knowledge as have men. As already discussed, the curriculum in public schools and in higher education continues to reflect primarily the nature of the world as men have imagined it.

Academic women, including increasing numbers in the South, have begun to address the question of women's place in the curriculum, a "fabric" that certainly and ultimately would affect the "growing centers" of girls and boys, women and men. Since the 1960s, a resurgence of concern about the role and status of women has occurred. Scholars have been asking how much is really known about the nature and experience of women, about the structure of the family, about the development of "femininity" and of "masculinity," about the effect of male-oriented curriculum on the development of individuals and their civilization, and about the effects of diverse cultural aspects associated with race, ethnicity, and socioeconomic status on all these questions.

Each region of the United States has a unique history associated with a particular economic base and population mix. The South began as predominately crop-based agricultural and has bypassed in large part (except in some of the coastal areas) the mercantile and the heavy industrial development of the North and Northeast. Though some areas east of the Mississippi River have a history associated with the extractive economic functions — forestry and mining and oil — the predominant economic bases in the West have been just these extractive functions in addition to herd-based ranching. Populations and cultures have varied by region, from differences in Native American Indian tribes to differences in immigrant groups, whether forced or voluntary, and whether north or south European, African, Asian, or South and Central American. Intergroup conflicts interacting with socioeconomic development have affected the status of women of diverse backgrounds in different ways according to region. Thus, the consciousness and perspectives associated with living and working in the South that southern scholars bring to their enterprise, whether these scholars grew up in the region or moved into and/or out of the region, doubtless have their counterparts for scholars living and working in other regions of the country. The following analysis should provoke scholars of other regions to ask the same kinds of questions of their own region's effect on their studies and teachings concerning women.

The South, once the bastion of a black slave – based plantation and farm economy, now an area experiencing the expansive stages of social, economic, and political development, is the most rapidly urbanizing region of the United States.[11] The breakthrough of the black protest movement, whose roots are in the South, is being followed by breakthroughs for the women's movement. Though a disproportionate number of the states still failing to ratify the Equal Rights Amendment are in the South, southern society has not been left untouched by the women's movement. The women's movement directly and indirectly has encouraged many women to be part of the group pushing to take advantage of new opportunities occurring as a result of regional development. The South, then, is the region where the interaction between the women's movement and other relatively rapid socioeconomic and political change can be observed and felt quite readily.

Many scholars living and working in the South and attuned to the interaction between the women's movement and changes in racial and socioeconomic status have observed an impact on themselves as well as their students and the wider community. The scholars who participated in the conference, "A Fabric of Our Own Making": Southern Scholars on Women,[12] were asked to comment on the validity of this proposition for their own work. Most of those who responded agreed with the premise that the South, like other regions, has some unique characteristics; some went on to confirm that the region affected their approaches to the development of knowledge about women.

A common theme in the responses was that growing up in the South, moving out and then moving back, or growing up outside the South and then moving to the South, heightened one's awareness of regional differences and southern characteristics. One white woman scholar responded:

> I agree that our surroundings shape perceptions of reality. More importantly, they affect or should affect how we approach solutions to problems perceived within the reality. A year outside the South [in a southwestern state] forced me to realize and reevalutate how we approach women's issues and problems in the South. . . . I perceive southern women as much more submissive and accepting of the status quo. The "protection" of southern women by society and their mates/children prevents a realistic look at many of the issues women need to address.

A black woman scholar noted, on the other hand:

> Living and working in the South has shaped my perception of the realities of women's lives. The traditional southern concept of upper class white women as creatures to be put on pedestals and forgotten is in dire contrast to the concept of Black women as toilers and open prey. It is true that these concepts are changing. But in the South, as elsewhere, traditions die hard and often leave lingering pain. I have felt that pain.

From a midwestern feminist scholar came this response:

> Living in the South, for me, has made me have to confront the reality of inequality . . . and to recognize that a sense of independence and self-esteem are not necessarily widely shared by women and often are nurtured at a great cost and pain to the individual.

Some of the effect of living and working in the South derives from the ways in which scholars must try to relate to their students. For example, one scholar says that her insights combining Marxist theory and biblical examples derive primarily from having tried to make sense of the relationships between sexism, racism, and classes while living in the South and from having to make sense to students whose intellectual categories come from fundamentalist churches and who would not accept a number of popular assumptions I brought from my liberal Eastern education.

The scholar quoted above on the effects of coming from the Southwest also has been affected by her relationships with southern students:

The students' lack of experience and knowledge about feminism and "liberation" forces me to stress this aspect of my life . . . [family and profession] for the student — it may be their only exposure to such a view! This is a tragedy in itself. Stressing the family framework for this is due to the major importance family plays in the southern culture (at least in their heads), as does "religious" belief and practice.

Finally, the effects of the region on the content or approach to one's research can be seen in the responses of two other women scholars. The first scholar states:

Since moving to the South, I have become more aware of Black-white relations and how they affect health care delivery. For this reason, I focused on Blacks as well as Hispanics in my examination of maternal and child health issues. . . . This proved to be an enlightening experience: for the first time I recognized the racism inherent in many scientists' interpretations of interethnic variation in health status indicators. And I have begun to move within my own agency to make other health professionals aware of the dangers of accepting these views.

The second scholar observes:

Living in the South has affected my visions of women's lives. I think this has both positive and negative connotations: positive in the sense that women's lives seem to be more clearly rooted in tradition in the South, and negative in the sense that much of that tradition has been exploitative, sometimes in very subtle ways. What makes the issues so subtle, if not insidious, is that class and gender are so clearly defined, and seem to be so rarely challenged, that it is hard to sense how rigidly these categories determine our awareness, and experience, of Southern culture. There seems to be a greater danger here of reactive analysis, both feminist and anti-feminist, because issues pertaining to gender and class are so narrowly defined. This becomes evident in those gatherings which are multi-racial, working and middle-class, male and female. It is very difficult to hold discussions that address problems or issues felt by all the participants. . . . Which women's lives are we really talking about?

Both of these last two women's responses draw together threads of thought and action that form the fabric, the dialectic of knowledge inherent in transforming the curriculum: the development of new knowledge — research — within an acknowledged sociopolitical context and the transmission of that knowledge as a corrective to both theory and practice that are either overtly racist and sexist or insensitive to the differences in condition of women and men because of differential treatments on the basis of race and sex.

From Feminist Visions to Feminist Transformation: Turning Theory into Practice

The stage has been set for using the sources in this book as aids to transforming the liberal arts curriculum. In Part II, a keynote address from the 1981 conference, "A Fabric of Our Own Making": Southern Scholars on Women, provides an overview of the theoretical aspects of bringing about feminist transformations of the curriculum.

Part III contains selected conference papers introduced by an analytical essay that points out some common themes among the various authors. These papers represent some of the new knowledge of and about women developed by scholars living and working in the South. These scholars are based in many different disciplines of the liberal arts or in a profession. They bring to their particular research the perspectives of women and/or men, blacks and/or whites, middle and/or working classes.

Taken together the essays provide an interdisciplinary approach to feminist theory, which in turn, as a growing body of new knowledge, raises new questions whose consideration can lead to transformations in each of the disciplines. As a first step, each essay can be integrated as material into a course or courses within a particular subfield of the author's discipline. But each essay also suggests implications or new paradigms for reassessing given knowledge or generating new knowledge of women in any of the disciplines. For example, Ochshorn's historical analysis raises questions about how some pieces of Western literature are interpreted; Harper's political analysis provides another context for the study of human sexuality. The book is designed to spark and feed the imagination of scholars/teachers along many pathways. A short bibliography of selected sources on feminist curriculum change is provided at the end of the book.

Part II
Theoretical Perspectives

Chapter 2

Women as Knowers

CATHARINE R. STIMPSON

I write out of contradictory feelings. I am apologetic, for I will not be explosively original, but yet I am overweening, for I will try to amass some general statements about a massive enterprise: the new scholarship about women.[1] The new scholarship assumes both that women can be knowers and that women have yet to be fully known. We have bibliographies and review essays about the research on a single subject, or in a single discipline. For example, in 1979, Natalie J. Sokoloff published a bibliography. Although it covered only the research in the sociology of women and work in the 1970s, and although it was representative rather than inclusive, it had seventy-four double-columned pages of entries. It also had a solid feminist perspective, that is, it wanted to show how sociology might help to explain "women's disadvantaged position in the contemporary labor market."[2] Such work reminds us of how much the new scholarship about women has achieved. Nevertheless, we perhaps need a sense of the questions that unite us, of the matrix of ideas that organizes us.

Obviously, such questions, such a matrix, must exist within a context, or, more accurately, within a multiplicity of contexts. First, the new scholarship about women has a historical context. The pressures of the modern period are altering what it means to have been born a man and what it means to have been born a woman. Among those pressures are the entrance of women of all classes and races into the public labor force, the democratization of American education, a partial decline in religious definitions of masculinity and femininity and a rise in supplementary ideologies that support equality and self-realization, greater access to divorce and to reproductive control, and a lessening of the prejudice against women in positions of public power. Such changes call out for understanding, for study, for clarification. Simultaneously, women want to be formal knowers — of their own experience and the world at large. Increasingly they seek the opportunity to do so: in 1965 women earned only 10.5 percent of all the doctorates in the United States; in 1979 they took 28.6 percent of them.

Next, the new scholarship about women has a political context. The very historical pressures that I have outlined have helped to create the women's movement, a force that articulates and supports beneficial change in women's lives. Feminism and the new scholarship about women are obviously related. It is no accident that in 1966 the National Organization for Women was founded in the United States, and Juliet Mitchell published her influential essay, "Women: the Longest Revolution," in England. Nevertheless, the relationship is complex and often vastly oversimplified by those who would reduce women as knowers to women as crude propagandists.

For some, scholarship, inseparable from action, clarifies a political task. Theory and practice are profoundly conjoined. For example, Joan Kelly, the distinguished historian, in making a superb public/private sphere analysis, writes: "ours may be a historical moment . . . not only to 'see' how the patriarchal system works, but also to act with that vision — so as to put an end to it."[3] For others, the women's movement is a source of the questions they ask, a generator of the problems they wish to ameliorate. Nancy Chodorow, the sociologist, says of her recent book: "This project owes its existence to the feminist movement and feminist community and its origins to a group of us who, several years ago, wondered what it meant that women parented women. Many of my ideas were first developed with the members of the mother-daughter group."[4] As people select the problem that will be theirs, they often try to choose one that matters to large numbers of women. If their work is successful, those large numbers will benefit. An economist, then, may try to explain the mechanisms of occupational segregation in order to find some structural relief for the women whom inequitable salaries so badly hurt. A biochemist may examine reproduction in order to suggest new forms of birth control. Still others deny any direct connection between the women's movement and the study of women. Primarily in the more quantitative social sciences, they still subscribe to the theory that being a researcher means being immaculately free from the taint of morality or ideology.

Despite accusations to the contrary, most people doing the new scholarship about women do pay attention to the unexpected finding, to the rules of logic and evidence, to primary and secondary sources. The fear that women's studies is a Trojan mare, shod in footnotes, sneaking bias in its belly into the vulnerable City of Thought, is dangerously unrealistic. Rather, much research about women belongs to a pragmatic tradition that Emerson lyricized in "The American Scholar" in the nineteenth century and that agronomists who developed more fertile strains of rice and nurtured the Green Revolution personified in the twentieth.

Finally, the new scholarship about women has an intellectual context, for it represents certain features of contemporary consciousness. Restless rather than contemplative, relativistic rather than absolute, it is skeptical of tradition rather than submissive to it. One of its poets might well be Wallace Stevens, who in "Poems of our Climate" tells of the "never-resting mind." Among its sociologists of knowledge are Thomas S. Kuhn, the author of *The Structure of Scientific*

Revolutions, and Peter Berger and Thomas Luckman, the authors of *The Social Construction of Reality*, who write of the mind's ability to define and redefine our sense of what is true. Among its compatible schools of thought are black studies, Marxist studies, family history, French deconstructive criticism, such interdisciplinary enterprises as American studies, and the new social history that investigates the lives of the powerless, the ordinary, and the ignored.

So placing the new scholarship about women, I have written of it as if it were unified, monolithic, even serene. In part, this description is accurate. In every discipline, since the 1960s, people who have sought to know women have had three consistent ambitions. First, they have wanted to deconstruct error and banish the demons of falsehood. Among the most famous acts of repudiations has been that of a vulgar, derivative Freudianism that has, in its devotion to the phallus, made the female a maimed male. Next, they have wanted to add knowledge about women to our self-conscious mental life and to our curricula. For example, they have asked to have suffrage campaigns integrated into courses about civil rights. So doing, they have said that the refusal to include women both repeats and initiates vast misunderstandings. Gradually some people not identified with the new scholarship about women have recognized that bad things can happen if it is ignored.[5] Third, people doing the new scholarship about women wish to build theories. They legitimately suggest that as we generate large ideas about women we can illuminate immense fields of general experience as well. We can show how we have, over time and in many cultures, responded to the fact that our species consists of females and males by organizing sex/gender systems. One of the most provocative theories is that of the reperiodization of history. Several thoughtful historians believe that the way in which we have labeled history—to call a certain period the Renaissance, for example—distorts the female experience. During the Renaissance the lives of women may have been constricted rather than enhanced, hurt rather than reborn. If so, we must rename historical periods so that our language and our past will be congruent. Simultaneously, we will embody our theory that historical processes move differently for men and for women.[6]

Accompanying such ambitions—the deconstruction of error, the reconstruction of fact, the construction of theory—is a persistent, sad assumption: that many men cannot be objective about women, that their picture combines projection, distortion, and the discharge of desire. To be sure, some men can think about women accurately, including some who practice the new scholarship about women with welcome humility and zeal. However, too many men are like a nineteenth-century Englishman, Arthur J. Munby. Like other nineteenth-century Englishmen, Munby was infatuated with an invention of his time, the camera. He took a series of photographs of Hannah Cullwick, the servant woman who was first his mistress, then his wife. He shot her as a servant, with her great, raw, toil-burdened hands; as a slave, in grotesque blackface; as a lady; as an angel; and finally as a man.[7] Munby did to Hannah what many men, personally and impersonally, have done to women: to costume them according to their fancy. Of the academic disciplines, anthropology was among the first to understand that women might know more about women than men. Not only might women better avoid gender-bound error, but they would have psychological and physical access to women's hidden worlds, to experiences behind veils and walls.

Despite such shared ambitions and assumptions, the new scholarship about women is not wholly unified, monolithic, and serene. People pursuing it disagree about ideas, methods, and the governing structures of women's studies programs in various institutions. Major concepts have shifted. One idea has not tap-danced off the stage of discourse to have another sashay on. However, the new scholarship has gone through a process in which it has developed four major, interdisciplinary arguments that have had cogency, appeal, and power. Each represents an important path toward knowledge about women.

At first, in the late 1960s, an enormous amount of attention was paid to women's sufferings, to sexual discrimination, to female invisibility. Literally and symbolically the most compelling text was Simone de Beauvoir's *The Second Sex*, published in France in 1949. Scholars, particularly anthropologists, vigorously quarreled over whether or not men were universally dominant, women universally subordinate. However, no one fought over the existence of subordination—only over its universality. Every discipline produced crucial documentary evidence of the presence of sexism.

Quickly, scholars developed a second, more complex set of ideas. They postulated the existence, with local variations, of two related, interdependent, intersecting worlds. Although members of one world could cross into the other, under certain circumstances, scholars could map distinctive contours for both worlds. The first world was that of the male. It contained production, public activity, formal culture and speech. It was the domain of power and of the father. Because it had decided what history was, it had forged our collective memory — with all its repressions, omissions, and stutters. Perhaps inevitably, ambitious American scholars found fascinating the performance, the competence, and the success of the women who, like themselves, had crossed into the world of men to work.

The second world was female. It contained reproduction, private and domestic activity, informal culture and speech. It was the domain of love and of the mother. However, not all women in the West were good mothers, who modeled themselves on Mary. Some were bad mothers, even whores, who perpetuated the legacy of Eve. Because this female world had lacked control over the codification of collective memory that we call history, it had no known history except in family gossip and old wives' tales.

A great deal of energy in the past decade has gone into the mapping of female worlds. At first, this effort provoked anxiety about discovering and being associated with lesbianism. Though still present, such fears have diminished. Indeed, some less homophobic theoreticians and historians are excavating causal links between a homosexual life and much modern female creativity, power, and self-esteem. For many women, being with women released energy and potential.

In the study of the female world, feminist theoreticians, especially in Europe, began the great debate about housework — its functions, value, and changes. Literary critics and art historians asked if there were such a thing as a female aesthetic, imagery, and art, and if there were, what caused it. Psychologists and sociologists studied mother-daughter bonds. As they did so, they often worried about the distorting effects of Nancy Friday's popularizing explorations of the same subject. Reconstructing prehistory, anthropologists began to speculate about the importance of groups that a female anchored. Woman the Mother and Woman the Gatherer took on the interest that Man the Hunter had previously arrogantly claimed. Economists graphed the rise of the female-headed family, the most rapidly increasing unit in the United States in the 1970s. Historians examined Victorian female friendships and such women's institutions as the women's colleges and the convent. They began to speculate about the relationship between women's institutions and women's strength. In all disciplines, scholars began to look at the women's movement itself.

Like the new social history, the study of the female world demands the redemption of the everyday: the letter, the quilt, the stove, the common gesture, the daily toil, the cooking and the washing and the cleaning of it all. Ordinary as well as extraordinary lives compel scrupulous attention — a French laceworker as well as a George Sand. To understand them both, interpretations of their subjective experiences matter.[8]

Because understanding can command respect, the redemption of the everyday can become the basis of a more democratic theory of heroism. That theory construes as heroes those who endure as well as dominate, those who weave as well as rip the fabric of our lives, those who are female as well as male.

Accompanying such research has been a set of attitudes about women. First, scholars have tried to extend affection and esteem toward their subjects.[9] Next, scholars have assumed that their subjects are vulnerable, that their testimony is to be treated gently. Obviously, not all women deserve affection, esteem, and the assumption of vulnerability. The new scholarship about women cannot treat elite women who abuse their power or slave-holders or aggressively fascist women in this way. Indeed, some of the most tormented researchers in the new scholarship about women are studying fascism, for they must see an active coconspiracy between women who might literally be their mothers or their grandmothers, and evil.

Finally, whether or not the scholar can approve of her subject, she tends to believe in her own capacity for sincerity. A woman is less the chatty fiber of legend than a reasonably reliable personal witness. This assumption has influenced—among other things—our response to rape. We no longer so quickly think of the rape victim as a liar, or as a fantasist, or as a devious manipulator, but as a victim telling of traumatic suffering. When a Virginia Woolf talks about her half-brothers' assaults upon her, she is neither slandering them nor writing a destructive fiction but reporting her pain, anguish, and shame.

The study of female worlds, and of their intricate connections with male worlds, has necessarily been political. "Political" has had two meanings. The first is the insistence that politics take account of the private sphere, of the household, of sexuality. In brief, politics must become a more capacious term. The second meaning is that the relationship between the female and the male worlds is itself political, that it involves questions of power and governance. This relationship, in turn, entails exploring three fertile, festering, still unresolved questions.

That such questions remain unanswered is a tribute to their difficulty and importance, not a tocsin to be sounded about the weakness of the new scholarship about women. After all, a mark of any intellectual inquiry is the seriousness of the questions that it keeps.

First, if the female and male worlds are unequal, how are they unequal? In what ways? How do we measure patriarchy — in the family, in the state, and in a set of impersonal institutions? Next, what are the origins of inequality? If male dominance is not universal, where does it begin? In the formation of private property? Of the state? Of modern industrial societies? Finally, how do discriminatory systems maintain and reproduce themselves? Through what mechanisms, through what relations between female and male spheres, do they keep themselves going? What is our psychosexual and cultural and socioeconomic DNA?

Interestingly, during these political queries, the pervasive picture of women that had been held by the new scholarship about women began to change. Accurate images of woman as victim remained. People published crucial studies of rape, of wife abuse, of sexual harassment, of economic hardship. Yet, a supplementary image also emerged. In it, women were tough and active as well as weak and passive. If they had been subordinate, they also had developed patterns of resistance, protest, and shrewd adaptation. Women were no longer the epistemological blanks, the existential weaklings, the servants of socialization that they had been in *The Second Sex*. As a result, Gertrude Stein became less the fat tyrant of a famous salon than a brilliant modernist who presided over a charmed circle. The authors of nineteenth-century sentimental novels were less advocates of mealymouthed submission than senders of coded messages of rage. If librarians were exploited in genteel fashion, they were also proud professionals. In the hands of such scholars as the sociologist Bonnie Thornton Dill, black women, despite their multiple oppressions, became models of strength.

In the midst of such developments, people began to articulate the third of the four major arguments that I have mentioned. As scholars unearthed more and more squirming facts, as they grew in number, as they fell under the spell of dialectical reasoning, they began to scrutinize the universal validity of knowing women through analyzing them as citizens of a world consisting of female and male subworlds. Some suggested that such a paradigm inadvertently perpetuated older patterns of dualistic thought that divided reality into a series of polarities.[10] Others legitimately argued that the paradigm failed to account for the specifics of their lives. In the United States, blacks, lesbians, and students of working-class women found the model incomplete. Outside the United States people called for a far greater recognition of the role of national characteristics. To understand an Israeli woman, one would have to understand the power of the religious courts; to understand an Australian woman, the presence of an overwhelming, empty landscape; to understand a Latin American woman, the terrible power of United States economic practices.[11]

In brief, the new scholarship about women learned the importance of *differences* among women. Rhetorically, this lesson meant the abandonment of easy cries of sisterhood. Formally, it meant the acceptance of the need for multiple empirical studies of specific situations. Yet, even as people recognized how valid the third stage of inquiry was, a fourth phase appeared. Joining the awareness of differences among women was a renewed interest in the debate about differences between men and women.

During the 1960s and 1970s the new scholarship about women hardly had ignored sexual differences. However, across all the disciplines, most people had adopted a particular, minimalist theory. They had acknowledged, as only a fool or a fabulist would not, that men and women are not biologically identical. Obviously, women bear children, men do not. However, they went on, social and cultural and economic conditions have created what other differences there are. Such forces decree, for example, that women will rear as well as bear children. Scholars offered a number of phrases to summarize this conviction: relations between the sexes are largely social relations; nurture means more than nature; gender controls sex, not sex gender. Inseparable from such an idea was the belief that history is a mutable record of conditions that we can change. If we wish, we could alter the role of woman as mother. So a Nancy Chodorow could reassure her readers that we can reconstitute parenting as one step toward establishing a sexually egalitarian world.

Then, particularly in the late 1970s, some scholars revived the argument that profound, permanent, sexual differences exist. Combined with their maximalist theory was a commitment to several feminist principles. They spoke out against history's maltreatment of women. However, they argued, we must destabilize that bad response to difference rather than refuse to recognize it. We must release rather than repress the female; honor rather than sentimentalize and dishonor the maternal; applaud women's rich, special sexuality rather than mourn the lack of phallus. Inseparable from these ideas was the belief that history has some continuities that we ought not thoughtlessly to touch.

Such advocates belong to several groups that are otherwise theoretically and stylistically incompatible. One group includes American social scientists. Of special importance is the illustrious sociologist, Alice S. Rossi. In a long, speculative essay in 1977 she suggested that we regard relations between the sexes from a "biosocial perspective." If we do so, we will see that physiological factors in the bonding of mother and child have facilitated the survival of our species. If we want, then, to rearrange parenting, we will have to give men "compensatory education." Though Rossi is no reductionist, she is attempting to restore the body as a lawgiver for our sex/gender systems.[12] A second group includes American cultural feminists. Often hostile to the academy, this group consistently has celebrated a vision of a separate, happy world in which women hold in common their biology, sensibility, and virtue. A third group, increasingly influential, consists of such French theoreticians as Julia Kristeva, Helene Cixous, and Luce Irigaray. Divided among themselves, often sharing very little but brilliance, they nevertheless seek to reground our sense of the distinctiveness of female and male.[13]

The argument about sexual differentiation — its past, present, and future — is analogous to the quarrel about sociobiology as a discipline and to contemporary efforts to show that we, as human beings, are subject to the overwhelming imperatives of nature's laws.[14] Unhappily, the argument also has arisen as the political battles about women's status have become increasingly ugly. In the United States three issues provoke the most open bitterness: the Equal Rights Amendment, which some claim will kill "the family" and breed in its place a unisex civilization, the minimalist dream turned nightmare; legal abortion, which gives women a degree of reproductive freedom and choice; and finally, gay liberation, in which people seek to divorce their sexuality from reproduction and from heterosexual rules and stigmatizing. Together, these issues ask whether or not we support traditional patterns of child rearing, work, sex, and gender. Within the new scholarship about women, then, is an argument about sexual differentiation that seeks to ally difference and equality, while outside the new scholarship are arguments and struggles that seek to ally differentiation and, at best, an indifference to equality.

Given such a public response to women in general, it is hardly surprising that many people resist the vitality, the exuberant volatility, of the new scholarship about women in particular. Recently, a pervasive voice of opposition has adopted a new, sad, mournful tone. People who do women's studies, the lament goes, are to be pitied as well as judged. Because they know they are in academic life *only* because of affirmative action, they understand that their place is unmerited and unearned. That situation does them "spiritually speaking, no good."[15] As condescending as it is wrong, such criticism fails to note some of the real reasons for contrariness. One is the fact that the new scholarship about women has had its polemical or cozily lyrical moments. If one wishes selective evidence with which to condemn it, one can rummage about and pick up some. Another, and more important reason, is the extent of the challenge to what we think we know about women and to our claims that we think fairly, efficiently, cleanly, and logically. Still another reason is the fact that the new scholarship about women asks us to consider difficult, even intractable material — brutality, domination, the terrors of childbirth — that surely must call up some unconscious resistance.

A final reason is that the new scholarship entails institutional as well as intellectual claims. It asks that women, audacious though it seems, be incorporated equitably into the academy. It seeks the presence of women as knowers. Moreover, it asks for an academic style in which people are cooperative, helpful, supportive colleagues; in which we strip our speech of any jargon that entwines members of a discipline together in a mysterious cult that mystifies others; and in which we travel with some grace among the disciplines. We now fumble badly as we approach each other's field. In part this situation reflects United States graduate training and in part it reflects the reward system of American higher education in which tough-minded specialists get more praise than curiosity-ridden generalists. Nevertheless, the desire remains that a linguist listening to a historian talk about periodization will remember that a period is more than a grammatical mark; that a social psychologist listening to an economist talk about "crowding" (Barbara Bergman's explanation for occupational segregation), will know that it means more than jostled space.

I suspect that the ideas of the new scholarship about women — though perhaps in a diffuse, defanged, even corrupt form — will be more acceptable than women themselves, particularly those women who study women. The commitment that most scholars have to their professional identity will force them eventually to read about women. The "harder" the discipline, the more difficulty its members probably will have in admitting that they have erred, that they have omitted a critical variable, that their tests of verification have failed. In contrast, to hire a woman means to dissolve lingering skepticism about women as colleagues, to ward off a churlish resentment of affirmative action, and to resist the temptation to play it safe in a harsh job market that one can use to justify unfortunate employment decisions.

I fear, too, that people will integrate content about women more quickly than more benign scholarly methods. Obviously, felicity is not wholly absent from the academy. Yet, prevailing notions of academic success stress efficiency, impersonality, productivity — at their worst the features of a deliberately bland rat race. In theory, the demands of success sort out the less able, but in practice they punish those who would have a modicum of a decent private life. Unless higher education has the wit and will to change utterly, which it cannot do unless American society changes, it will continue to be easier to footnote an article about the history of child care than to insist that universities have enough child care facilities to enable men and women to combine professionalism, affectionate parenting, and more than a dab of domesticity.

Despite my suspicions, fears, and skepticism, I sense how vast the movement
is to redeem women as knowers, to rewrite what we know about them. I know
how lively the minds are, how generous the ambitions can be, of those people
who have conjoined their work and that movement. Perhaps a poet, Adrienne
Rich, has best inscribed their epigraph and my hopes for them. Writing in 1968,
Rich is thinking of Carolyn Hershel, the astronomer. Born in 1750, dead in 1848,
the sister of the far better known William Hershel, Carolyn Hershel discovered
eight comets and became one among the galaxies of women who have been
impetuous and daring and who have done penance for it. Then Rich says — of
Carolyn Hershel, of herself, and of so many others now:

> I have been standing all of my life
> in the direct path of a battery of signals
> the most accurately transmitted most
> untranslatable language in the universe
>
> . . . .
> I am an instrument in the shape
> of a woman trying to translate pulsations
> into images for the relief of the body
> and the reconstruction of the mind.[16]

Part III
Reassessments,
Rediscoveries,
New Paradigms

Chapter 3

Women Knowing: Feminist Theory

and Perspectives on Pedagogy

CHARLOTTE S. McCLURE and DIANE L. FOWLKES

Scholarly efforts to address the deficiencies in knowledge of and about women have been analytic, interdisciplinary, and theoretical and have resulted in a rethinking and reconceptualization of ideas inherited from men as well as a creation of new ideas. Sheila Tobias observes that scholars have gathered interdisciplinary information on the history of women's experience in public and private spheres, on the question of innate or learned characteristics of female personality, and on the effect of patriarchy on women's lives.[1]

It was soon recognized that the study of women, as articulated by Joan I. Roberts and others, would mean a reassessment of the nature of knowledge through rediscovery of women's heritages, through the construction of new paradigms or "new explanatory systems."[2] That Roberts's call for "some of us" to engage in a dialectic process of knowledge and curriculum development is being heard by scholars/teachers in the South is evident in the research papers presented at the 1981 conference, "A Fabric of Our Own Making": Southern Scholars on Women, and published here.

We have collected in this section selected essays in which the writers as feminist theorists and researchers address basic issues involved in educational equity for women. As feminist theorists, they try to explain the condition of women as a class and the source of women's oppression, reassess inherited ideas and facts, and point out avenues of change. The essays address the issues from both interdisciplinary and single discipline perspectives. The writers' disciplines are noted below in parentheses following their names.

Women Knowing: Feminist Theory and Criticism

Several essays under the general topic "Feminist Theory and Criticism" reassess the role of language as a means of naming reality or of excluding people from an already defined reality. Three researchers on women's communication explore the concern that the power to name, traditionally enacted by the male in Western cultures, perpetuates customary sex-role stereotypes and elevates male concerns, contexts, and communication behaviors as the standard forms of behavior. Julia T. Wood, Eva M. McMahan, and Don W. Stacks (speech communication) collaborated to question the male-centered assumptions underlying sixty years of research on women's communication. They call for future research in communication that reflects equal interest in women's and men's business, topics, and settings; they suggest research based on a constructivist theory of person perception in order to overcome the current communicative discrimination toward women. In their essay, "Darwin and Sexism: Victorian Causes, Contemporary Effects," Sue V. Rosser (biology) and A. Charlotte Hogsett (French) challenge whether Darwin can ask questions of female evolution given the Victorian social norms regarding the sexes. They claim that this use of the theory of sexual selection would affect his evolutionary theory by excluding women's reality and that his imaginative conception of the cosmos would affect his choice and use of metaphor to explain his theory. Their reassessment of the effect of Darwin's Victorian milieu on his evolutionary theory with respect to the reality of women's lives results in a new understanding of how bias in a scientific investigation can distort a search for truth. Marie Tedesco (history), in her essay, "A Feminist Challenge to Darwinism: Antoinette L. B. Blackwell on the Relations of the Sexes in Nature and Society," records her rediscovery of a feminist's use of language in 1875 to challenge Darwin. When Judith Ochshorn (history) found that theories that supposedly explain women's historical secondary role in polytheistic cultures in the early Western tradition failed to account for several opposing factors verifiable from other sources, she used different conceptual language to produce an alternative working hypothesis. Her research shows that early Western patriarchy, which supposedly would explain women's secondary role, coexisted with a more androgynous world view and at times a more sexually egalitarian type of social structure. Ochshorn claims that the key to understanding earlier eras is to try to see them through the eyes and experience of those who lived then. Thus scholars in different disciplines, through their reexamination of conceptual language, redefine and rediscover the realities of human experience. Sandra L. Langer (art history) also recognizes that language can be used by those in power as a tool of exclusion, restricting those outside a special status or class from participating in the naming of what constitutes good art (or bad art) in a given period. In her essay, "Against the Grain: A Working Feminist Art Criticism," Langer maintains that social conditions influence the creative process, and she creates a new language of art criticism, "gynergenic criticism," to overcome the traditional male-centered language of art theory and criticism.

Other scholars address the social, historical, and existential factors that invade basic concepts and distort statements about women and therefore about humanity. As art historian Langer claims that social conditions influence the creative process, Jane Flanders (English) assumes a close and direct relationship between the novel and its social context, especially in power relationships between the sexes, which is frequently the focus in fiction. In her essay, "The Fallen Woman in Fiction," Flanders explains the use of the theme of woman's fallen status in fiction by a patriarchal mentality as a promotion of submission of women and as a symptom, through the rendering of a primitive level (primarily sexual) of the relationship between the sexes, of the alienation of all people in the modern world. Such a thematic characterization of a "fallen woman," the fall estimated by others rather than by woman herself, scarcely "names" the real woman's condition, which a study of the social milieu from which the novel evolved would reveal. Dealing with another kind of stereotype from a cross-cultural perspective, Mary Anglin (anthropology) analyzes the changing existences of Appalachian mountain women and shows the dynamics that develop when women, responding to new socioeconomic conditions, work inside and outside the home. Historians and political scientists have studied the impact of sociohistoric factors on the lives of women worldwide, recording how feminists' concerted action to achieve equality frequently has been stalemated by historical phenomena at a particular time. Black women's development in South Africa is being stymied by the oppressive, long-prevailing ideologies of sexism and racism. As Mamie Locke (political science) analyzes the origins of these sexual-racial obstacles to women's development, she joins with other scholars in building new paradigms for understanding the condition of women in many nations and cultures.

Checking the set of assumptions of the nature of the existence that underlies knowledge in their disciplines, other southern scholars have discovered new primary sources of women's knowledge as well as rediscovered women's historic roles and ways of transforming their socially expected roles. In her essay, "Of Paradigm and Paradox: The Case of Mary Boykin Chesnut," Elisabeth S. Muhlenfeld (English) examines the diary and writings of a nineteenth-century aristocratic southern lady, finding them a valuable resource for evaluating historical and sociological aspects of other writings on the antebellum and postbellum South. More importantly, Muhlenfeld discovers in Mary Boykin Chesnut a startling paradox, a feminist and abolitionist in an aristocratic environment hostile to both those philosophies. Chesnut's diary, along with other examples of nontraditional materials being recovered from obscurity in various fields, needs to be explored responsibly, Muhlenfeld explains, in order to deal with the complexity of the writers' views and of the human existences revealed. Delving further back in the history of her discipline, Catherine M. Howett (environmental design) rediscovers women who were successful in the early years of landscape architecture. Howett suggests changes in structure and curriculum that can help to return women to fuller participation in the schools and profession of landscape architecture.

Feminist Perspectives on Transforming Pedagogy

A common observation of many people is that institutions communicate traditional cultural and social ideologies through different media, for example, the curriculum and textbooks. In the essays in this section, feminist perspectives on the means and ends of the educational process provide valuable material on curricular and structural change in the service of gender-related educational equity. To offset the institutionalized sex-related attitudes and behaviors that prevail in the teacher education colleges, the curriculum, and the textbooks from kindergarten through college, feminist scholars advise examination (1) of the way that women's colleges and male-dominated institutions of higher education educate students and prepare them for the professions, (2) of the differences between the sexes in terms of brain lateralization and the implications therein for teaching methods and curriculum change, and (3) of human sexuality as a basis for determining what sex education ought to be. Debra Herman (history), asking, "Does equality mean sameness?" analyzes various philosophical arguments about women's education and preparation for the professions. In addition, her historical perspective on women's colleges raises the question of what might be missing in the male-dominated educational process. Two essays focus on the effect of the curriculum on women's full development. Ina Jane Wundram (anthropology) explores sexual dimorphism in order to understand differences between the sexes in the development of the human brain and the implications therein for curriculum change. Wundram proposes that culture can affect the manner and rate of development of the two hemispheres of the brain and may be responsible in part for some of the observed differences between the sexes and between races. She concludes that girls and boys should be given a greater variety of learning techniques in order to develop cerebral potential according to individual need and to attain individual variation and population diversity. Anne L. Harper (political science) calls for sex education based on a study of the question of what sexuality is. In her essay, "Human Sexuality: New Insights from Women's History," Harper recommends that such a study include anthropological, historical, political, and economic aspects of sex relationships to offset or balance the past and current emphasis on the physiological, biological, and personality aspects of sexuality. Then sex education, she claims, could be not only education about the sex organs but education about relationships between the sexes.

Chapter 4

Research on Women's Communication:

Critical Assessment and Recommendations

JULIA T. WOOD, EVA M. McMAHAN, and DON W. STACKS

Research on women's communication, that is, the form and content of communication employed by women, dates back at least to 1924.[1] Since that time sporadic reports have surfaced both in academic journals and popular forums.[2] Research on women's communication, then, is not a product only of contemporary interest. However, heightened sociopolitical awareness growing out of the resurgence of feminism casts the topic of women's communication in a new light—one that calls for revisions in the assumptions, methods, and interpretations characteristic of traditional research. It is the nature of these revisions that we will address in this essay. We will examine critically the set of assumptions that undergird the bulk of sixty years' research on women's communication. Based on this critique are our recommendations on directions for future inquiry that might be more fruitful than those pursued in the past.

Critique of Traditional Research

Research is not a neutral, value-free enterprise. Valuative assumptions infuse the entire process from conceptualization of questions to interpretation of results. Attention to basic assumptions is a necessary first step in evaluating past research and in forming future work. Review of studies of women's communication reveals four consistent assumptions, three that are substantive and one that is methodological. All four, we will argue, have undermined the caliber of past research and thus merit revision.

Assumption One: Male Communication Is Standard

It certainly is not new to note that research assumes male behaviors as the standard or normal form of behavior. Yet the issue is sufficiently important to merit repeated attention. The assumption of male standardness so thoroughly pervades research in the social sciences that gauging its impact becomes difficult. To take but a single specific example, consider the research on leadership communication. Male-defined criteria guide the conceptualization and implementation of studies of leaders' communication; further, assessments of leadership effectiveness are based (often implicitly) on leadership characteristics derived from studies of male leaders. It should come as no surprise that women generally meet these criteria less well than men, especially in view of preliminary evidence of sex differences pertinent to leadership communication.[3]

Unthinking and automatic reliance on male standards seriously limits understanding of the phenomena under study. Potentially there is a wealth of leadership communication not previously identified because it is not typically enacted by males. We need to broaden analysis to include the widest possible range of leadership communication, not all of which may be routinely practiced by men. This kind of expansion promises to enhance our understanding of the options open to individuals attempting to exert influence.

The problem of distortion in conceptualization runs throughout research. It is as pervasive as the assumption that male communication is standard. In assuming male standardness researchers have limited their study to the kind of communication employed by less than half of the population.

Rejecting the assumption of male standardness would open important avenues of research on women's communication. A first order of business would be examination of women's communication in its own right to identify its characteristic form and content.[4] We need to know not only how women's communication compares to men's (more on the comparative focus later) but also whether women's communication includes qualities not present in men's communication.[5] Recent studies of leadership communication offer preliminary support for the distinctiveness of female and male styles of influence.[6] Once we identify distinctive qualities of women's communication, we may move on to probe implications and to assess appropriateness in various settings. Researchers might evaluate communication by the criterion of functional utility (i.e., impact vis-à-vis specific goals) rather than the criterion of male standardness. For instance, investigations might focus on identifying communication effective in directing work (e.g., coordination, feedback, information giving), fostering cooperative interpersonal climates (e.g., supportiveness, listening, acknowledgment), resolving conflict (e.g., analysis, questioning, collective orientation), or personnel counseling (e.g., openness, receptiveness, empathy, listening). Using a functional criterion, the researchers' goal is to discover what types of communication advance particular outcomes; this objective is quite different from the goal of matching observed communication against a priori and arbitrary standards, that is, maleness. Given a functional perspective, researchers likely would find that women's communication includes a variety of behaviors useful in achieving specific goals.

Abandoning the assumption of male standardness not only would expand our knowledge of communication behaviors but also might alter evaluations of particular communication strategies. For example, several researchers describe the leadership style typical of women as low-profile or nondominating.[7] Too often this finding is interpreted as rationale for advising that women become more assertive, a predictable response given the assumption of male standardness and the tendency of male leaders to be assertive. Rejecting the equation between male communication and correct communication would allow researchers to ask whether low-keyed leadership is particularly effective in some situations and/or with certain kinds of subordinates. Researchers also might investigate the impact of low-profile leadership on subordinate initiative, development, satisfaction, and investment in work. We suspect such research would find that in some settings low-keyed leadership is more effective than an assertive style. Whether or not this speculation is borne out, researchers need to begin asking the kinds of questions illustrated here — questions that do not presuppose male communication as the standard by which effectiveness is judged.

Assumption Two: Women's Behaviors Determine Their Effectiveness

Research on women too often assumes that the crucial influence on personal effectiveness is women's behaviors. Women who are effective managers, for instance, are so because they enact the appropriate behaviors, while ineffective managers are those who have not mastered (an unfortunate word) the requisite behaviors. The pragmatic implication of this assumption is that women are viewed (and view themselves) as having major responsibility for their effectiveness. If they succeed in traditionally male arenas, they are entitled to pride; if they fail or are only marginally successful (more typical outcomes), they must look within themselves for the causes.

Certainly we do not wish to argue that women's behaviors are inconsequential to effectiveness. Neither, however, do we accept the assumption that overt behaviors including communication are the only — or even the primary — influence on individual impact. Behaviors per se are neutral. Their value and impact derive from the interpretations placed upon them; in turn, interpretations arise out of frameworks of expectations, perceptions, and values that exist prior to the behaviors. These evaluative frameworks have *at least* as much to do with an individual's effectiveness as do an actor's behaviors. Women have responsibility for their behaviors, yes. What they do not have and cannot be held accountable for is absolute control over how others will perceive and respond to those behaviors. The distinction is substantial.

The practical implications of this distinction can be easily demonstrated. Consider the studies documenting negative male attitudes toward female managers.[8] We also remind you of a survey, dated but still noteworthy, in which 660 of 1,000 male executives and 180 of 900 female executives reported they would not feel comfortable working for a woman.[9] Attitudes such as these clearly influence how women executives' communication will be interpreted. Even the efforts of women who have formal authority and the incumbent behavioral skills can be thwarted by reluctant subordinates.[10]

Research in the years ahead should move away from the assumption that a woman controls her effectiveness by her behavior and should move toward the more reasonable position that effectiveness is a product of negotiation between interactants. The latter view provides clear rationale for specific kinds of inquiries: (1) How do various expectations influence perception of women's communication?[11] (2) How do alternative views of women affect perceptions of women's communication?[12] (3) How does self-concept of perceiver affect judgments of women's communication?[13] In short, research should attend to the fact that communication is played out against and judged by a backdrop of assumptions and expectations, generally beyond the control of the individual actors. Research of this sort would promote in women more realistic views of their latitude of responsibility and control over personal effectiveness.

Assumption Three: Identification of Differences between Female and Male Communication Is a (the) Significant Research Focus

A traditional goal of research is generalization. To generalize it is necessary to define and think in categories. In the area of women's communication the basic categories are women's communication and men's communication, represented as (a) distinct from each other[14] and (b) relatively homogeneous within classes. A large portion of research on women's communication begins by separating subjects into two realms of humanity: women and men; next some designated behavior of the subjects is observed and measured; then the observed behaviors of the female subjects are compared to those of the male subjects; finally, findings are noted, laced with value judgments. From this prototypical form of research comes identification of differences characterizing women and men's communication.[15]

While we do not disapprove of this genre of research in its own right, we do argue that it provides insufficient insight into women's communication. Studies of the form described above tell us more about how women's communication differs from men's (standard) communication than about the nature of women's communication per se. Several problems inhere in the comparative approach to women's communication. First, as we suggested earlier, it is of questionable appropriateness to compare women's communication to that of men. Because of probable differences in form, content, and function of the sexes' communication it is difficult to make accurate comparisons—we lack criteria that can be applied equally to women's and men's communication. If women and men employ divergent communicative strategies to achieve like goals, comparisons are inaccurate or meaningless. Similarly, if women and men use their communication to accomplish very different ends, comparisons of process or product are problematic. A second danger of comparative research is that comparisons between two classes inevitably invoke evaluations. When women's communication is compared to men's communication (we challenge readers to identify a group of studies that reverse the order), women often are judged as somehow inferior, an interpretation preordained by the assumption of male standardness. Third, comparative research elevates the dichotomous variable of sex (sometimes gender) to a position of primary importance in explaining various outcomes; consequently, attention is deflected from other, potentially pertinent variables such as experience, position, status, expertise, and power.[16] The tone of comparative research often suggests that sex is *the* factor that explains impact. A fourth problem growing out of the first three is that focus on comparisons between categories (in this case women and men) distracts attention to possible differences within each class. To borrow a statistical metaphor, it may well be that there is as much or more variation within each class as between them. In any case, we will not know unless we conduct thorough analyses of the communication within each class. In the effort to identify distinctions between women's and men's communication researchers have neglected or glossed over the variety within women's communication. We suspect women are not as homogeneous a group as they often appear in research reports. Rather, it seems likely there is tremendous diversity in how women communicate; if so, we need to recognize it. Assertive behavior, for instance, may be manifested in countless ways, not all of which are evident from male-defined standards. A closer examination of women's communication—its versatility and range—should prove useful in informing us of possibilities as well as probabilities.[17]

Serious, thorough study of women's communication in its own right (rather than in comparison to men's communication) not only should increase understanding but, more fundamentally, would argue the importance of women's communication, a point sorely lacking in the extant literature. The assumption that women's communication is best understood in comparison to men's communication limits and distorts knowledge about how women communicate.

Assumption Four: College Students in Laboratory Settings
Approximate "Real Life"

The final assumption we will critique concerns research design and methodology. The majority of research on women's communication (as well as other topics
of study) is conducted in artificial, laboratory conditions with that ever-popular
subject—the college sophomore. There is a substantial gap between the simu-
lated and carefully controlled environment of an academic laboratory and the
real world; further, there is little basis for believing college students' attitudes
and actions are representative of the general population. Because college students tend to be upwardly mobile, younger, better educated, and often more
liberal than the general population, student attitudes and behaviors cannot be
readily generalized beyond the ivory tower—especially in reference to attitudes
and actions relevant to values that are in flux, such as those concerning women.

We see these design problems as quite serious because they bear directly on
the external validity of easily 90 percent of the research on women's communication. In her forthcoming book on women executives Linda Keller Brown reports
finding over 300 studies of women in managerial roles—an impressive amount
of research.[18] However, nearly all of these studies were conducted in laboratories
using students as subjects—not even business students in most cases. Brown
found it impossible to make useful extensions to the real world from such
research. Because researchers typically rely on student subjects, we know very
little about populations that are uneducated or less educated, not socially mobile,
not career-oriented, or over age twenty-five—that is, the majority of the
population.

But use of students as subjects is only half of the problem with the design of
the preponderance of research. Equally serious is reliance on laboratory settings.
The great advantage of laboratory studies is that the researcher can control
carefully the variables present in a situation and can trace the effects of selected
ones. In theory this control is valuable because it allows study of pure relationships between variables without contamination by extraneous factors. In the
"real world," however, few people can select which variables will and will not
impinge on a situation. Most of us live our lives and conduct our work in the very
messy matrix of social interaction where unwanted variables constantly abound
and must be managed. Knowledge of the pure relationship between variable A,
say tag questions used by a woman, and variable B, say dominance of conversation by a man, is of minimum use in situations "contaminated" by power
differences, established role relationships, and particular organizational philosophy and norms.

The assumption that college student subjects in laboratory environments
approximate real life underlies much of the research on women's commuunica-
tion. This assumption should be abandoned so that future research may provide

more useful and accurate information about women's communication and may offer more applicable guidelines for expectations and actions beyond academe.

Since 1924 researchers have compiled an impressive amount of data on women's communication. The value of this work, however, is severely limited by four assumptions that seem amazingly consistent across the bulk of sixty years: (1) Male communication is standard. (2) Women's behaviors determine their effectiveness. (3) Women's communication should be compared to men's communication. (4) College students in laboratory settings approximate real life. Our critique of these assumptions argues that the majority of existing research limits and sometimes distorts knowledge about how women communicate and may lead to inappropriate advisories regarding how they should communicate. It is of course far easier to point out deficiencies in past work than to propose viable alternatives for future study. We turn now to the more difficult task of recommending directions for future research.

Priorities for Future Research on Women's Communication

Avoidance of problems characterizing past research is important, but that alone provides insufficient direction for future study. We also need to declare new frontiers for research. If we were to identify a single priority for scholarship it would be this: eliminate the defensive tone that permeates previous research on women.

Research and thought about women's communication reflects and perpetuates defensiveness in women. Ways in which women's communication differs from men's communications are translated from differences to inferiorities. Explanations for the differences/inferiorities center on the oppressive, subordinating socialization of women. (Those who accept the explanation simultaneously endorse the value judgment of inferiority.) When researchers move into advisories they typically suggest ways to "improve" women's communication, to help women "overcome" their learned styles and to learn "more appropriate" (read male) styles of interaction.[19] This defensive-inducing posture, arising primarily from the assumptions we have criticized, is further evidenced by researchers' focus on women's problems, disadvantages, or handicaps in, for example, executive positions.[20] The cumulative impact of this orientation is a portrayal of women as deficient, aberrant, somehow impaired and in need of remedial treatment to bring them up to acceptable (male) standards. To the extent that people, particularly women, buy this portrayal, women cannot affirm their qualities as women and often find themselves apologizing for these qualities. It is this defensive tone that must be exorcised from future research. To elaborate this recommendation we will suggest two focuses for future work: first, research should establish a perspective that affirms women and their communication; second, it should legitimize women's concerns and settings as topics of study.

Future Research Should Affirm Women's Communication

Frequently we are asked by women's organizations to conduct communication workshops for which a requested topic usually is differences between women's and men's communication. Description of differences reported in the literature invariably is met with two responses: How can we eliminate our undesirable (female) communication patterns? How can we develop more effective (male) styles of communication? In our classes a number of students write papers on such topics as women in management, career-oriented women, and women in professions. After reviewing the available literature, replete with the assumptions we have criticized, our students generally conclude with statements such as: "Contemporary women can be successful in nontraditional roles by learning the ropes of these roles. They must be sensitive to the norms of their situations and be willing to adapt behaviors accordingly. In this way they can fit into areas that have been dominated by men in the past." Thinking of our students and participants in our workshops we ask ourselves, "Are women so willing to disown their styles of communication? Should they be?" We suspect the answers are, respectively, "Yes, many women are ready, even eager, to disown their communication styles and adopt male styles," and "No, they should not necessarily do so."

At first glance these issues seem removed from recommendations for research; yet we believe they go to the very crux of what research is about: assumptions and implications.

Like all research, study of women's communications is guided by basic assumptions, some of which we criticized earlier in this essay. To return briefly to this point, the bulk of work on women's communication reflects a set of assumptions that argue (a) women's communication differs from men's communication, (b) therefore, women's communication is somehow inferior to men's communication (after all, the standard for effective communication is male), so (c) one task of researchers is to identify and test methods (raising awareness, training, skill development, etc.) that have potential to help women learn appropriate (male) communication styles. These assumptions are ingrained in research that either examines sex-role behaviors (and in so doing explains why women haven't learned effective communication due to their socialization) or documents sex differential communication (and implies valuations of the differences).[21]

Research erected on these assumptions has the pragmatic effect of depicting women primarily in terms of inadequacies, problems, non(sub)standard behaviors. It is, then, small wonder that women in workshops and classes ask how to overcome their female style of communicating and how to acquire a male style.

The research underlying teaching and popular advice predisposes that perspective.[22]

What is needed is a radical turn in research, one that redefines the fundamental approach we take in doing research. Along with Adrienne Rich we believe research should affirm the value and significance of women's experience, traditions, and perceptions in and of themselves.[23]

In order for research to affirm women as women there must be clear deviations from past work. An initial priority is identification of strengths, values, and positive functions of women's communication.[24] Research reports should enlighten readers about the unique strengths of women's communication, an objective that is most difficult within the assumptive framework of past investigation.[25] Such an affirmative approach would represent a long-missing and needed complement to the volumes of work on weaknesses of women's communication. As women increasingly enter nontraditional areas, surely they must modify some of their old ways of behaving and cultivate some new ways. It is equally true, however, that women already have a wealth of skills and perspectives worth retaining and teaching to others.[26] This point has too seldom been made.

Existing research, premised as it is on sexist assumptions, encourages in women and men perceptions of women's communication as weak, ineffective, substandard. In turn, this view promotes in women a willingness to adopt male-associated styles of thought and action, an outcome with at least two undesirable repercussions. First, equating male behaviors and attitudes with correctness obscures discrimination among the range of male-associated behaviors, some of which may be unworthy of admiration, much less emulation.[27] The false dichotomy between male behaviors as effective and female behaviors as ineffective not only is unrealistic but also perpetuates some of the less laudable behaviors of men while obscuring some of the more valuable behaviors of women.

There is a second and more pernicious outcome of research that predisposes women to value and adopt male standards of thought and action. In so doing women must reject their own experiences, perceptions, values, and codes of conduct. Ultimately this attitude leads to rejection of self.[28] Research plays a powerful role in shaping perceptions of what is and of what should be. Future research, we hope, will provide positive views of women that encourage women to take themselves seriously and to appreciate their unique perspectives, insights, and styles of behavior as women.

There is little question that women successfully can imitate men, but there is substantial doubt as to whether emulation is a goal worthy of pursuit. Would such imitation improve the quality of life in professional, interpersonal, and private areas? This question must be raised and dealt with; it should not remain an unarticulated assumption in research.[29]

One priority of future research is affirmation of the heretofore neglected strengths of women's communication. Research from this perspective will encourage more realistic and more critical thought about the wisdom of wholesale adoption of male standards and simultaneous denial of female standards. It also should encourage women to think more carefully about the implications of trading in their ways of knowing, being, and doing for those advocated by males. Such an exchange, in the long run, may be more costly than envisioned or warranted. It is possible that women will discover that the trade-off is not confined to specific compartments of existence, that it gradually infuses all aspects of their lives and in so doing precludes significant experiences.

Before leaving this issue we must note, albeit briefly, the broader implications of women's adoption of male standards. Not only does such a move compromise individual women, it also reinforces the rules, values, and hierarchy that have dominated our society to date.[30] Acceptance of male standards and values can only perpetuate the very social structure that legitimizes oppression, competition, divorce of emotion and reason, and other features in need of revision. We remain unconvinced of the accuracy of an equation between effectiveness and a masculine orientation to living. A more realistic position is that social and political history renders masculine orientations the dominant approach to existence but not necessarily the best, and certainly not the only one.

Future Research Should Legitimize Women's Concerns and Settings as Topics of Research

For the most part this essay has focused on the ways in which researchers go about the task of answering questions, particularly how assumptions guide decisions about conceptualization, methodology, and interpretation of findings. In this final section we address the even more fundamental issue of the kinds of questions posed by researchers.[31] We argue, first, that existing research has pursued questions that elevate and ennoble masculine concerns and contexts while neglecting (and thus demeaning)) women's issues; second, we argue that future research should devote greater attention to women's concerns and settings.

The majority of research in the social sciences focuses on male-defined topics, concerns, and environs.[32] This approach should come as little surprise, given the facts that there have been and are far more male than female researchers and, further, that male issues are assumed more significant than female ones.[33] An obvious, albeit less noted, fact is that women's issues and environments have been virtually ignored by researchers in most disciplines. Researchers essentially have ignored the contexts in which the majority of women live out their lives. In so doing they have implied that women's settings are trivial, not meriting serious study.[34]

Women's settings have been neglected by researchers, but this omission is only part of the problem. It is compounded by the fact that the contexts for the bulk of study on women's communication are invariably male contexts: task groups, businesses, organizations. The tendency to study masculine activities and environments, then, achieves two outcomes. First, it constitutes an implicit argument for the importance of masculine issues, enterprises, and settings and a corresponding argument for the unimportance of feminine concerns, activities, and contexts. Second, it distorts descriptions, assessment, and understanding of women's communication by consistently observing it in alien environments.

Future research should refuse to award exclusive attention to masculine arenas. Instead, it should reflect an equally strong interest in women's business, topics, and settings. Researchers should make a serious commitment to the study of domestic issues, social settings, jobs such as secretary and homemaker. And research on business and professional contexts should probe into how interpersonal networks positively affect these business and professional activities.[35]

By the very settings chosen for study, researchers make statements about which topics and contexts merit study and which are so insignificant that they may be ignored. Future research should pursue nontraditional kinds of questions and thus locate important absences in research.[36] In this way future work will acknowledge the legitimacy of woman-defined concerns and contexts. Such acknowledgment is a necessary step in the overall struggle for a transformation of social values that will encourage redefinition of human society and reassessment of human values.

Research operating from the perspectives advanced in this essay should, to quote Arlene Kaplan Daniels, "restructure the boundaries of knowledge" and broaden our world view.[37] If this objective seems more difficult than those that guided past research, it is also one more worthy of pursuit and far more exciting if achieved.

Chapter 5

Darwin and Sexism:

Victorian Causes, Contemporary Effects

SUE V. ROSSER and A. CHARLOTTE HOGSETT

Scientists, like all scholars, hold, either explicitly or implicitly, certain beliefs concerning their enterprise. Most scientists believe, for example, that the laws and facts gathered by scientists are constant, providing that experiments have been done correctly. As Hilary and Steven Rose put it, scientists seem to feel that "Science is the pursuit of natural laws, laws which are valid irrespective of nation, race, politics, religion, or class position of their discoverer."[1] If the observations of science reflect natural law, they stand outside historical context. Both the facts and the theories based on them are, according to this kind of view, affect- and effect-free, having come from sheer attentiveness to the outside world unshackled by opinion or desire and leading only to applications that others might wish to make of them.

Historians of science are making us aware that, quite to the contrary, the individuals who make observations and create theories are people who live in a particular country during a certain time in a definable socioeconomic condition, and that their situations and mentalities inevitably impinge on their discoveries. Even their "facts" are contingent. Aristotle "counted" fewer teeth in the mouths of women than in those of men — adding this dentitional inferiority to all the others.[2] Galen, having read the book of Genesis, "discovered" that men had one less rib on one side than women did.[3] Clearly, observation of what would appear by today's standards to be easily verifiable facts can vary depending upon the theory or paradigm, to use the terminology of Thomas S. Kuhn, under which the scientist is operating.[4]

The paradigms are far from value free. The values of the culture, historical past and present society, heavily influence the ordering of observable phenomena into theory. The world view of a particular society, time, and person limits the questions that can be asked and thereby the answers that can be given. Kuhn has demonstrated that the very acceptance of a particular paradigm that may appear to cause a "scientific revolution" within a society depends in fact upon the congruence of that theory with the institutions and beliefs of the society.

The theories of Charles Darwin constitute such a paradigm. Scientists today question the relevance and validity of many of his ideas, which no longer seem to us to explain biological phenomena. Yet his ideas are not of antiquarian interest only. They have deeply influenced the thinking of both natural and social scientists from his time to our own. Further, contemporary sociobiologists use many of Darwin's observations and paradigms to support their constructs. In this essay, we as feminists examine the theory of sexual selection in particular. Sexual selection is a theory that assumes and provides a scientific explanation for female inferiority. Insofar as the attitudes imbedded in it still remain with us, it calls for our critical understanding.

In the *Origin of Species* Darwin brings in the theory of sexual selection as a secondary agent to explain how descent with modification, or evolution, has taken place.[5] The primary agent of change, in that first version of the theory, was natural selection, a paradigm laden with the values of nineteenth-century England. As Rose and Rose suggest, "its central metaphors [and we shall have occasion to return to the idea of theory as metaphor] drawn from society and in their turn interacting with society were of the competition of species, the struggle for existence, the ecological niche, and the survival of the fittest."[6] These metaphors reflect Victorian society and were acceptable to it because they, and the "social Darwinism" quickly derived from it, seemed to ground its norms solidly in a biological foundation.[7] When Darwin depicts the fittest as the individuals who pass on their genes to the greatest number of offspring, one thinks of the importance of passing on property in this society. One can hardly overlook an upper-class perspective and appeal when, in the *Descent of Man,* Darwin implores that "both sexes ought to refrain from marriage if they are in any marked degree inferior in body or mind; . . . All ought to refrain from marriage who cannot avoid abject poverty for their children, for poverty is . . . a great evil."[8] The upper class of Victorian England had self-serving reasons for finding Darwin's theory attractive: it gave biological rationale for their position in society. Nor was Darwin's own position a matter unrelated to the acceptability of his theory. Even though Darwin himself was not aggressive in advancing it, he had wealthy and influential friends such as Thomas Henry Huxley, Sir Charles Lyell, and Sir Joseph Dalton Hooker who championed the theory for him. One wonders if Alfred Russel Wallace might not have fared better in receiving credit and publicity for his contributions had he had such friends and been from an equally prominent social class.

In like manner, the theory of sexual selection reflected and reinforced Victorian social norms regarding the sexes. By this theory Darwin set out to explain a phenomenon still not fully understood, that of the existence of secondary sex characteristics. He claimed that "when the males and females of any animal have the same general habits of life, but differ in structure, colour, or ornament, such differences have been mainly caused by sexual selection."[9] Expanding considerably on the theory first presented in the *Origin*, Darwin specified, in the *Descent of Man*, how the process functions and what roles males and females play in it:

> The sexual struggle is of two kinds; in the one it is between the individuals of the same sex, generally the males, in order to drive away or kill their rivals, the females remaining passive; whilst in the other, the struggle is likewise between the individuals of the same sex, in order to excite or charm those of the opposite sex, generally the females, which no longer remain passive, but select the more agreeable partners. [P. 64]

According to the theory, the males who triumph over their rivals will win the more desirable females and will leave the most progeny, thereby perpetuating and increasing, over numerous generations, those qualities that afforded them victory. The females who succeed, by the seductive means they employ, in being chosen will also procreate best and pass on their characteristics. As a result, by the time evolution has produced modern man and modern woman, the two are considerably different, men being superior to women both physically and mentally. Not only are they "taller, heavier, and stronger than women, with squarer shoulders and more plainly pronounced muscles," but also they attain to a "higher eminence" in whatever they take up.[10] The theory reflects the Victorian age, with its depiction of active males competing and struggling with each other for passive females. That depiction of male-female interaction would have seemed quite obvious to most segments of Victorian society and its grounding in scientific fact most reassuring.

However, the process of selection involved in the theory encountered much resistance. Biologists of Darwin's time came up with numerous counterexamples. Alfred Wallace, who independently had arrived at the theory of natural selection, fundamentally disagreed with the theory of sexual selection. Even Darwin himself gives proof, in *Descent of Man*, of considerable difficulty with many of the assumptions and necessities of his theory and admits that, especially as applied to the history of man, it "wants scientific precision" (p. 605). Antoinette Blackwell attacked his theory on a number of points.[11] In her understanding that a central problem of the theory was Darwin's limited perspective as a male observer, she may be said to have made the first feminist criticism of it. Today, the phenomena that Darwin set out to explain, namely secondary sex characteristics that distinguish the sexes, are seen in an entirely new light because of the discoveries in the field of genetics, although indeed much remains unexplained still. But the way of thinking behind Darwin's theory has not, we believe, been sufficiently exposed.

To make an adequate analysis of the theory of sexual selection, one must ask why Darwin needed such a theory. Where, in his enterprise of affirming, proving, strengthening the principle of evolution in the mind of the reader, does sexual selection, as an agency of such change, fit in? Indeed, Darwin asserted and demonstrated, both in *Origin of Species* and in *Descent of Man,* several means by which species advance and differentiate, sexual selection being a quite minor one in the former work and yet taking on primary importance in the latter. Why did he invent such a theory in the first place? Why did it acquire more prominence in his mind over the nearly thirteen years that passed between the publication of the *Origin* and that of the *Descent?* In examining that question, one begins to understand the patterns of thought, both manifest and covert, that characterize Darwin's theory.

In order to arrive at that understanding, one needs that which, for example, Blackwell, the first feminist critic, lacked: distance from the theory sufficient to provide critical perspective. To be sure, we have today the distance that only the passage of time affords. Beyond that, we want to establish another kind of distance by looking at the theory, as Darwin expressed it in his two major books, through the methodology of a discipline not ordinarily applied to works in the field of science: that of literary criticism. We ask that the reader suspend whatever disbelief the announcement of such an outlandish approach might evoke in order to move with us toward the insights it may bring into the generation and the nature of the theory of sexual selection.

Let us look, then, at Darwin the writer. Although certainly Darwin chose his words with considerable care and did not lack rhetorical skill, he is not particularly renowned as a stylist. However, especially in the *Origin,* Darwin's writing is extremely interesting. It takes on a strength that comes only when an author reflects while composing on the nature and limitations of the medium that of necessity is being used. Darwin reveals that he feels suspicion regarding the role of language in the elaboration of thought. In using language one names things. Once one has named a thing, one inevitably has fixed it into a category, has provided a definition that rigidifies around the thing and freezes it into place. For Darwin, the denominating power of language is harmful to his undertaking. He wishes to demonstrate the "slow and gradual" process by which species develop.[12] The history of that process is obscured by the fact that the human mind retains only those entities that have been distinctly named. Neither the linguistic record nor the geological record (which Darwin compares to an imperfect language) will preserve that history.[13] Languages themselves are like species in that "they can hardly be said to have had a definite origin"; rather, both dialects and varieties as well as species pass from one to the next by graduations that language is unable to capture.[14]

In chapter 2 of the *Origin,* "Variations under Nature," Darwin quite cleverly plays with definitions of the words "species" and "varieties" in order to demonstrate the impossibility of adequate definition and the problems that impossibility poses: "To discuss whether they are rightly called species or varieties, before any definition of these terms has been generally accepted, is vainly to beat the air" (p. 49). From this demonstration he can move easily to his own point: "These differences blend into each other in an insensible series; and a series impresses the mind with the idea of an actual passage" (p. 51). In this way Darwin replaces the mere systematic naming of things in static language with what he calls an "actual passage" or, in other words, a dramatic and dynamic story. In moving from series to passage he is able to recount a tale that bursts through the limitations of language.

However, the tale he tells is not a radically dynamic one. His narration of the past is full of movement and energy, but not until the end of the *Descent* is his story notably future oriented. We do not suppose that, had he been asked, Darwin would have asserted the immutability of the Victorian natural and human world; yet certainly his language betrays a tendency to arrest the process of development at that point. He speaks in the *Descent* of the "perfection of structure and coadaptation which most justly excites our admiration" (p. 3). Or again, he asks, "How have all those exquisite adaptations of one part of the organization to another part, and to the condition of life, been perfected?" (p. 60). He also asserts that we need not be surprised if not all of nature's "contrivances" seem perfect to us, indeed if some are even "abhorrent to our ideas of fitness," for we must reflect that "as natural selection acts by competition, it adapts the habitants of each country only in relation to the degree of perfection of their associates" (p. 472). Continuing natural and social change in the future would seem to be the inevitable consequence of the story Darwin tells. Yet he shrinks from that consequence. In the *Origin* he states that domestic instincts are "far less fixed or invariable than natural instincts" (p. 213), thus implying that change in society is possible. But by asserting that natural selection can make "an occasional habit permanent, if of advantage to the species," he provides a way to stop development at a given point. Moreover, at the end of the *Descent,* his discussion of the future takes the form of eugenic recommendations for the controlling of humanity's future. The story of evolution is apparently not, according to his wishes, to be an ongoing one, certainly not in the human realm.

His story is, then, a conservative one in which social change is limited. He ends by arresting the dynamics of his story by reestablishing stasis. The characters of his story, theoretically an innumerable cast, undefinable in their infinite variety, eventually are classified into groups subordinate to groups. They cease to be separately coexisting individual entities but rather are ordered into a familiar hierarchy. Having destroyed the language of the systematists, Darwin establishes his own, unwilling or unable to remain faithful to the radical implications of the thoroughly dynamic story he suggests.

To be sure, in so doing Darwin was, as we all are, the victim of language itself, which, as he very well understood, forces us into definitions, denominations, orders, if we are to speak at all. But he was the victim as well of his own conservative nature, his own commitment to established order. The nature of the social order that Darwin seems instinctively to have wished to maintain comes to light as we further examine Darwin as writer.

Darwin was not only a storyteller who repugned to tell the story to the end but also a poet whose poetry led him toward both fertile suggestion and threatening vision. Just as his writing was made stronger by his awareness of the limitations of language, so also was it enhanced by his sight into language as metaphor. Let us define metaphor as the application by analogy of terms ordinarily associated with one realm to another. It was by metaphor that Darwin chose at least some of his key terms — natural selection, to take a first notable example. "I have called this principle, by which each slight variation, if useful, is preserved, by the term of Natural Selection, in order to mark its relation to man's power of selection. . . . Natural Selection . . . is a power incessantly ready for action, and is as immeasurably superior to man's feeble efforts, as the works of Nature are to those of Art."[15] Variation under domestication, Darwin claims, provides the best clue to variation under nature. In so claiming, he proceeds metaphorically to generate a concept of nature from a concept of art.

The term "struggle for existence" is also, by Darwin's own assertion, metaphorical: "I should premise that I use the term Struggle for Existence in a large and metaphorical sense."[16] The sort of case in which one might apply the term literally would be that of two dogs struggling with each other to get food and live during a time of dearth, Darwin explains. Or, one might say literally, truly, or properly that several seedling mistletoes close together on the same branch struggle with each other. But Darwin states his intention to use the term in many other sorts of situations.

> As the misseltoe [*sic*] is disseminated by birds, its existence depends on birds; and it may metaphorically be said to struggle with other fruit-bearing plants, in order to tempt birds to devour and thus disseminate its seeds rather than those of other plants. In these several senses, which pass into each other, I use for convenience sake the general term of struggle for existence.[17]

That Darwin spoke metaphorically is one way to explain the easy passage even in his own time from Darwinism to Social Darwinism, for indeed Darwin himself was much given to the passing or transferring of terms from realm to realm, including, notably, the natural to the social and vice versa. The adaptations of which he spoke (in the *Origin*) in the natural world are readily seen at work in society: "In social animals it [i.e., natural selection] will adapt the structure of each individual for the benefit of society" (p. 87). We will not be surprised to see, then, that Darwin's presentation of nature is a metaphorical or poetic vision generated by his own conception of the cosmos, itself formed by that inexplicable interaction of self with world that creates in all people an imaginative universe. We may understand something of Darwin's mental representations by studying

those metaphors by which he presented nature. We must be aware that he
inevitably was ordering his observations according to these representations and
that both facts and theories will be deeply imprinted by them. Nor should we be
surprised to see how overwhelmingly Darwin's views bear the mark of the
Victorian world in the use of the metaphors of competition, selection, struggle,
battle, and war to which we already have referred. Certainly he was reading
society into nature when he spoke of the latter as an economic or political
system.[18]

The metaphors by which Darwin in the *Origin* describes the process of sexual
selection also are borrowed from human society. Indeed, even as he speaks of
separation of the sexes in plants he immediately brings in a principle of economics, claiming that the separation becomes advantageous because it is a "physiological division of labor" (pp. 93 – 94). As he moves toward the animal realm,
the relationship between the sexes is depicted in a quite anthropomorphic
manner. In the case of some animals, such as stags, cocks, and alligators, the
relationship is warlike, the animals being described as equipped with weapons
and shields. In the case of birds, the metaphor is that of a theatrical performance
on the part of the males, a performance designed to charm and seduce the
females. The seduction itself is a male prerogative; the females wait until the
battle or the act ends, finally choosing the males who have performed most
valiantly or most delightfully. Having described animals in human terms, Darwin goes on, and at much more length, in the *Descent* to differentiate between
male and female human beings in those same terms that he "discovered" in the
animal world.

In the *Descent* Darwin expands his theory considerably, attributing more
importance to it in the process of evolution than he had in the *Origin* and
amassing an impressive amount of detail in order to demonstrate it. But detail
notwithstanding, his highly favored theory encountered difficulty not only because of the criticism it evoked but also in his own mind, though he did not
admit the latter in any overt way. He does confess at least twice in the *Descent*
that it is difficult to affirm whether given structures have been developed
through natural or sexual selection (pp. 210 and 615). Natural selection operates
"in relation to the general purposes of life," whereas sexual selection comes into
play "in relation to the propagation of the species. . . . Hence secondary sexual
characters, when equally transmitted to both sexes can be distinguished from
ordinary specific characters only by the light of analogy" (p. 615). Again Darwin
proceeds metaphorically. Only by metaphor can one discern the action of sexual
selection at all. That Darwin appeals to metaphor as a last resort at a moment of
difficulty in his theory is not surprising, inasmuch as the whole theory is
grounded on metaphorical procedures. In doing so, he points out the profoundly
metaphorical nature of his thought process. But when metaphors function
poorly, as they do in the *Descent,* the comparisons become mere examples. This

weakness is perhaps why the *Descent* is a long, tedious recital of cases that never quite seem to reinforce the theory adequately.

Why, then, one wonders, did Darwin insist on the theory so much? What role did it play in his total conception of change in nature? Initially, in the *Origin,* Darwin used the theory as a secondary agent to explain the means by which evolution takes place: "Amongst many animals, sexual selection will give its aid to ordinary selection, by assuring to the most vigorous and best adapted males the greatest number of offspring" (p. 127). The reader understands readily that sexual selection is a minor support to natural selection. But the reader may be surprised to see that males only are mentioned as the bearers of the desirable characteristics that are sexually selected. At this point in the text Darwin adds a second benefit of sexual selection: "Sexual selection will also give characters useful to the males alone, in their struggles with other males." Again, the focus is entirely on the male half of the species. The only activity envisioned in this expression is bound up in a masculine world.

Later in the *Origin* Darwin stresses the variability of secondary sexual characteristics. He wonders why there is more variability in these characters than in those of other parts of the organization. Sexual selection has "wide scope for action." At this point, Darwin expands on the possible benefits of sexual selection.

> Variations of this part would, it is highly probable, be taken advantage of by natural and sexual selection, in order to fit the several species to their several places in the economy of nature, and likewise to fit the two sexes of the same species to each other, or to fit the males and females to different habits of life or the males to struggle with other males for the possession of the females. [Pp. 157–58]

The verb "to fit" is used three times in this society-oriented view. Darwin speaks as if places have been somehow previously marked out for the species and the sexes. As the sentence continues, he increasingly stresses the differences between the sexes and again depicts a world in which the males actively struggle for passive females who become the property of the winning males.

What seems to have struck Darwin most when he observed males and females of species throughout the natural world was the tremendous difference between them: "How enormously these sometimes differ in the most important characters is known to every naturalist."[19] What amazed him was the fact that such different beings belong to the same species. When viewing the human world in the light of other natural realms, he was even surprised to note that even greater differences still had not been evolved. "It is, indeed, fortunate that the law of the equal transmission of characters to both sexes prevails with mammals; otherwise it is probable that man would have become as superior in mental endowment to woman, as the peacock is in ornamental plumage to the peahen."[20]

At first view it may seem strange that Darwin stresses the differences between the sexes. In the *Origin* he depicts the struggle for existence as a mainly intraspecific conflict, claiming that competition is fiercest among those closest in the scale of nature (p. 76). Yet when he comes to those beings most closely related, namely the males and females of a given species, he does not speak of competition at all but rather of an entirely masculine struggle for females. Indeed, as he depicts male-female interaction it seems that the males constitute something like a separate group, interacting mainly with each other in relation to another quite separate group, the members of which have relatively fewer secondary sex characteristics. In order to make the differentiation between males and females as strong as possible, the theory of sexual selection is needed. The theory is the agent of differentiation, that which assures an ever-increasing separation between the sexes and their operation in two quite distinct realms that touch only for the purpose of procreation.

Thus whereas the functioning principle of Darwin's thought is metaphor, whereby beings are constantly compared with each other and analogies are constantly established, when Darwin comes to the intraspecific sexes he abruptly stops the process of metaphor. Just as Darwin the storyteller puts an end to his dynamic story when continuing change might have been the result of it, so also Darwin the poet suddenly eliminates metaphor as a way of thinking the moment it would suggest that analogies drawn from the male world might apply to the female and vice versa. Here he proceeds by contrast rather than by comparison. Likenesses between males and females seem to be as threatening to him as social change.

The desire to distinguish came to be an increasing obsession with Darwin after the *Origin*. Nor is the context in which he places his agent of differentiation in the *Descent of Man* a coincidence. That book consists of two major parts, the first a discussion of human evolution that ends with a consideration of whether the different races should be classified into the same species. He stresses that it is difficult to accept that one should do so, because of the prodigious differences among them. He decides that in fact they should be considered as subspecies. At this point in the book he begins to introduce the second topic, sexual selection in the natural and human realms. This juxtaposition of ideas—classification of the races and sexual selection—suggests that Darwin was as reluctant to view the races metaphorically as he was to so view the sexes. Here is a second area in which he dislikes to think of analogies, gradations, similarities, where he introduces instead a procedure to explain differences. His familiar agent of differentiation, sexual selection, makes a second and even more prominent appearance here than in the *Origin*. Darwin provides an excellent locus to study Shulamith Firestone's claim that "racism is sexism extended."[21]

A rather bizarre and apparently gratuitous passage in the *Origin* takes on some meaning in the light of Darwin's difficulty with metaphor in the case of race and sex. It is in his chapter on the importance of descent or family in the establishing of categories (chapter 13) that Darwin remarks specifically on the vast differences between the sexes of species. Having made that remark, he introduces an imaginary interlocutor who asks him how, inasmuch as he emphasizes the importance of descent in classifying, he would classify a species of kangaroo that had been "produced by a long course of modification from a bear." Darwin calls this imaginary objection "preposterous" and states, "I might answer by the *argumentum ad hominem,* and ask what should be done if a perfect kangaroo were seen to come out of the womb of a bear?" Darwin repeats the word "preposterous" in his characterizing of that "reductio ad absurdum."[22] What is all this talk about bears and kangaroos? Who would have made such an objection? What made Darwin think of it? He had just been commenting on the differences between the sexes. Perhaps it seemed as absurd to him that a male should be born of a female as that a kangaroo be born of a bear. We have seen how, in the *Descent,* he shows the same repugnance to identify himself with other races as with the other sex. "The astonishment which I felt on first seeing a party of Fuegians on a wild and broken shore will never be forgotten by me, for the reflection at once broke into my mind—such were our ancestors. . . . For my own part, I would as soon be descended from that heroic little monkey, who braved his dreaded enemy in order to save the life of his keeper" (pp. 618–19). We maintain that the theory of sexual selection was necessary for Darwin in his attempt to arrest the consequences of his own metaphorical procedures, necessary because of his desire not to compare himself with beings (members of the other sex, members of other races) he could not consider his equals and because of his repugnance in contemplating his ancestral ties with them.

Sexism, racism, and reluctance to entertain the possibility of change were part of Darwin's way of viewing the world. They deeply influenced the elaboration of his theory, in fact keeping him from following his own insights to certain of their conclusions that threatened his world view. This retrenchment may have played a part in making his later work less creative than his early work. Instead of pursuing the implications of his theory, he arrested its development at crucial points, attempting to fix history at a given moment and to set the sexes into predetermined roles, the races into discrete categories.

Historians might advise us not to be excessively upset by this character of Darwin's work and urge that we try to understand theories in the context of their times only, not to judge them. Darwin himself, by way of justifying his forays into the extrascientific and the nonverifiable, in the *Descent of Man* claimed that, whereas false facts may be harmful to the progress of science, false views are not. We disagree. It is unfortunate that a scientific justification for sexism and racism can be found in such a creditable source as the father of modern biology. And this father does not lack descendants. A reflection of the same manner of thinking is to be seen in the work of sociobiologists today. "Sociobiology is the study of the biological basis of behavior. It attempts to show that human social institutions and social behavior are the results of biological forces acting through prehuman and human evolution. The theory is based on Darwin's theory of evolution through natural selection, which sociobiologists claim to extend and amplify."[23] Sociobiologists describe human sex roles and behaviors as innate and programmed into the genes. They base these roles and behaviors on examples of social interaction in lower animals, which, not coincidentally, remind us in their turn of the human world: "aggression," "selfishness," "male dominance."[24] In following a procedure like that of Darwin, current sociobiologists tend toward a rigidifying of social structures, as Darwin did. It is therefore important now as always to analyze critically the influence of social and psychological context on the scientific observation of natural phenomena and the generation of scientific theory. Feminists in particular must stand ready to question and to reinterpret applications that are unfavorable to women and to the improvement of women's status in the world.

Chapter 6

A Feminist Challenge to Darwinism:

Antoinette L. B. Blackwell on the Relations

of the Sexes in Nature and Society

MARIE TEDESCO

In 1875 American feminist Antoinette Louisa Brown Blackwell published *The Sexes Throughout Nature* (hereafter cited as *STN*). This book was a product of the nineteenth-century debate on woman's nature. By the 1870s the acute interest in biological science, engendered by the controversy over evolution theory, made the study of woman's nature a subject of scientific inquiry.[1] *STN* disputed the commonly held idea that the laws of evolution caused the female sex to develop as the physical and mental inferior of the male sex. Focusing on the functions of the sexes in animal species, Blackwell endeavored to prove that evolution produced sexes that were equivalent, that is, different yet equal, in mental and physical traits.

This essay investigates Blackwell's work as it emerged from her life experiences and as it related to and departed from contemporary scientific and feminist thinking. The core of the essay focuses on Blackwell's understanding of natural and sexual selection, her ideas on the origin of the sexes' mental traits, and her feminist application of those scientific conceptions.

Blackwell's family circumstances and early life closely resemble those of many other antebellum feminists. These circumstances and experiences contributed to making her a feminist and played a part in her developing interests that surface in *STN*. Antoinette Louisa Brown was born in 1825 in upstate New York. Her parents, descendants of Puritans, were native New Englanders who instilled in her the orthodox values of duty and education. But her parents were not religiously strict until converted to Presbyterianism by Charles G. Finney. The family's conversion greatly affected young Antoinette. Religion became the focus of her life, so much so that by the 1840s she resolved to become a minister.[2]

In 1847 she entered Oberlin College. Her parents' concern for education and the antebellum democratization of education had allowed her to attend a local academy and thus to acquire the academic preparation necessary for her to enter college. The Oberlin experience was crucial. Oberlin was a hotbed of reformism and as such attracted to it various "radicals." It was at Oberlin that Antoinette met Lucy Stone and through her became involved in temperance, abolition, and feminism. These reform activities, particularly the abolitionist and feminist, instilled in Antoinette egalitarian values.[3]

Egalitarianism caused her to question accepted ideas of woman's proper sphere.[4] This questioning became especially important in light of the resistance she encountered at Oberlin to her attempt to enter the male sphere of theology. The Oberlin faculty, after much ado, permitted her to study theology but would not grant her a degree. Subsequently, after leaving Oberlin in 1850, she had difficulty securing a pulpit. Thus, again, her feminist egalitarian values collided with those of the male-controlled religious establishment. Her feminism was strengthened by these experiences, but by the mid-1850s her religious convictions began to waver, and she underwent a severe crisis in faith.[5]

During this crisis Antoinette probably first came into contact with speculative evolutionary theory as proposed by English scientist Herbert Spencer in his 1850s *Quarterly Review* essays. It appears that philosophy helped unsettle her faith and that at the same time she turned to speculative theory as a substitute for religion. Subsequent to the 1850s she broadened her interests to include the positivistic evolution of Charles Darwin. More than likely, she read Darwin's *On the Origin of Species* after its publication in the United States in 1860.[6] She then attempted to reconcile her egalitarianism — particularly as it related to widening woman's spheres of activity — with an evolutionary theory that posited the inherent mental and physical inferiority of woman. The results of her efforts were the essays that make up *STN*.[7]

Comparatively, evolution theory had a greater influence on Antoinette Blackwell than on other feminists of her generation. That evolution theory had such an impact was not surprising. In the 1850s evolutionary speculation was commonplace, most notably in England. Spencer's works, for instance, are good examples of that decade's evolution theory. After 1859 Darwin's theory of natural selection caused a tremendous controversy that was reflected in the scientific and popular presses of the United States and England. Thus during the 1860s and 1870s numerous books and articles aimed at a middle-class audience debated the "evolution question."[8] As an educated middle-class person, Blackwell had access to such publications.

Although Blackwell's book was unique for the 1870s in that it was one of the few full-length works to try to correlate evolution theory with feminism, Blackwell was not alone in using science to support women's rights.[9] Both advocates and opponents of women's rights esteemed science and thought it was the arbiter of truth. Thus both groups looked to science for answers to the question, "What is woman's real nature?" As Blackwell wrote, "It is to the most rigid scientific methods of investigation that we must undoubtedly look for a final and authoritative decision as to woman's legitimate nature and functions."[10]

Blackwell intended that her study provide a new, comprehensive view of female nature. She believed that *STN* contained "the germs of a new scientific estimate of feminine nature, from its earliest dawning . . . up to developed womanhood." She thought her study was necessary because previous research on the topics of the origin and development of female capabilities were, she complained, wholly inadequate and inaccurate.[11]

In particular Blackwell criticized the work of English scientists Herbert Spencer and Charles Darwin. Both men, she said, failed to think deeply and intently on the question of woman's place in nature; consequently they neglected to provide sufficient evidence for their claims of woman's inherent inferiority to man. Spencer, for example, had written three pieces in which he discussed woman's evolution. In *Social Statics* and *Principles of Biology*[12] Spencer analyzed the relations of the sexes in evolution. But, because he became preoccupied with formulating a grand evolutionary scheme that would encompass the evolution of all organisms and institutions, he did not adequately support his claims of woman's inferiority. In his 1873 article, "The Psychology of the Sexes," Spencer clearly set forth his proposition that reproduction retarded the mental development of females, but once again he failed to support his thesis with necessary data.[13]

Blackwell contended that in the *Origin of Species* and *Descent of Man* Darwin was so concerned with settling the question of the origin of all species and the descent of man through the ages that he failed to examine properly both sexes' roles in evolution. Specifically, Darwin did not investigate whether females developed feminine traits that were equivalent to masculine traits.[14]

Blackwell proposed to correct the flaws common to Darwin's and Spencer's works by demonstrating that in all species the sexes were equivalents. "It is the central theory of the present volume that the sexes in each species of beings compared upon the same plane, from the lowest to the highest, are always true equivalents — equals, but not identicals in development and in relative amounts of all normal force."[15]

Three related mechanisms produce equivalence: the working of force, natural selection, and transmission of traits from generation to generation. These mechanisms ensured the equivalence of the functions and traits of the sexes within species and thus guaranteed the survival of species. Throughout the natural world conservation of force and the convertibility of like modes of force guaranteed a perpetual readjustment of the expenditure of force. Therefore, among all species and between the sexes within species equivalence of force was the rule. *"Nature is forced to provide for a balanced expenditure between the sexes of all the greater divisions of force — to maintain not only a differentiated moving equilibrium in each, but also a still wider equilibrium between the two."*[16] As organisms evolved to a more complex state, and hence as the sexes became more complex and divergent in structure and function, the different classes of activities of the sexes balanced one another.

Blackwell's use of force as an explanatory device may seem naive today, but in the nineteenth century it was by no means unusual. Concepts of force and energy were popular in that century, especially after 1847 when Hermann von Helmholtz wrote his famous essay on the conservation of energy. Force thus appears in many scientific works of the day. Spencer, for example, frequently utilized the device in his evolutionary scheme. In the *Descent of Man,* Darwin, too, discussed the expenditure of force by the sexes.[17]

To secure equivalence, however, force worked with natural selection. Blackwell's interpretation of natural selection differed significantly from that posited by Darwin, especially in that her theory included evolution of secondary sexual traits that Darwin attributed to sexual selection. In light of the serious disagreements between Blackwell and Darwin, it is important to know Darwin's ideas on natural and sexual selection.

According to Darwin, in nature there was a constant struggle for existence that resulted from the high rate at which organic beings reproduced. Without the struggle for existence the numbers of plants and animals would increase so tremendously that no country could support them. Beings that survived and procreated, then, had to have some advantage over their rivals.[18] Using the analogy of domestic selection, Darwin asked:

> Can it, then, be thought improbable, seeing that variations useful to man have undoubtedly occurred, that other variations useful in some way to each being in the great and complex battle of life, should sometimes occur in the course of thousands of generations? If such do occur . . . that individuals having any advantage, however slight, over others, could have the best chance of surviving and procreating their kind? On the other hand, we may feel sure that any variation in the least degree injurious would be rigidly destroyed. This preservation of favourable variations and the rejection of injurious variations, I call Natural Selection.[19]

Although natural selection caused the transmutation of species and accounted for most variation, Darwin recognized that many phenomena could not be explained on the basis of natural selection — especially those characters of beauty and ornamentation, which conferred no survival advantage. Darwin thus was led, via the process of elimination, to the theory of sexual selection.[20] Sexual selection depended on the advantage certain individuals had over others of the same sex and species solely in respect to reproduction. The best examples of characters developed by sexual selection, and unconnected with the primary organs of reproduction, included weapons of offense and means of defense used by males to drive away rivals; courage, strength, and pugnacity of males; males' gaudy coloring and various ornaments; and the males' contrivances for producing vocal sounds.[21] Darwin concluded in the *Descent of Man:* "It is clear that these characters are the result of sexual and not of ordinary selection, since unarmed, unornamented or unattractive males would succeed equally well in the battle for life and in leaving a numerous progeny, but for the presence of better endowed males. We may infer that this would be the case because the females, which are unarmed and unornamented, are able to survive and procreate their kind" (p. 570).

Sexual selection depended especially on the will, choice, and rivalry of the individuals of either sex. Thus, Darwin contended: "When we behold two males fighting for the possession of the female, or several male birds displaying their gorgeous plumage, and performing strange antics before an assembled body of females, we cannot doubt that, though led by instinct, they know what they are about, and consciously exert mental and bodily powers" (p. 570). Although Darwin thought the precise manner in which sexual selection operated was uncertain, he thought it uncontestable that among almost all animals there was a struggle between males for possession of the females. In this process the females chose their mates (p. 571).

In summary, Darwin's analysis in the *Descent of Man* of sexual selection and his comparison of it with natural selection are instructive. He emphasized that sexual selection acted in a less rigorous manner than did natural selection, because the latter produced its effects by the life or death at all ages of the more or less successful individuals. While battles among rival males sometimes resulted in the death of the combatants, in general the less successful male simply failed to obtain a female or obtained a less vigorous one. The vanquished male also might leave fewer, weaker, or no offspring (p. 583).

Blackwell's interpretation of natural selection differed noticeably from Darwin's theory. She thought natural selection promoted balance and equivalence throughout the natural world and, in particular, ensured equivalence of the sexes. Equivalence had to be guaranteed from the higher vertebrates and up because there differentiation of structure and function between the sexes became most marked.[22] Differentiation implied some opposition, and thus the maintenance of equivalence between the sexes was mandatory if individuals and species were to survive. Blackwell theorized:

By the survival of the fittest, the nearest approximations to equivalents in the sexes would leave the greatest number of offspring, and those best adapted to survive. The higher the development of the species and the more differentiated in structure and functions, the greater need would there be of a complex opposite polarity of activities in the uniting elements. Therefore natural selection, acting during immense periods of time, would be able to maintain through the survival of the fittest, an approximate equality between the sexes at all stages of their development. It would be a differentiated and mutually adjusted equivalence.[23]

Natural selection also worked on differences in nutritive functions that initially were brought about by the distinction of sex. Divergence of functions and traits and the evolution of sexual modifications to a great extent could be traced to nutritive functions. Blackwell observed that throughout the natural world *"The male never affords direct nutrition to offspring: the female always affords direct nurture to offspring"* (italics in original). Because nutritive functions related specifically to survival, they had to be subject to natural selection.[24]

From the insects through the humans, the demands of nurture caused the sexes to develop different roles and acquire unique traits. In the insects, for example, division of functions was relatively simple and exclusively revolved around reproduction. Female insects provided direct nutrition through laying of eggs, while the equivalent male activity centered on his greater powers of locomotion. Thus females acquired modifications for efficient laying and storing of eggs, whereas the male acquired modifications for locomotion.[25]

As organisms become more complex, division of functions necessarily increased. But the sexes' relations to nutrition logically followed the general development of the species. Blackwell agreed with the English physiologist William Carpenter, who pointed out in *Principles of Comparative Physiology* (1854) that the parents of "higher" animals spent more time supervising and assisting the young. But she contended that roles still would be apportioned along the lines of direct and indirect nurture. Blackwell noted that among the terrestrial carnivora, for example, the female supplied direct nutrition by nursing the young, while the male supplied indirect nutrition by foraging for food. As a consequence of his role the male usually exceeded the female in size and strength. Conversely the female developed a capacity for "maternal love."[26]

With humans the same nutritive distinction held true. The human mother contributed much more toward the sustenance of offspring than did females in any other species. For many months before and after the birth of a child, the mother's system was geared to providing nutritive support for the child. The growth and activity of the child were supplemental to that of the mother. But nature modified the female body so that its frame was small and able to withstand the expense of nurturing.[27]

If the human mother provided direct nurture, then the father, in accordance with "nature's highest law," evolution, was bound to contribute indirect sustenance. For the father this meant providing edible, cooked food for the family. Thus, nature dictated a reassignment of present allocation of domestic functions. Sharing of domestic tasks would allow, Blackwell claimed, what nature demanded: prolonged maternal supervision of offspring.[28]

For Blackwell, then, the one agency for developing all modification was natural selection. Masculine and feminine physical and mental traits evolved solely because of natural selection. In essence, Blackwell contended that there was no such process as sexual selection.

> The evolution of secondary sexual characters developed in the male line, which Mr. Darwin had recognized and followed out extensively, assigning their origin chiefly to sexual selection, we may attribute chiefly to the broader natural selection, *which securing both the survival and the advancement of the fittest, gradually selects secondary or indirect characters which enable average males, equally with average females, to contribute to the general advancement of offspring.*[29]

Here Blackwell made a serious mistake. She confused natural and sexual selection. Her idea that the origin of secondary sexual characters should be attributed chiefly to the "broader natural selection" indicates that she interpreted sexual selection, as Darwin proposed it, as being subsidiary to natural selection. But Darwin made it clear that natural and sexual selection were two different agencies. The former accounted for variations that allowed an animal or plant species to develop and survive, while the latter allowed individuals to procure a reproductive advantage over their rivals of the same sex and species.

In analyzing Blackwell's explanation of sexual selection, it is interesting to note that she did not comment on one of the most controversial aspects of sexual selection, that is, on the role Darwin assigned to the will and choice, especially of the female.[30] In most instances, Darwin said, it was the female who exercised choice of mate. One might have observed that in nineteenth-century American society the roles had been reversed: males exercised choice over females. Was this situation not contrary to the "laws of nature"?

The final mechanism, or agency, Blackwell thought, for ensuring equivalence of the sexes was the transmission and inheritance of traits. Here Blackwell agreed with Darwin's theory that as a rule all characters were transmitted equally to the sexes but that any trait might remain undeveloped in either sex or might be subject to sexual modification. Secondary sexual traits developed only in one sex.[31] What Blackwell really objected to was Darwin's emphasis on the evolution and transmission through sexual selection of male characters and his consequent neglect of equivalent feminine traits. Such treatment, she complained, relegated the female to inferiority throughout nature.

> The facts of Evolution may have been misinterpreted, by giving undue prominence to such as have evolved in the male line; and by overlooking equally essential modifications which have arisen in the diverging female line. . . . average males and females, in every species, always have been approximately equals. . . . the extra size, the greater beauty of color, and wealth of appendages, and the greater physical strength and activity in males, have been in each species mathematically offset in the females by corresponding advantages — such as more highly differenti-

ated structural development; greater rapidity of organic processes; and larger
relative endurance.[32]

Blackwell also attributed to natural selection the evolution of the unique but
equivalent mental qualities of males and females. But at most these qualities
derived from the differentiation of sex, which caused divergence in the nutritive
functions of the sexes. Thus, in animal species the male's role in supplying
indirect nurture made him mentally aggressive and guileful. On the contrary, the
female's maternal role, which demanded that she supply direct nutrition to
offspring, enabled her to acquire an intuitive ability to respond quickly to the
needs of her progeny and, consequently, to all external stimuli. In the human
species these mental qualities evolved into reasoning (indirect method of inquiry) in the male, and intuitive, direct perception (direct method of inquiry) in
the female.[33]

The differentiation of sex had another important effect: it modified the
nervous systems of man and woman. In woman, the necessities of reproduction
caused a greater special development of the nervous system. The female organism was provided with a graduated supply of blood vessels and their closely
attendant nerves. These nerve ganglia, partially automatic in their functioning,
were yet allied to consciousness and hence exerted a profound influence over the
whole sentient nature, elevating or depressing the entire mental activity. This
complex nervous development lacking in the male enabled the female to make
quick, insightful evaluations.[34]

The special evolution of the sexes' nervous systems determined that the brain
also would be modified and that as a result males and females would think and
act differently. "The nervous system is the brain system. Its greater special
development in relation with the reproductive functions would probably involve a
commensurate less development in the brain for women. . . . The mental
development of men and women must . . . be differentiated, as they act through
fundamentally differentiated nervous systems."[35]

Although Blackwell thought the brain occupied a special place because it was
the center from which nerves extended throughout the body, she denied that
mental capacity could be indicated solely by size of brain or cranium. Using
brain size as the index of intelligence, and ignoring the rest of the nervous
system, was the error commonly made by male scientists: "how incredibly
singular, blind and perverse, then, is the dogmatism which has insisted that man's
larger brain, measured by inches in the cranium, must necessarily prove his
mental superiority to Woman."[36]

Of extreme importance was the fact that the distinctive development of the
sexes' nervous systems affects the body's most essential force, nerve force.
Blackwell supposed that nerve force originated in the brain as a chemical force.
This chemical force was transformed into nerve force in the blood and was

accumulated in the organs of the nervous system, where it helped produce equivalent masculine and feminine mental manifestations.[37]

The total of nerve force was equal for the sexes, but, because the female's reproductive demands caused a shifting of nerve force to the reproductive organs, there was a consequent delay of mental development in that sex. Although mental progress was postponed in females, it was not, as Spencer (and others) insisted, arrested because of reproduction. Blackwell contended that just because force might be changed in its sequence of development, force was never lost or destroyed.[38]

Blackwell's views on readjusting and shifting of nerve force within the body, like her previously discussed views of force in the natural world at large, were common in the mid- and late nineteenth century. The Romantic tradition of vitalism remained influential in the United States, England, and on the Continent, despite the opposition of physiologists who attempted to devise a physicalist model of the body. Blackwell's adherence to vitalism (as well as her belief in design) can be seen in her statement: "Nowhere is there higher evidence of Design, and of the existence of a *true sentient force co-operative in every organism*, than in the wondrous instincts of insect-life."[39] Carpenter combined vitalism with conservation of energy, thus formulating a system whereby force within the body could be transferred and readjusted as needed. Blackwell read Carpenter and, because her concepts closely resemble his, it is probable that his work was a source of her theories.

Throughout *STN* Blackwell voiced her opposition not only to scientists' suppositions about the evolution of females' mental abilities and traits but also to their pejorative evaluation of these traits and abilities. Blackwell specifically attacked Darwin and accused him of sanctioning an unfair judgment of woman's mentality. True, the mental characteristics assigned woman by Darwin in the *Descent of Man* were not, from his perspective, admirable. Woman displayed powers of imitation, intuition, and rapid perception, but man had an inventive genius lacking in woman. Man had the ability to reason and possessed keen imaginative powers. Thus he, not woman, attained a high eminence in, for example, literature, science, and the arts.[40]

Despite Darwin's generally low opinion of woman's mentality, his views in this regard were not entirely negative, and in some respects they coincided with Blackwell's estimations. Woman's mental disposition, shaped by her maternal role, was marked by tenderness and altruism. Man's mental disposition, shaped by competition, tended toward ambition and selfishness. These two traits, Darwin lamented, "seem to be his natural and unfortunate birthright."[41]

More importantly, though, Blackwell correctly reasoned that a "Darwinian" perspective unjustly and unscientifically deemed that woman's evolutionary mental development had progressed only to a level above that of the child, but below that of man.

There is a convenient hypothesis that the intellect of the female, among all the higher orders of beings, has acquired a development intermediate between the young of the species and the males, as their women's bodies and brains are intermediate in size. It is a theory closely akin to the time-honored assumption that the male is the normal type of his species; the female the modification to a special end. Also, it is nearly allied to any scheme of Evolution which believes that progress is affected [sic] chiefly through the acquirement and transmission of masculine characters.[42]

The low opinion men held of women's mental abilities encouraged, indeed justified, continued repression of women. But this repression adversely affected not only women but the whole "race," because females were unable to develop beneficial mental traits that they could transmit to future generations.

Feminine [mental] deficiencies, when acquired, are entailed as heirlooms to the sons as to the daughters. Thus has Nature been forced to maintain the average equality of sex. Defrauded womanhood, as unwittingly to herself as to man, has been everywhere avenged for the system of arrogant repression under which she has always been stifled hitherto; the human race, forever retarding its own advancement, because it could not recognize and promote a genuine, broad . . . equilibrium of the sexes.[43]

Yet, despite her contention that the difference of sex produced distinctive organisms with unique physical and mental capabilities and her recognition of feminine mental deficiencies, Blackwell refuted Edward H. Clarke's charges, set forth in *Sex in Education* (1873), that the female mind was unsuited for the kind of education males received and that the female body was too weak to withstand the strain of this education. The female intellect, characterized by its naturally quick insight and perception, was not superficial, Blackwell insisted, but only judged so by males. Moreover, the sharp perception of the female mind did not prevent it from comprehending complex and abstract theory.[44]

The female body, far from being weak, was strong in its capacity to endure pain, especially that associated with childbirth. Blackwell admitted that the female body was delicately balanced and needed respite from mental work in order to prevent the overtaxing of the reproductive system. But the necessity for rest would not make study impossible. Because the female's mental processes operated rapidly, she required few hours of study. Women, denied full access to education, thus had succumbed to mental idleness. Such forced idleness, Blackwell claimed, violated the laws of nature. Nature demanded habitual mental and physical exercise. Only with habitual exercise could a balance be retained between the mental and physical.[45]

In addition to using scientific theory to prove that denying women education contravened the laws of nature, Blackwell recounted her personal experiences to show that physically and mentally women could withstand the rigors of, and benefit from, mental exercise. She pointed out that she had been a student and a teacher and that for many years she had been setting aside three hours a day for mental work. These activities, she stressed, had not debilitated her, nor had they prevented her from marrying and having children.[46]

Theory and personal experience notwithstanding, Blackwell had to explain why in general women had failed to achieve intellectual eminence or to demonstrate a high degree of abstract reasoning. For her the answer was simple: "Fettered by conventionality," as she expressed it, women were not allowed or encouraged to pursue mental activities. It was not surprising, then, that women had not achieved intellectual eminence or developed high powers of abstract reasoning.[47] Anti-feminists and male scientists, she said, too often confused lack of opportunity with lack of ability: "When the vast weight of past social conditions is considered, that women thus far have failed to acquire large powers of abstract thinking . . . affords no reason for supposing that there is a corresponding lack of ability in this direction."[48]

Analysis of Blackwell's application of evolution theory to the development of mental capacity and disposition in the sexes reveals that she linked thought and action to physical development and by so doing advocated a materialist interpretation of human nature and capabilities. The physical fact of sex, for example, molded the mental being of males and females. As Rosalind Rosenberg points out, Blackwell's materialist stance represented an important departure from the eighteenth-century natural rights theory that was still endorsed by feminists in the 1870s.[49]

It is obvious, however, that Blackwell accepted as true many qualities that nineteenth-century observers thought innate to woman and responsible for her mental inferiority to man. For example, Blackwell agreed that woman's emotions impelled her thoughts. This link, the result of woman's maternal function of dealing directly with children, caused her frequently to arrive at more unbalanced judgments and to develop warmer prejudices than did man. But Blackwell contended that the connection between thought and emotion had two positive, uniquely feminine results. First, it permitted woman to make unmediated, perceptive judgments. Second, because woman directed her thoughts and feelings toward others, she thus became selfless and altruistic.[50]

This image of altruistic, self-sacrificing woman was one shared by members of the middle class, both feminists and anti-feminists. To a great extent the image derived from ideas on how woman's maternal instincts controlled her everyday life. Driven by maternal concern, woman sacrificed her interests to those of her family. Or woman displayed her altruism in accepted fashion outside the home by tending the sick or poor. Self-negation and altruism were simply two of a cluster of traits that long had formed the basis for woman's supposed moral superiority to man. By the 1870s, however, these traits came to be attributed to the scientific laws of evolution.

Women's rights activists of the 1870s, members of the first generation of feminists, by and large always had accepted this idealized version of womanhood. From the antebellum period to the post-1865 era, what changed for such feminists as Blackwell was not their view of woman but the basis upon which women's rights should be granted. Abstract right was deemphasized, while women's special needs and capabilities were emphasized. Thus feminists contended, for example, that suffrage should be granted because differences between the sexes made it impossible for men to understand or represent the needs of women.[51]

Evolution theory, as interpreted by Blackwell and subsequently accepted by other feminists, proved advantageous in two respects. It allowed feminists to disavow the idea that woman was a "lesser man" and to champion a scientifically based female superiority. Yet feminists did not, as Rosalind Rosenberg maintains, abandon the effort to maintain the "separate-but-equal-balance" by emphasizing separateness at the expense of equality.[52] From the antebellum period through the end of the nineteenth century, most feminists continued to pursue the contradictory goals of separate-but-equal spheres and equality with man.

To evaluate the influence and success of Blackwell's challenge to Darwinism, her work must be judged separately as a work of science and as a feminist treatise. As a work of science Blackwell's book is weak. It is flawed by a confusion of ideas and approaches. Although Blackwell advocated a materialism that accepted evolution as a valid explanation for the origin of species and variations, she insisted on viewing the natural world as harmoniously balanced because it was created and run by intelligent design. While Blackwell did not support a simple biblical creation, she nonetheless accepted design, nomothetic creation, and a teleology which considered that natural laws worked toward some final purpose.[53]

As a feminist work STN was typical and unusual, successful and unsuccessful. Although Blackwell, showing her continued interest in the spheres question, urged women to break conventional social restraints, and though she decried the oppression that kept women from realizing their mental potential, she, like other feminists, typically upheld the sanctity of the home and was careful to stress that wider spheres for women would not destroy the home.

> Morally certain it is that she will neither forego, nor desire to forego, her domestic relations; nor will the average woman seek to evade an equitable share of the burdens or disabilities or her station, or shrink from sharing honorably all the main duties which arise within the home life. Evolution has given and is still giving to woman an increasing complexity of development which cannot find a legitimate field for the exercise of all its powers within the household. There is a broader, not a

higher, life outside, which she is impelled to enter taking some share also in its responsibilities.[54]

Yet Blackwell's book was unique in a number of ways. For one thing, it presented a dynamic view of evolution. She assumed the continuing evolution of the sexes and linked this evolution to the progress of the "race." In this respect her ideas differed markedly from, especially, social evolutionists who had transformed evolution into a static theory that they used to justify the status quo of Victorian sex-role divisions.[55]

But perhaps the most important facet of Blackwell's book, despite her dangerous advocacy of separate spheres and unique abilities for the sexes, was her attempt to present a "woman-defined" system of values by urging reevaluation of a value system that put positive emphasis only on traits and activities termed "masculine."[56] If feminism can be said to advocate a readjustment of values and eventually a synthesis of what is termed masculine and feminine, then Blackwell's work indeed was a successful feminist one, even by present-day standards.

That Blackwell's book was both a success and a failure can be seen in the consequent acceptance by other feminists of the views she espoused. *STN* alone did not cause feminists to use evolution theory to uphold female superiority. Certainly it is true that because evolution was "in the air," so to speak, and because anti-feminists used it to deny feminists' claim to equality, women's rights activists would find a way to use evolution to their advantage. Yet it is nonetheless true that views later expressed by such feminists as Carrie Chapman Catt, Eliza Burth Gamble, and Charlotte Perkins Gilman strongly resemble those first enunciated by Blackwell.[57]

Yet neither Blackwell nor those who followed her could overwhelm the opposition. Anti-feminist tracts using evolution theory continued to be published and to receive approbation from the American public. Such evolutionary works sanctioned the status quo and perhaps provided comfort in an increasingly changing society. Not until the end of the nineteenth century and the beginning of the twentieth century would there be a reevaluation of the use made of evolution theory. Then the demise of craniology and the rise of Franz Boas's culture concept, with its consequent emphasis on environmentalism, would contend with, for example, the newly founded sciences of genetics and mental testing for reevaluation of woman's evolutionary role.[58]

In the final analysis, Blackwell thought that because women had not left adequate records of their lives the question of woman's nature would be settled by evolutionary physiology. Although today's feminists do not have the same faith in science that characterized Blackwell and her contemporaries, today's scientists surely think they can find the "real answers" to sex differences. In the nineteenth century evolution theory promised to find the irrefutable basis for sex differences. In the latter part of the twentieth century, research into chemical, hormonal, and genetic differences holds out the same promise.[59]

Chapter 7

The Contest between Androgyny and Patriarchy

in the Early Western Tradition

JUDITH OCHSHORN

It is by now part of the current history of women that the revival of feminism in the 1960s affected many of us personally. Its influence also was felt with varying impact in most of our major institutions, among them the fiefdoms of the creators and guardians of knowledge. Their sovereignty was threatened when group after group of women in academic and professional associations, whom they had trained in traditional fashion, separated themselves into women's caucuses, asked questions never before heard in graduate schools, and began to frame answers that might have been predicted once women were granted access to higher education, almost 150 years ago, after their prior exclusion for 500 years.

In response to the omission or trivialization of the serious study of women in virtually every discipline, and with a growing sense of pain and outrage at the sexual and cultural bias that permeates so much of what we had been taught as "fact" — not only distorting interpretations of data but impeaching the reliability of conventional methodologies and therefore even the accuracy of the data — the scholarly arm of the women's movement took shape. At universities, women's studies courses and programs proliferated. In the new research on women, some of the most sacred intellectual cows were exposed as wearing only the emperor's new clothes.

Assumptions were reexamined, new kinds of sources explored, new questions formulated, new data assembled, and the efficacy of an interdisciplinary approach was asserted, all designed to yield new information about women. To many, it became apparent that anything less, which excluded or ignored significant information about half the human race, was open to criticism as at least over-simplistic, at most only partially accurate.

Above all, this scholarly ferment affirmed the power of education to shape our lives by socializing both sexes to gender-appropriate roles, implicitly legitimizing, with all the authority of "expert" knowledge, the various means used by every culture to reward conformity to and punish deviance from these roles. Hence, beyond the usual motives that up to now served to spark innovative research was the conviction of many feminist scholars and teachers that any social change in the direction of a more humane, sexually egalitarian society that might provide expanded options and choices for women as well as men would remain forever impossible so long as the theory and content of our education remained, at base, androcentric.

The last point is crucial. Consider for a moment what usual interpretations of some of the most familiar and finest poetry in English, which we all read at one time or another, conveys about the "nature" of women and men and how new questions asked of this great literature might tell us things quite different from what we all have learned and so neatly internalized.

For example, is *The Taming of the Shrew* really a "comedy"? In what sense is Kate initially a shrew? Does the account of how a witty, intelligent young woman is psychologically manipulated and brutalized into submission to her husband, who is concerned only with dominance over her, end happily or well for Kate? More generally, those of Shakespeare's plays in which women act to change or escape the adverse conditions of their lives often feature them traveling around in drag, achieving true happiness and the fulfillment of their destinies only at the end when they discard their male apparel, abandon their independence (or male behavior), and fall into the arms of their actual or future husbands.[1]

Whose is *The Tragedy of Othello*, the Moor's or Desdemona's? Of course, both; but what does it tell us when we realize that Othello's character is flawed not by jealousy but by his concurrence with Iago's belief that *all* women are shot through with lust; that Othello has some choice over whether or not he is to fall from power; and that Desdemona, in her innocence deprived of choices, and as a sacrificial lamb to her lord's opinions about the nature of all women, dies while protesting her love for her husband and murderer?

Is Marc Antony, as we are told, torn between his love for Cleopatra and his desire for imperial power, while Cleopatra merely consumes herself for love of him? Does Egypt really govern itself while its queen moons and primps? Was it Cleopatra's sexiness alone that prompted three rulers of Rome, in turn, to make pilgrimages to her court, or was it rather that her political ambitions as well as her possession of Caesar's son not only posed a threat to Rome but also that the latter converted rich Egypt, prospering under her reign, as the eastern linchpin of its empire?

Multilingual, the only ruler of the Greek house of Macedon fluent in Egyptian, and far more educated than Antony, Cleopatra dealt with him on the only level he knew, meanwhile keeping in reserve some of her military forces from support of Antony's aspirations. In fact, Octavian declared war only on Cleopatra, not Marc Antony, and like a true Hellenistic queen she led her fleet into combat.[2] Until recently, who would presume even to think in such terms about the beauty of Shakespeare's plays or the wisdom of Aristotle's theories?

To be sure, this woman-centered stance did not originate twenty years ago. One has only to remember the arguments of Mary Wollstonecraft, Sarah Grimke, Elizabeth Cady Stanton, Charlotte Perkins Gilman, Virginia Woolf,

Mary Beard, Simone de Beauvoir, and others, whose brilliant insights contributed so substantively to the present climate of thought.[3] However, the large difference between their experiences and our own seems to lie in their essential marginality as thinkers and women, many of them moving in their work and lives at the outer edges of consciousness of most of their contemporaries. Today, the radical challenge in every field to how we know and what we know has been broad and deep.

To feminist historians it has become clear that a denial of knowledge about our past conveys a potent message, namely that women (or any other group) left out of history obviously did not contribute to it in any significant ways, and this message functions as a potent mechanism of oppression. By the early 1960s this notion had become so commonplace that even as sedate a body as President Kennedy's Commission on the Status of Women, in its widely disseminated report, concluded that American women exhibited the characteristics of a minority group, in part because they had no sense of their own history.[4] The close link between the present social position of women and the new scholarship of women's history is apparent in Joan Kelly-Gadol's definition of the dual aims of the latter, "to restore women to history, and to restore our history to women."[5] Historical amnesia not only dooms us as a sex to reinvent the wheel in a personal sense each time we opt for nontraditional roles but more basically it ties us to our own culture's vision of our "nature" simply because we lack any other.

Hence, for more than a decade much energy has been poured into recovering and redefining the obscured history of women, with a view toward nourishing the impoverished historical record by rendering it more inclusive and accurate. Coincident with (but not quite identical to) the accelerating interest in social history, oral history, family history, and the like, all of which have moved us away from an exclusive concentration on the relationships and confrontations of powerful male elites, historians of women have produced some breathtakingly original work.

In the field of American history, some use new kinds of sources, for example, diaries and letters by women,[6] or hitherto uninvestigated public documents,[7] or contemporary literature written by and about women.[8] Others break with traditional methodology altogether and use daringly new conceptual approaches. For example, Gerda Lerner abandons political and military chronology as irrelevant to the female experience in America. In her edition of writings by different classes and kinds of women, Lerner leaps back and forth in time, organizing their voices around the female life cycle, the entry of women into male-dominant institutions, and the efforts of women to create new images and roles for themselves in their passage toward autonomy.[9]

Still others maintain, along with Lerner, that although women have suffered from patriarchal constraints they hardly have been only passive victims. Just as Lerner contends that women lived and functioned within these constraints "on their own terms," so Carroll Smith-Rosenberg demonstrates how nineteenth-century, white, middle-class American women developed a feminine subculture, highly satisfying to their personal, affectional needs and at times astutely political, even morally autonomous in its organizational manifestations.[10] Nancy F. Cott shows how these same women both embraced and transformed the limitations of normative feminine passionlessness in order to suit best their own interests and enhance their claims to full personhood.[11] By now, so much of real value already has appeared that it was possible recently to publish a collection of what have come to be regarded as "classics" of the current research on women.[12]

Much of this work has been paralleled by equally original research on European women, on women in other cultures, and on women who lived in distant times and places. Conventional periodization and theories of social change have been found wanting. There is convincing evidence that periods that saw dramatic transformations in Western civilization were vastly different, even opposite, for women and men.[13] While some of the new research reveals that in some cultures certain classes of women played a more important role than has hitherto been acknowledged, other cross-cultural data seem to indicate the opposite.[14] However, what ties together the new research on women's history is the belief that gender must be added to all of the other basic categories of historical analysis if we are to understand our past. Thus, data on female sexuality and reproduction, familial relationships and the socialization process, the work done by women and men and the value placed on it, all have come to be seen as windows on the past.[15]

Not unsurprisingly, simultaneous with specific, microhistorical research has been an ongoing concern for the development of a comprehensive and coherent theory that will permit all of this new knowledge about women to be incorporated into a more accurate and meaningful human history.[16] That effort is what I would like to discuss here, for as valuable as the new data and insights are, they are like pieces of a puzzle that eventually will have to find their place and pattern.

There is hardly a monolithic consensus among feminist historians about the dynamics of social change. Despite differences among them in their assessments of the actual status or power of different classes of women in various societies, and whether or not the establishment of partriarchy is seen as an outgrowth of the possession of private property and the sharpening of class divisions, as Friedrich Engels conjectured, it would appear that the "given" for many feminist scholars is that ultimately, whatever degree of independence or influence groups of women might have enjoyed, for most of recorded history it was only temporary and finally ephemeral. Women either could not or would not assume leadership, even when that seemed a real possibility for them (e.g., during the late Middle Ages in Western Europe); or, in very early times, women were thrust from preeminence to a subordinate position by men, who came to hold political and military power as society underwent basic structural modifications in the development of a centralized state; or, later, families and women within them suffered a diminution of power as more specialized, extrafamilial institutions evolved and supplanted their public functions; or, women have always been consigned, in a "nonnecessary" but nevertheless universal manner, to the inferior domestic sphere, in an assignment of value by all cultures to "nature" along sexual lines.[17]

Certainly, much of the domestic assignment is congruent with the physical and mental anguish suffered by a number of great and therefore deviant women like the Abbess Heloise, Margery Kemp, Joan of Arc, Teresa of Avila, and, much more recently, Florence Nightingale, Charlotte Perkins Gilman, Virginia Woolf, and Sylvia Plath, enabling us to measure the price paid, in one way or another, by those women who exercised their mighty talents in the public sphere.[18] However, it should be remarked that all of these women lived in fairly recent times when patriarchal values were either ascendant or consolidated.

Another point of view accepts the importance for the history of women of the separation of the public from the private sphere and incorporates it into Engels's analysis of the subordination of women as the result of acquisition of private property by men, the movement of men into the public sphere to work for profit while women remained in the domestic one, and the development and sharpening of class divisions whereby some men and all women became the property of more affluent males. Conversely, it is held, in subsistence economies where the public and private areas of production were fairly merged, property was communally owned, and the social structure was relatively classless, it is most likely that the status of women was high.[19]

All of these theories seem to be predicated on the assumption that either a patriarchal system always has existed in every culture, or that it emerged at a very early or unsophisticated stage of civilization, extremely different in most ways from our own, or that the social roles of women more than men were circumscribed by their family affiliations.

Useful as these theories are for conceptualizing attitudes toward women or determining the parameters of their existence for the past several hundred years in Western societies, they fall short in explaining many of the representations of femininity in the early Western religious and literary traditions, as well as much of what we are able to reconstruct about women's lives in those early times. Specifically, these theories fail to account for the following:

1. There was an enduring religious tradition, lasting from about the third through the first millennium B.C.E. (Before Christian Era) across polytheistic cultures in the religion-dominated societies of the ancient Near East, characterized by an outlook that can be identified as androgynous — that is, it was marked most fundamentally by a cluster of beliefs that did not ignore the differences between the sexes so much as it regarded them as of lesser significance than the satisfaction of community and, later, personal needs for an

abundant food supply, victory in battle, protection from natural or social disasters, assurance of the possibility of immortality, and the like.[20]

2. There is a long literary tradition, lasting from the late Bronze Age in the ancient Near East up to the late Middle Ages in northern and western Europe, which, in its portrayal of powerful or independent women of various classes who functioned as did men in the public sphere of their own times, is significantly different in content and effect from what we normally associate with patriarchal images of the feminine.

3. During this same long period, at different times and places, there are records of women who engaged in nondomestic occupations and played conspicuously public roles, both in those cultures marked by a clear division between the domestic and public arenas, and typified by the accumulation of private property and the presence of class differentiation, and in those cultures marked by their absence. These women did not live and function "on their own terms" within a male-defined culture, nor did they develop a feminine subculture to meet their needs within patriarchal constraints (as was true of middle-class women in much later times). Rather, they helped to shape the culture, as did men, and exhibited a high level and wide scope of activity within many of the same areas of the public sphere that engaged the activities of men.

Therefore, those theories noted above that attempt to incorporate the new data on women into their framework simply do not suffice for earlier times, important as they are for later periods and fundamental as the political and social consequences have been of the distribution of wealth by class and sex.

I would like to propose an alternative working hypothesis. Though Western patriarchy as a value system and an institutional/legal structure began to emerge fairly early, probably by the second millennium B.C.E. in some parts of Mesopotamia, the course of its evolution was very long, complex, and difficult. Fluctuating through periods of ascendance and decline, for about three millennia patriarchy coexisted and conflicted with and finally suppressed and replaced another more androgynous world view and, we yet may find, at times a more sexually egalitarian type of social structure. (There are suggestions of the last, for example, in fourth-millennium Sumer and in second-millennium Elam and Egypt, at least among the upper classes.)[21]

When and where that androgynous view held sway, it legitimized the possession of power and influence by persons of both sexes. Therefore, women prominent in the public sphere were not considered deviant, nor did they so consider themselves. This attitude was reflected in the literature, though obviously there are all kinds of disjunctions between the visions of art and social reality, and, though the two are inextricably linked, neither one can or should be collapsed into the other.

Also, it goes without saying that definitions of the private and public sphere vary from culture to culture. At times the two seem confused, as in the tenth and eleventh centuries in western Europe. However, in most societies there were aspects of community life that encompassed activities most highly valued in their own time and place, participation in which was linked with the exercise of power or the accoutrements of prestige. These activities were critical to the creation and maintenance of the culture that most centrally distinguished those societies — and that is the public sphere.

At this point, it seems to me that patriarchy did not come to prevail in western Europe, in either the public or private sphere, until the late Middle Ages. The anomalies and contradictions in the medieval era perhaps may be understood in part as expressions of the tensions surrounding the contest between patriarchal ideology and practices and those attitudes and customs of a nonpatriarchal nature that persisted, under various guises, until fairly late. The economic, political, and social changes set in motion by the thirteenth century were to help resolve this contest decisively by the time of the high Renaissance and Reformation in the sixteenth century. Both periods proved to be far more expansive and liberating for men than for women, and both, probably not fortuitously, coincided in time with the peak of the witchcraft mania directed against women and the pitiful remnant of their prestige and power in community life.[22]

Due to constraints of space, this hypothesis can be dealt with here only by way of illustration, suggestively rather than comprehensively, and much more detailed research remains to be done in order to test its validity and, if I read the historical record right, its possible implications. With these caveats, let us turn first to some examples from literature and then compare part of what we know about women's lives in those early times with a paradigm of patriarchy.

Like most of the secular literature dating from the late Bronze Age on, the Homeric epics are replete with ambiguities about women. To be sure, there are instances of even princesses and prophets like Cassandra routinely taken by men as the spoils of war, and Odysseus' Penelope personifies the docile female side of a double sexual standard. But there are also portraits of strong, independent royal women — Hecuba who ransoms her sons, Andromache's mother who is designated by title as a ruler, Nausicaa who appeals to her mother the queen rather than her father to determine the fate of Odysseus.

In addition, there are some explanations of the origins of the Trojan War that see beneath the expansionist designs of the Argive host the need for Menelaus to recover his wife Helen in order to retain his right to the throne of Sparta. It must be remembered that Menelaus became king only as the husband of Helen in a matrilocal, matrilineal marriage, consummated while her brothers still lived. (Interestingly, this mythic motif of the male leader who is compelled to redeem his bride in order to rule is found also in the Ugaritic *Epic of Kret* and in the biblical story of Abraham — Gen. 12:10 – 20 and 20:1 – 18.)[23]

The scene on the walls of Troy, often referred to as a model of domestic felicity — Andromache, cradling their baby in her arms while she bids a tearful farewell to Hector as he leaves for his last battle with Achilles (*Iliad*, bk. 6, 11. 409–96 University of Chicago Press, 1951, pp. 164–66)—is altered somewhat when we learn that part of their conversation in the original version consisted of military advice given to Hector by Andromache, lines excised by later translators who apparently believed that women could not or should not know about such matters.[24] Because Troy was a warrior-society, it seems significant that Hector did not think it strange that his wife should have knowledge of military matters or should advise him.

When classical Greek dramatists refashioned the Homeric material, again there are representations of powerful women, shown as perhaps even more autonomous than their foremothers. For example, though Medea's awesome magic derives from her alien place of origin, it is curious that, on the whole, the Greek chorus is sympathetic with her fury over Jason's behavior. Even her horrible murders literally are removed from the jurisdiction of the community by the fantastic ending of the play when she is simply carried off.[25]

In *Agamemnon*, Queen Klaitemnestra defiantly confronts the chorus alone after she murders her husband upon that hero-king's return from Troy. She autonomously establishes a moral code for the community by identifying her murder as just retribution for Agamemnon's sacrifice of their daughter to further the aims of male militarism, thereby assserting the primacy of the mother-daughter relationship over the marital bond and, in passing, defending her sister Helen from calumny. She even decrees a final and most awful punishment for Agamemnon, namely that on his arrival in the world of the dead he shall be greeted first and embraced by the daughter he killed, Iphigeneia.[26]

Antigone also autonomously asserts her right to fulfill her religious obligations to her dead brothers, placing those obligations above her future status as a royal wife even in the face of the life-threatening prerogatives and force of the male-dominated state. In choosing to act publicly according to her own moral standards, and in accepting full responsibility for her choice, she symbolically brings that state to its knees by her own death.[27]

There are several things worth mentioning about these female protagonists. All act very much in the public sphere in defiance of community standards, sometimes accusing the community of moral hypocrisy as does Klaitemnestra when she insists on her own notions of what is just and right. The portrayals of their moral autonomy, involving the community in the consequences of their decisions and choices, coincided roughly with the period of time in which great philosophers also were concerning themselves in part with ethical issues and with setting norms for social and familial behavior.

Given the large audiences that regularly attended the performance of these plays, it is a bit difficult to imagine as totally foreign to the mentality of those times the depictions of women who behaved with such authority, who not only publicly expressed but also acted on their anger, sense of moral outrage, and responsibility. And all of these qualities were balanced against the heroism, military prowess, or aims of their consorts. In a very real sense, then, these dramas were publicly voicing alternative conceptions of appropriate feminine behavior to those found in most of the writings of Plato and, later, Aristotle.

Furthermore, if the literary tradition that included these strong women was confined to only a few hundred years of Greek history, one might look for local circumstances to explain it. However, in the literature that spanned about 2,000 years and was to originate in western and northern Europe as well as in the ancient Near East, the multiplicity of accounts of women as well as men who were prominent in the public sphere tells quite another story. And their descriptions of active, powerful, independent women present an image of the feminine at considerable variance with patriarchal ideals.

For instance, the literary acceptance of the importance of the feminine as well as the masculine may be found in sources as diverse as the Nag Hammadi texts, including those recovered from the Christian gnostics; the Icelandic sagas that depicted powerful females as well as males; and the *Nibelungenlied*, which pits strong, heroic men against strong, heroic women like Queen Brunhild, and in which the initially passive Criemhild finally matures when she gains the last victory over the assassins of her hero-husband. She becomes, in fact, a fitting consort for Attilla.[28]

If this literary tradition included accounts of only upper-class or royal women, something might be made of that. But the many-faceted late Middle Ages, which produced both the theological "proof" of women's inferiority by Saint Thomas Aquinas and the female paragon of patriarchy, the patient, suffering, passive Griselda, was to produce simultaneously a body of tales that described lower-class women, who refused to leave the taverns where they congregated to cook dinners for their husbands (in turn shown as henpecked) and who returned the verbal and physical assaults inflicted by their mates in kind — in other words, the medieval version of the shrew.[29] And Chaucer's tale of the wife of Bath permits us to see the world through the eyes of a well-traveled, shrewd businesswoman, who certainly did not suffer sexually from a double standard and who knew well that

> . . . if women had but written stories
> Like those the clergy keep in oratories,
> More had been written of man's wickedness
> Than all the sons of Adam could redress.[30]

Even sharper divergence from the gender-based requirements of a patriarchal system may be seen in the roles of various groups of women in different societies during this long period. Thus, it would seem that the close involvement of women as well as men in some of the central concerns of community life, described in part of the literature, might not have represented mere fantasy, or that it reflected something other than projections of male fears of powerful women (Philip Slater's Freudianism notwithstanding).[31] On the contrary, it appeared to express a countervailing, androgynous outlook that contested with patriarchal ideology.

This outlook is attested in a fairly wide range of female activities. As different from patriarchy, which supports political rule only by men, there are scattered instances of female sovereigns dating back to the second millennium B.C.E. — for example, Hatshepsut, pharoah of Egypt for several decades during the Middle Kingdom. About half the time she is pictured as male, even with a beard. However, this depiction probably had more to do with the Egyptian conception of kingship, or the belief that the pharoah was the god Horus incarnate who at his death became Osiris, rather than with any absolute proscription of female rule, for Hatshepsut was followed more than a millennium later by Cleopatra, who ruled Egypt in her own name.

In Greece there is a record of strong Hellenistic queens from the house of Macedon. Before the common era in Britain and Gaul women along with men helped to adminster their tribes, sometimes acted as military or civilian judges, shared in communal decision making, and are said to have negotiated settlements of disputes between Hannibal's troops and their own tribes when he crossed Aquitaine.[32] Later, as part of their "domestic" duties, Carolingian queens administered the imperial domain. Two generations after the time of Charlemagne, Hincmar of Rheims gave the queen, assisted by the chamberlain, control over the royal treasury because her husband had to govern the whole kingdom and could not take the time to deal with such petty matters.[33]

Indeed, in the tenth and eleventh centuries in western Europe, the public power of women from wealthy families is well documented. As Suzanne Wemple and Jo Ann McNamara document, during the Carolingian period women gained the right to own land and took on a variety of powerful roles in the public and private spheres, including jurisdiction over the administration of justice, the administration of the royal treasury, participation in secular and ecclesiastical assemblies, and the like.[34]

It has been maintained by some that women could exercise such power then because the private and public spheres were so indistinguishable. Because women could inherit land and bring it to their marriages, their power within their families carried over into the public sphere. Nevertheless, it should be pointed out that the same was also true for men of powerful families. Likewise, beginning by about the twelfth century, when the power of great families began to be diminished by the growing centralization of power within the Church and state, thus curtailing the public influence of women, this process also affected many of the men within these great families as well.

In other words, it is not as if only women but not men of the upper class suffered a constriction of power. At first, women and many men of the upper class endured a similar fate. Indeed, it was only by the end of the Middle Ages, with the institutional strengthening of patriarchy, that distinctions based on gender hardened and that men rather than women of the middle and upper classes came to dominate public life.

Yet even this change proceeded unevenly. As late as the sixteenth century in Norway, the historical model for Henrik Ibsen's *Lady Inger of Ostrat*, Fru Inger Ottisdatter Gyldenlove, was the wealthiest and most powerful person in her country.[35] And the achievements of Elizabeth I of England were so outstanding in so many areas that well into the twentieth century reputable historians were attributing her greatness either to her wonderful male advisers or to the fact that she was really a man, which explained why she went bald and never married.

According to the values of patriarchy, men dominate religious life and cult. However, apart from the solid evidence for the participation of women as well as men in virtually every aspect of near Eastern polytheistic cult for three thousand years prior to the birth of Jesus, for much of the first millennium C.E. (Christian Era), in the Near East as well as in western Europe, persons of both sexes were actively involved, some in leadership roles, in a number of the non-Christian as well as Christian gnostic sects until they were effectively suppressed by the Church.[36] In Britain and Gaul, women and men held religious offices.[37] Women as witches played a large role in popular religion. In the late twelfth-century southern France one of the "heresies" of the first target of the Dominican Inquisition, the Cathars, was its attitude toward women in leadership roles. And this Christian "heresy" of female independence and leadership was to surface again in seventeenth-century dissident Protestant sects, mercilessly persecuted by Calvinists and Lutherans alike.[38]

In addition to the cultic prominence of women in polytheistic cultures and heretical enclaves in western Europe from the fifth to the twelfth centuries, there was a long tradition of powerful, highly educated, independent lady abbesses. They came from royal and noble houses that dowered and enriched the Church even as some of their female members, as abbesses, administered large estates and double monasteries, not infrequently subsuming male ecclesiastics under their jurisdiction in exchange for their offering of the sacraments. In Britain, France, and Germany, these abbesses variously encouraged and consolidated Church power, held fiefs directly from the king, fielded armies, excommunicated, sat in the German Diet, wrote tragedies in the classical manner, compiled highly artistic and erudite encyclopedias containing the most current knowledge for the education of their female students, and corresponded with emperors and popes.[39]

More than that, they often dressed in gorgeous-colored silks, took no vows of poverty, chastity, or obedience, and enjoyed a measure of personal sexual freedom that was to compare favorably with that of upper-class women in succeeding centuries who experienced a considerable restriction of those liberties. A glimpse of the lifestyle open to them is revealed in part of a letter by a friend of many "cloistered" upper-class women, Saint Boniface, when he wrote to Cuthbert of Canterbury in disapproval of continental travel for women in general and Anglo-Saxon nuns in particular. The heart of his objection lay in the sexually free life led by monastic women.[40]

These options for women, even for those in the Church, continued for centuries after the early church fathers stigmatized women as inferior in the body, valuable only for their reproductive abilities, and capable of achieving spirituality only through celibacy. Or these options coexisted with an expression of tremendous ambivalence toward women, characterized largely by a contempt for femininity in the flesh and an abstract adulation of femininity in the form of Mary.[41]

Again, as different from the patriarchal order in which all, or most, positions of prestige and power are monopolized by men, we read of many women who not only shared in the governance of their people but also were publicly visible in the many areas usually associated with male predominance — war, politics, culture, economic life. Examples up to the late Middle Ages are so numerous that only a few can be cited here.

There is a long history of women closely involved in military campaigns. Leaving aside the military exploits of Deborah and Jael recounted in the Old Testament, and what may or may not be the products of male fantasies and fears in the many tales of Amazon warriors in the ancient Near East, the example of Teutonic women who rode to war with their husbands, marveled at by Tacitus for their size and strength, is especially significant inasmuch as wars were not merely incidental but basic to the Teutonic way of life.[42]

In western Europe during the late Middle Ages, the baron's wife managed the economy of the manor and militarily defended it while her husband was off on the Crusades, sometimes for years.[43] Joan of Arc not only heard voices but also led the dauphin's troops to victory. In Renaissance Italy, Caterina Sforza militarily defended her family's holdings, Forli, against even Cesare Borgia, and for this behavior earned the accolades of her compatriots. She was praised by them as the "prima donna d'Italia" and a "virago," then a complimentary term used to designate the woman who had the mind and courage of a man (note that the standard for excellence was male by then).[44]

At different times and places in this 2,000-year period, there were few areas of public life in which women did not either distinguish themselves or move with relative ease. Quite early, during the Archaic Age in Greece, there were widely known and admired female lyric poets who flourished in non-Athenian parts of the country, nine of whom were later thought the finest of their own time. Of that group, Sappho was probably the greatest and is undoubtedly the most familiar to us.[45] Later, the *hetairai* were the intellectual and sexual companions of some of the leading men of Athens as their wives never were. Some maintain that a number of them cofounded important schools of philosophy — for example, Stoicism and Epicureanism — and delivered public lectures to women and men. Whether all of this influence indeed existed is still disputed. However, at a time when learning was most highly valued, it is clear that some of the *hetairai* were well educated and involved in the intellectual life of Athens. During the period of the Roman Empire, under Greek tutelage, what upper-class Roman women knew and publicly displayed may be gauged by the virulence of Juvenal's attack on educated women in his sixth Satire. Some Roman matrons were orators and poets, some presided over literary salons.[46]

With the revival of classical culture during the Italian Renaissance, the *hetairai* tradition was resurrected. From his Victorian perspective, Jakob Burckhardt refers to them as courtesans, indeed discusses them in virtually the same breath as street prostitutes, and attributes their talents and taste in art to the desire to please their cultured male companions; they seemed to rival in wealth, lifestyle, and patronage of the arts the well-educated noblewomen of Italy.[47]

Furthermore, the female humanists, scholars, and painters of the Renaissance — Marguerite of Navarre, Fulvia Morata Olympia, Cassandra Fedele, Sofinisba d'Anguiscola, Artemesia Gentileschi, to name but a few — all worked in the public sphere of learning and the arts most highly valued in their own time. By then, if they represented a model far more sexually deviant than their more numerous male contemporaries, it may be that their presence at all in the male-dominated universe of the Renaissance is evidence of an earlier and other precedent.

If the murder and destruction of the works of the reputedly great Alexandrian scholar, Hypatia, by early Christian zealots have forever deprived us of her thought, some centuries later, it apparently was not considered too extraordinary in medieval Paris for the merchant-class uncle of a gifted young woman, Heloise, to hire as her tutor the most celebrated and controversial church scholar, Abelard. And that these were not merely isolated instances of a few women who were privileged to receive an education (and of course the vast majority of women and men were then uneducated), it must be recollected that women helped create the courtly love literature, a major genre of that era.[48]

Another touchstone of patriarchy is that men own the land or wealth, and the economic dependence of women is reflected in their lack of political or civic rights. There is a long history of exceptions to this rule. By the fourth century B.C.E., Spartan women owned two-fifths of the land outright. Likewise, under the conditions of war in Imperial Rome, and in the contest between the male heads of great families and the growing, centralized state, upper-class Roman women were in large measure to gain control over their wealth.[49] In neither instance was political power a concomitant of independent possession of land and wealth.

Moreover, inheritance did not pass exclusively through the male line, from fathers to sons or to husbands of their daughters. Both the sixth-century Burgundian laws and the fifth- and sixth-century Visigothic code permitted daughters as well as sons to inherit land.[50] There were many informal but binding provisions for daughters to inherit fixed property in the absence of sons, even after the first Salic law in France denied women the right to inherit land. The twelfth-century Scandinavian *Eddas* describe the right of women as well as men to inherit land. In thirteenth-century Spain both sexes were treated equally in matters of inheritance. And in that same century in Germany legal agreements could be drawn up between husbands and wives so that either survivor of a spouse's death could inherit from the other.[51] Thus, it was possible for Eleanor of Aquitaine to bring more property into her first marriage to the king of France than he already ruled over, and upon their divorce the duchy of Aquitaine was returned to her.

Perhaps nowhere was the nonpatriarchal model so striking as in the areas of trade and commerce after the commercial expansion of the thirteenth century and in the wake of the Black Death and the famines of the fourteenth century that produced a critical need for labor. Irrespective of their marital status, women in London were to be found working in a wide variety of trades usually thought of as male, for example, as armorers and shipwrights. When they married, women often worked so closely in business with their husbands that upon the death of the latter the wives could inherit all of it, including apprentices. Though married, women also could work as "femmes soles," which meant they could work at trades different from those of their husbands, could keep their profits, and were held solely responsible for contractual obligations and debts, as though they were single. In addition, women entered many guilds and even dominated some.[52]

Thus, the evidence seems incontrovertible that, at least in medieval London (and much of this activity was replicated elsewhere), women traders played a prominent and often independent role in that city's industrial life. In fact, in fourteenth-century Genoa the wives of artisans led a far freer life than Genoese noblewomen. The former tended to marry later, have fewer children, frequently earned the respect of their husbands by their economic contributions to the family business, and when widowed escaped the pressures exerted by an extended family and, unlike their noble counterparts, were more able to determine independently their own futures.[53]

The patriarchal view assumes that husbands are entitled to several wives, concubines, mistresses, or access to prostitutes, while wives are sexually restricted to premarital chastity, marital fidelity, and monogamy. Beyond the hard evidence from some ancient Near Eastern cultures that indicates the lack of a double sexual standard at least in religious life, these older, egalitarian attitudes toward sexuality seem to have persisted for some time in parts of western

Europe.[54] The patriarchal distinctions drawn between "good" and "bad" women on the basis of their sexual behavior, while no such distinctions were applied to men, may have developed fairly late.

Well into the first millennium C.E. among the polytheistic tribes of Scandinavia, Germany, and Gaul, while the commission of adultery by women was severely punished, it also was discouraged for men. For example, among the Burgundians of the sixth century the following law prevailed: "If adulterers are discovered, let the man and the woman be killed."[55]

Furthermore, the long practice of witchcraft in western Europe was in many ways extrafamilial, and its attitudes toward female sexuality were certainly nonpatriarchal. Witchcraft was engaged in largely by women who were believed to possess magical powers needed to sustain the agricultural economy and to ward off all kinds of personal and social disasters, and witches often lived apart from their communities. Until the fifteenth century, the Church held to its position that the practice of witchcraft was largely "illusory."[56] However, by the fourteenth century the economic and social dislocations and turmoil caused by the Hundred Years' War, the Black Plague and its attendant famines, and the complicity of the Church in maintaining the feudal status quo even as it became more secularized and corrupt, all contributed to the transformation of the witches' Sabbaths into the more explicitly anti-Christian Black Masses.

It was perhaps especially in the Black Masses that the patriarchal insistence on female chastity and fidelity was most openly flouted. The body of the witch served as the demonic altar after she sexually committed herself to Satan. With the Church's prohibition of marriage by cousins within the fifth degree of consanguinity, among the many other functions served by the Black Mass, it provided an opportunity for related rural women and men of the same or neighboring villages, who otherwise might have married, to express their affection for each other sexually. And it was believed that pregnancies did not ensue, which of course enhanced the power of the witch.[57]

That most witches were women, that they were made scapegoats for the enormous social, political, economic, and religious convulsions that were to change the face of Europe by the end of the sixteenth century, and that the accusations hurled at them were at bottom sexual in nature, all are really not too surprising given the fact that patriarchy was by then becoming firmly entrenched in every aspect of Western society, beginning with the nuclear family.[58]

Moreover, for hundreds of years marriage was not a sacrament for most people in Europe, especially for those of the lower classes. Indeed, "clandestine" marriages (as the Church was pleased to call them, though they were by no means secret) began to be outlawed in England, for example, only by the eighteenth century. Such marriages consisted of vows taken by a woman and man to each other, sometimes in the presence of witnesses. They were pronounced illegal but not invalid by Peter Lombard in his formulation of canon law, and they continued well into the sixteenth century in Renaissance Europe until outlawed by the Council of Trent.[59]

And that is just the point. In upper- and middle-class families, marriages most often were contrived not for love (for centuries the legal age for marriage for girls was a scandalous twelve) but for purposes of enhancing the families' fortunes or achieving upward social mobility or contracting political alliances. In those cases it is likely that the patriarchal code of premarital chastity and marital fidelity for women was strictly enforced, and there are many instances of harsher punishments for discovered adultery by women than by men. For example, during the Italian Renaissance it was not uncommon for upper-class women to raise the illegitimate offspring of their husbands along with their own, but we do not read of the reverse.[60]

By way of contrast, among lower-class Europeans (i.e., most of the people), where "clandestine" marriages were entered into for reasons other than material or political gain, it is most likely that familial restrictions on female sexuality were far less rigid. In some peasant communities, even until quite recently, the bearing of an illegitimate child by an unmarried young woman was not always considered an insuperable obstacle to marriage because it demonstrated her fertility, and premarital sex often served just that purpose. As late as the nineteenth century in England and France, urban working-class people, who had migrated from the countryside to find industrial employment, held far less judgmental opinions about female sexuality than did middle-class moralists. Women in their own communities who were forced into occasional prostitution because of financial need, or who lived with men in the absence of their husbands or the fathers of their children, were viewed rather neutrally.[61]

Hence, even the power of the patriarchal moral code over women's lives for much of Western history apparently was very much a function of class. As we move into the early modern period, along with enlarging patriarchal constraints imposed on women's sexual behavior in middle- and upper-class marital relationships, older, more egalitarian attitudes toward sexuality abided among some of the lower classes.

Finally, Western patriarchal ideology sees women as the property of their fathers and husbands and values them mostly as reproducers, especially of sons, even as their sexuality is viewed as dangerous to men. But this point of view was largely irrelevant to the experiences of *hetairai* in both Greek and Italian renaissances, to women prominent in those Christian sects recurrently suppressed as heretical, to powerful lady abbesses who chose their vocation as an alternative to marriage or who preferred it after having been married, to women who expressed their sexuality freely in Black Masses, to "femmes soles" traders, to unmarried peasant women who had illegitimate children or engaged in premarital sex, to wives in "clandestine" marriages, and to lower-class urban women who found themselves in difficult economic straits.

It was, perhaps, in the control over their own sexuality and reproduction that some women most conspicuously acted in contradiction to patriarchal values. During the Archaic Age in Sparta, it seems likely that husbands not only lent their wives to other men for childbearing purposes (as Athenian writers claimed) but also that married Spartan women also initiated their own love affairs. In any event, Spartan women were not bound to marital fidelity, and by the fourth century B.C.E. their control over their own bodies precipitated a steep decline in the population.[62]

This nonpatriarchal attitude toward female sexuality was to be found later in Imperial Rome, and again it was articulated by women. For a few hundred years the decline in the birthrate among upper-class Romans was met by the state with material inducements to bear children and penalties for childlessness. Despite these official responses, the birthrate remained low, contraception was overwhelmingly practiced by women, and abortions were performed.[63] Centuries later, after the decimation of the European population in the fourteenth century, the low birthrate until the seventeenth-century increase was blamed on woman as witch. But it seems most likely that many nonsupernatural methods were employed by more ordinary women in order to control and limit their reproduction.[64]

What, then, might we conclude from all of the above? Though ideology never fully defines social reality, it would appear that patriarchy alone was not always with us in Western civilization. More certainly, when patriarchy was most influential, its constraints on women were not felt equally at all times or necessarily felt equally by women of different classes at the same time. Moreover, from the late Bronze Age up to the late Middle Ages, the portrayal of a strong, autonomous feminine as well as masculine presence in the literary and religious traditions and the prominence of women as well as men in what their own cultures regarded as the public sphere, with no indication that the women themselves or their own communities regarded them as deviant, all suggest that an outlook more androgynous than our own prevailed in competition with patriarchal ideology.

From the thirteenth century on, despite the persistence of superstitious beliefs, Europe underwent a long and gradual process of secularization and rationalization of institutional structures that saw the slow disentanglement of the divine and secular in everyday life. This process was accompanied by the growth of a cash economy, urbanization, the evolution of a centralized political state, the emergence of a powerful middle class, and the triumph of patriarchy both in the home and in society as a whole. It will not do, I think, to project backward in time the gender-based divisions between the private and public spheres and the class-and gender-based ownership of the means of production and distribution, both so important in more recent history.

In contrast with these later developments, it seems to me that the key to understanding earlier eras is to try to see them through the eyes and experiences of those who lived then, as nearly as we can recreate those experiences, rather than through our own more recent experience with a world view that makes pandemic and fundamental value judgments based on gender. It appears that up to the late Middle Ages the existence of an alternative, androgynous outlook, in coexistence and conflict with patriarchy, was grounded most basically in the central role played by religion in those early cultures — understanding religion through the people's own vision as a primary way of relating to the natural and social universe — and in the kinds of values the religions engendered.

Despite the official adoption of Christianity by Rome in the fourth century, the establishment of convents and monasteries, and the appearance of missionaries in northern Europe, I think conversion was slow, as attested by the long and pragmatic accommodation of Christianity to pagan beliefs and practices. Indeed, if pre-twelfth-century Europe was also "pre-Christian," as noted elsewhere, that is a euphemism for polytheistic.

The conception of divinity as female and male, and the widespread involvement of women as well as men in cult, or the integration of persons of both sexes into the most vital concerns of social life, all might have tended to lessen the overriding importance attached to gender and female sexuality in later, more patriarchal times, subordinating the two concepts to the assurance of community survival in accustomed, nonpatriarchal ways.

If I am right, it is obvious that this hypothesis raises as many questions as it answers. Among them are: Why was patriarchy or the denigration of women more congenial than an androgynous outlook to the economic, political, and social changes ushered in by the Renaissance and Reformation? What did the subordination of women accomplish? Why was it so essential for culture to be defined by men? And what part, if any, did the movement from polytheism to monotheism play in the modernization of Europe and the victory of patriarchal values?

Chapter 8

Against the Grain:

A Working Feminist Art Criticism

SANDRA L. LANGER

Since 1969 conscious women in art have attempted a systematic inquiry into literature of art history as it currently is taught through patriarchal texts in our institutions of learning. Needless to say, the revelations of the 1970s that once were shocking now are common knowledge.[1] Reflection on this problem in the intervening years has led some contemporary art historians and critics to undertake a partial revision of the discipline, while others still maintain the status quo is fine just as it is. My purpose in this essay is to undertake a multilevel analysis of a number of issues that have arisen in this context. The first part of the essay will examine the "woman question" within the confines of a sexist art history created primarily for a white male audience. This step requires an understanding that in traditional art history women's contributions and those of others outside the mainstream are devalued or classified as inferior to those of white males. Here I also will conduct a reexamination of the pertinent literature concerning women in art.[2] I will attempt to summarize representative examples through a survey of these contributions, showing similarities and differences among nineteenth- and twentieth-century art historians, critics, and writers.[3]

The problem of how to carry observations beyond these immediate issues is crucial for theorists, critics, and those making art. Required here is a methodology for the implementation of a revisionist history of art and its criticism. In an attempt to formulate some criteria relative to what I see as an emerging feminist practice in the field of art history, I once posed some fundamental questions that a self-consciously aware feminist revisionist might ask: "What implicit assumptions underlie my definition of a specific art historical problem? How do these influence my choice of method? Can the method I choose affect my conclusions? How does my language affect how my conclusions are read by others?"[4] Essentially the issue is: How can I practice art history and its criticism in such a way as to minimize its service to the continuation of sexist domination? Having roughed out a framework, I now pose the question: Can one practice feminist criticism and, if so, what might such a practice reveal in relation to the traditional practices of art history and criticism? Later in this essay I will attempt to carry this notion several steps further, that is, into the realm of a working feminist criticism. I will examine two well-known visual themes, eroticism and maternity. My aim in so doing is to show not only how female and male artists differ in their interpretations but how language might function in "gynergenic" criticism.[5] It is my intention throughout this discourse to use the term of Mary Daly and Emily Culpepper (*Gyn/Ecology*, p. 12), "gynergy," which I have transformed to "gynergenic," to characterize a working feminist critique. I will use this term interchangeably with "feminist" and "gynocentric." It is hoped that by taking a gynergenic perspective, which I understand to place emphasis on women's perceptions and experiences in our society, and comparing and contrasting it with male consciousness of these same events, some new insights may be gained. My interpretations are not intended as absolute feminist readings of these conceptions; none currently exists (nor would I wish the situation to be otherwise). Finally, I will address the difficulties, possibilities, and implications of such gynergenic criticism. Here again my intent is to offer not a closed system of interpretation but a new beginning.

In the last paragraphs of Kate Chopin's *The Awakening*, the heroine Edna imagines the concert pianist Mademoiselle Reisz laughing and commenting on what a high risk it is to be an artist.[6] This response is exactly what has been required of women artists, revisionist art historians, and feminist critics of our own generation.

Freedom fighters on the art front can look back on twelve years of struggle to free themselves from patriarchal art historians, curators, gallery directors, and arts professionals. "Patriarchal" and "patriarchy" in this context refer to the social system based on father-right that universalizes male experience, institutionalizes the values of that experience in all facets of social life, and presents these social norms based upon power relationships as objective truths. Thus reified, these values are expressed through a system of sanctions that reward upholders and punish transgressors of establishment conventions. The power of originating, of naming, is thus appropriated as a masculine prerogative, and with it comes the power of defining what is good, right, proper, and significant. Evelyn Reed suggests that a woman is defined as a husband's property and is legally bound to sexual fidelity.[7] An analogous situation exists in modern intellectual life. Rooted in the medieval university and for centuries shaped by male definitions of what constitutes legitimate intellectual inquiry, the modern academy unsurprisingly continues to reflect masculine bias. While the intellectual capacity of contemporary women is generally acknowledged, the legitimate exercise of that capacity has been defined and limited to those areas certified as valid by male practitioners of the past. Sanctions are enforced through administrative rules that grant or withhold status on the basis of scholarly criteria.

"Scholarly" in this sense, however, carries both descriptive and commendatory meanings. Applied to a process of methodological investigation as rigorous inquiry and rational ordering of information, it describes fact; but used to direct the proper focus of such activities or judge the significance of their findings, it conveys approval or disapproval of the subject itself as a legitimate object of investigation. Thus would-be feminist critics are discouraged from pursuing this avenue of inquiry. Adrienne Rich sums it up best in "Diving into the Wreck": according to the status quo, women do not have a history. [8]

The attempt to rid ourselves of sexist language, images, values, and aspirations has been and continues to be a daily battle requiring constant application of feminist theory to daily professional practice, whether that practice be art criticism, art education, art history, or the creation of art itself. With the recent publication of six explicitly feminist-inspired histories of women's art, it would seem that art historians and interested others have been particularly successful in pressing the cause of feminism in the visual arts. In this context, my purpose here is to explore this apparent praxis through a critical examination of this literature. [9]

In her essay "Why Have There Been No Great Women Artists?" Linda Nochlin predicted contemporary feminists would take one of two lines of argument in responding to the question. [10] The first would be the defensive assertion that, indeed, there had been great women artists but that they had been somehow excluded from art history by sexist male art historians. Having "swallowed the bait," as Nochlin puts it, these outraged defenders are then stuck with ferreting out the great women artists of the past, using their traditional patriarchal standards of value to justify their selection, thus perpetuating the form of the initial oppression they wish to combat. The second possibility lay in the suggestion of a different standard of measure to evaluate the work of women artists of the past, a position premised upon the existence of a discernible "feminine sensibility." Many women artists and a number of art historians and critics have explored this corridor of discovery; thus we have seen a proliferation of essays and art dealing with the search for female rootedness.

While the accuracy of this prediction is amply borne out by contemporary literature on the subject, I cannot help but be struck by a certain sense of déjà vu when I find variations on the same themes pursued by Elizabeth Freis Lummis Ellet, Clara Erskine Clement, and Walter Shaw Sparrow. [11] No doubt it will be suggested that there is an inherent flaw in any attempt to compare apples and oranges. The works discussed in my previous articles and summarized here are written on different levels and aimed at different publics; they vary greatly as do both the scope and depth of their enterprise, and in a very real sense the only thing they ultimtely share is their subject matter. Nevertheless, it has been my contention in this discourse and others that through examination of the premises underlying the pursuit of this common subject and the methods adopted in their application we might better comprehend the relationships among feminism, women's studies in the arts, and the more general context of the discipline of art history as a whole.

If there is an emerging pattern evident in these publications, it is the revelation of a shared consciousness of the fact that as presently constituted the discipline has either relegated women artists to inferior status or excluded their contributions altogether. In a sense, a pattern exists in that this common assumption underlies the fact that each author undertakes to fill in the void. Thus, they are all revisionist to a degree; but they differ in the extent to which this consciousness enables them to be critical of the field itself. These works, then, cannot be viewed in terms of linear development but rather must be seen in terms of their relationship to two polarities of disciplinary self-criticism. The more conservative formulation differs from traditional art history primarily in the focus of its attention. It upholds, if only tacitly, the same long-established categories of "high art," "great artists," individual genius, and the purity of formal aesthetic criteria. Its object is to prove that there have been great women artists worthy of scholarly consideration by the same standards applied to their male contemporaries. All these works are expressive, albeit in varying degrees, of this formulation by virtue of their unwillingness to challenge the status quo and rock the methodological boat in its totality. Ellet, Clement, and Eleanor Tufts are closest to the pole in terms of the established notion of "fine arts" and "creative genius" as the proper object of fine art historical investigation. Karen Petersen and J. J. Wilson, Elsa Honig Fine, and Eleanor Munro deviate from this traditional wisdom by suggesting that social conditions influence the creative process and by introducing the status and role of women in a given period as necessary augmentation of the study of their art.

A more aggressive and accusatory stance is taken by Ann Sutherland Harris and Linda Nochlin and by Germaine Greer. Fine and Greer, however, remain true to the concept of painting and sculpture as the highest expressions of artistic energy. In Greer's case one is obliged to say that *The Obstacle Race*, which the author styles a sociology of art and "feminist art history," is a far cry from the rigorous model provided by Harris and Nochlin. In fact, Greer's attempt is a case in point of how *not* to create gynergenic art history. As one astute reviewer suggests, Greer's book is less art criticism than opportunistic exploitation of the emotionality that surrounds women's achievements.[12] Remarkable indeed is Greer's insensitivity to the requirements of a feminist critique. Particularly painful from a gynergenic point of view is her use of patriarchal vocabulary and its implications in her text. More striking, however, is her blatant exploitation of women artists through her use of penny-dreadful sensationalism when it comes to their lives and art. Most astonishing of all is to see those who claim to "live in the tradition of the Furies" sidestep the requirements of feminist ethics in reviewing this book.[13] Women-centered thinking does not mean lack of integrity when it comes to "critique."

Gynocentric criticism is risky and in this sense Eleanor Munro's *Originals* is anything but risk taking. The author takes a sociobiographic and psychological approach to the lives of select women artists. In tracing the careers and aspirations of American women artists from Mary Cassatt to contemporary women artists of the 1970s Munro follows patriarchal form. She provides subjective information using the language of the ruling class and attempts no critique. It should be noted that her book is the outgrowth (much like Petersen's and Wilson's) of a media event, in this case a television series, "The Originals/Women in Art" (produced by WNET in New York City and assisted by grants from the National Endowment for the Arts and the Corporation for Public Broadcasting). As such the book has all the virtues and drawbacks of that inspiration.

Clearly, Petersen and Wilson, Munro, and most markedly Harris and Nochlin (who after all must be credited with setting the standard for this sort of analysis) differ from these other writers (e.g., Ellet and Clement) in recognizing that social conditions have resulted in the concentration of women's creative expressions primarily in the "minor arts" and include the decorative and applied arts. In practice, however, all of these writers should be viewed as gradualists rather than as active revolutionaries, reformers rather than radicals.

The radical formulation, by contrast, is not content just to add women artists to the existing honor roll of art historical judgments. In examining the social and institutional causes for women's "success" or "failure" in the arts, the radical formulation proposes to look at art and its language with new eyes and with the purpose of describing it in women-centered terms. By bringing a sociological perspective to bear upon the study of art, the radical view dismisses the idea of objective criteria for "artistic quality" and emphasizes instead the importance of such concepts as class, status, and power in the determination of what constitutes "good" art in a given period.[14]

I have titled this discourse "Against the Grain" precisely because of the nature of female art history and its criticism. For the purposes of this commentary and in the most general sense I should like to venture a distinction between "female art history" and "gynergenic criticism," understanding that these are not necessarily mutually exclusive categories. Filling in the gaps and setting the record right would seem to be practicing female art history, an effort that devotes itself to the examination of women artists and their visual contributions to culture. By contrast, I would define gynergenic criticism as a self-consciously aware and aggressively female-identified attack on the male-identified status quo, in this particular case the history of art as it is now known, taught, and practiced in our society. Although far from conclusive, this definition is a necessary first step. Thus, on the one hand, female art history may be viewed as the conservative formulation because it differs from standard art historical practice only in the object of its gaze. Gynergenic criticism, on the other hand, is the radical practice in that it demands active commitment to and participation in social change.

To summarize, in the creative arts, as in all patriarchally dominated endeavors, it is assumed that men originate ideas and women follow them. Moreover, it is a simple fact of sociopolitical and economic history that the rights of men generally do not incorporate the rights of women for the obvious reason that it is not to men's advantage to do so. It is evident that like socialism, Marxism, and anarchism, and other "isms," feminism may be practiced by both sexes provided they share the conviction that females have been oppressed by a sexist society. Historically this approach has meant addressing "the woman question," which is precisely what Friedrich Engels dealt with when he asserted, "The first class opposition that appears in history coincides with the development of antagonism between man and woman in monogamous marriage, and the first oppression coincides with that of the female sex by the male."[15] As a consequence of such political theory and its ensuing practice internationally, it is logical for woman-centered critics to investigate the implicit tensions inherent in relationships between two sexes. In this sense the obvious areas for a gynergenic critic to focus on are eroticism and maternity. It is to an exploration of these themes that we now turn.

One of the major issues to emerge during the last twelve years of art critical activity is the role that visual images of women play in shaping perceptions of women in the lived-in world. Certainly, the objectification of women in a sexist culture is such that it need not be substantiated by visual illustrations; they are all around us everywhere we look.[16] Turning to any standard history of art will provide ample support for this thesis. It is clear to any aware professional woman that her ideas of herself are influenced by these pictures. In a sexist society woman is a creature defined by her biological function and erotic possibilities, a thing that at once generalizes and condenses both male fear and fantasies. Any woman who refuses her proper place in the patriarchal scheme of things is immediately in danger of being labled a radical-feminist-man-hating-dyke. Thus is the lesbian evoked as a specter of things to come. The lesbian is unavailable to men and therefore no longer participates in a patriarchal assumption that all females are available to male needs. As a consequence, patriarchally trained women, who are all of us, run the risk of implicit penalties when we choose otherwise. In this case the rejection of our "femininity" results in our being made outcasts. The moral code, however, is strictly enforced only when it is to the advantage of the ruling class to make an issue of it. As Mary Daly points out: "Fear of the label 'lesbian' has driven many into matrimony, mental hospitals, and — worst of all — numbing, dumbing normality. In her own light the Self sees/ says her own light/insight. She sees through the lurid male masturbatory fantasies about made-up 'lesbians' who make out in Playboy for men's amusement."[17] The point that needs to be made here is that anti-patriarchal is not necessarily anti-male. Simply, women are free to emphasize the female experience as subject rather than as object. The results of this choice might be that for the first time it is possible to see what eroticism might be for both sexes.

In 1975 at Douglass College feminist critic Carol Duncan discussed the problem of love and beauty in terms of art's image of woman and noted the relationship between erotic art and the aesthetics of power.[18] Her point, that erotic art is culturally defined, was not new. It is obvious that women and men in our society are taught to respond and identify with the social interactions depicted in pictures. Duncan and a number of other feminists asserted that male artists, particularly those of the nineteenth and twentieth centuries, approach the female nude in a number of male-centered ways, none of which are realistic or reassuring from a female-centered perspective. A nude woman, Duncan and others argue, is for the majority of male artists a threat, an adversary to be conquered, or just plain property to be used in any way they choose.

The drama of portrayal that ensues from this approach is one of ritual subjugation of the female via various means that titillate both the male artist and the male viewer to whom these creations undoubtedly are addressed. Because identification with such themes as Delacroix's *Death of Sardanapalus* or more recent examples from popular culture (e.g., *Lipstick* or *Dressed to Kill*) do nothing for the female audience, who naturally have to identify with the female victim, it is obvious that these are male media events. Short of absolute masochism there is nothing erotic here for women. If death, brutality, violation, and sadism are erotic for the patriarchy when it comes to female bodies, what, one wonders, does this attitude say about misogynist culture in general? Clearly, violence and force are used by the male artist to show this ritual surrender that reinforces images of male superiority and power, no matter how sick or distorted from a gynocentric perspective. In looking at the majority of examples available to us in the history of the visual arts, it is clear that much high art, craft art, and popular media deal with exploring only male desires and fears concerning women. Female viewers, thinking of their highest aspirations, hardly would seek to imitate art consciously in their lives by partaking of relationships similar to those depicted in these works of art. The gynergenic critic is left asking: What is there for us?

This question was posed by Linda Nochlin at the 1969 meeting of the College Art Association when she made her point with a witty juxtaposition of a French dirty picture postcard and her own contemporary version of this same theme, manufactured for her presentation, showing a reversal. The French postcard featured a well-endowed young woman wearing a garter belt, pearls, and high-heeled boots. She presented a tray of apples upon which her full rounded breasts also were displayed. The caption read, "Buy some apples?" Nochlin's postcard featured a nude hirsute young man with his black garters, high-heeled loafers, and penis resting on a tray of bananas and bore the caption, "Buy some bananas?" The message was clear. While the audience of usually staid art historians roared with laughter, Nochlin made the point that there were simply no real equivalents for "Achetez des pommes?" for the female sex. The reactions of those same art historians were not nearly so cordial nearly a decade later when Alessandra Comini addressed them on sexism in art history at the New Orleans meeting.[19] Using Larry Rivers's phallic measures, which asserted that America's Number One Problem was size, Comini pointed out that 49 percent of the population had made it the problem of the other 51 percent too.

While male artists can be trusted to deal with the penis, the same cannot be said of female artists. The censorship afforded the works of Eunice Golden, Joan Semmel, Judith Berstein, and Sylvia Sleigh serves to underline the double standard when it comes to patriarchal morals and the sexual revolution. In his book *Eroticism in Western Art*, Edward Lucie-Smith describes the female qualities of the female *Odalisque* as "totally submissive" and a "beautiful blank."[20] Turning to Sylvia Sleigh's nudes of Philip Golub (figure 8.1) and Paul Rosano (figure 8.2) we see no "beautiful blanks." Instead she paints individual portraits of what she considers young and beautiful male subjects. Unlike contemporary male artists such as Mel Remos, John Kacere, and Allen Jones, to mention only a few, Sleigh's emphasis is on the alert, self-possessed, and sexy male. She is respectful of her subjects' individuality and does not objectify them as mere things. What we have here is not a simple reversal of this art historical cliché but instead, perhaps for the first time, a contemporary female expression of erotic appreciation. Not surprisingly, given the newness of it all, these visions have been met by male and patriarchally conditioned female audiences with titters of self-conscious derision. The irate male audience is particularly sensitive to the change in position from vertical to horizontal, from superior to object. Ironically, this same moral male hierarchy sees the objectification of wombs, vaginas, and breasts by men as perfectly acceptable in works of art and worthy of inclusion in its national presses and prestigious institutions. It is indeed a paradox that these same art lovers are capable of censoring the work of female artists who have the unmitigated audacity to use male anatomy in a similar fashion.

Even more provocative from a gynergenic critic's point of view is the debate raging around Judy Chicago's *Dinner Party*. Tokenism is, of course, alive and flourishing in the land of the fathers. As a consequence the *Dinner Party* is shown and written about. Apparently Chicago's is the most threatening sort of feminist vision because of its ability to project itself into the society at large, and the repercussion in male-dominated museums and presses has been predictable. Despite all of the derision and trivialization of this work, it is drawing record crowds and making uncomfortable waves. Of all gynergenic art theory, that of

Figure 8.1. Sylvia Sleigh, *Philip Golub Reclining,* oil on canvas, 42″ x 60″, December 1971, Private Collection. Photography, Geoffrey Clements, Staten Island, New York.

Figure 8.2. Sylvia Sleigh, *Paul Rosano Reclining,* oil on canvas, 54″ x 78″, February 1974, Private Collection. Photography, Geoffrey Clements, Staten Island, New York.

Chicago's central imagery remains the most controversial. It is a concept that patriarchal thinkers insist on reading as merely genital, which may tell us something about Freudian conditioning in a sexist society. Understanding, however, that Chicago's *Dinner Party* is an explicitly hagiological piece facilitates a more in-depth interpretation of it.[21] Obviously its iconography is a radical vision that attempts to restore revolutionary women to their rightful place in our shared inheritance. One instance of this attempt is Chicago's choice of Georgia O'Keeffe as a figure of homage. Chicago views O'Keeffe as a gynocentric being, as a woman who says no to men and yes to herself, and as the living artist most reponsible for giving birth to a language that provides a foundation for a female-centered art. The artist sees the original female being as genital. To her this being is one from whom all life emerged: "the primal vagina—her center dark and molten; all of her energy emanates from her bloody core. She is the sacred vessel, the gateway to existence and the doorway to the Abyss."[22] Once we have accepted this new gynocentric iconography, which many misogynist critics insist on ignoring or ridiculing, it is clear that Chicago's content and theme are explicitly and implicitly critical. Comprehending this fact facilitates a fair reading of her work. As a consequence it is no longer shocking that Chicago's symbolic portrayal of O'Keeffe emphasizes her undeniable "femaleness." It is not simply a matter of vaginal imagery but instead a sign of femaleness, a metaphor for female experience and aspiration. Most significant from a political perspective is the fact that such an image cannot be transformed into a male metaphor or co-opted by a sexist society. It is an affirmation of the new gynergenic hagiocracy.

A similar argument can be made in relation to maternity. Among the variety of ways this theme has been portrayed by artists, that of the "happy mother" is perhaps one of the most enduring images in traditional art history.[23] What such an image suggests to young women is that it is both natural and desirable for them to be mothers. When one examines this premise and its visual manifestation from a gynergenic critic's perspective, however, it takes on a somewhat different meaning.

Mary Cassatt has been soundly condemned by the male art establishment for her paintings of women and children. This criticism often has been pointed out as a justification for evaluating her art as inferior to that of her contemporaries. In point of fact, as Adelyn Breeskins's painstaking research has revealed, Cassatt, much like her male contemporaries, painted her environment.[24] Given her social class, upbringing, and the expectations of her parents, Cassatt was a remarkable woman. Her work depicts upper-middle-class mothers and children with extraordinary empathy. In these pictures she displays an individuality and unique lack of the sappy sentimentality with which so many of her male counterparts have treated the same subject. Astonishingly, until Breeskin insisted on the visual fact of Cassatt's point of departure, her work was either trivialized or forgotten altogether. Traditional art history insisted upon presenting her as a pupil of

Degas, which she was not, and as a female artist limited by her unambitious subject matter. Her childlessness was pointed to by patriarchal explicators as the reason for her choice of theme. Implicit in this interpretation was the notion that she was compensating for not having fulfilled her "natural destiny" as wife and mother by painting a wished-for reality.

Paula Modersohn-Becker is yet another case in point of a talented, innovative, and courageous woman artist excluded from patriarchal art history. Modersohn-Becker's statements about women's experiences, and particularly those of the toiling farm women in northern Germany, should entitle her to a place in any representative text; lamentably they do not. The artist presented one of the most striking portrayals of motherhood ever created in her *Reclining Mother and Child* of 1906, recapturing the impressions of the "heroic" giving of life that she jotted down in her diary of 1898.[25] With a magisterial sense of monumental presence this woman is at one with nature. The artist has given this age-old subject a new freshness and power. Unattractive and threatening as this symbol may have been to the polite bourgeoisie, it was nonetheless acceptable because it reinforced their conviction that woman's only natural role in the scheme of things is to procreate and nurture.

The most radical presentation of women and motherhood may be seen in the works of German artist Kathe Kollwitz. Her emphasis was on the urban working-class poor, especially women; she recorded how forcefully she became aware of the hardships of proletarian women.[26] In her art she attempted to capture the "full force of the proletarian's fate" in industrial society and nowhere with more impact than in her heroic mothers. In such stunningly powerful and moving works as *Das Opfer, Mutter, Saugling an irh Gesicht druckend* (ca. 1925) and *Die Mutter* (ca. 1919), Kollwitz pours out her outraged protective maternal instincts.

Kollwitz's mothers are not content merely to accept passively the rewards or lack of them that a patriarchal industrial society saw fit to give. Her toiling women cry out in desperation and rage, they rebel, are dangerous, and strike back with surprising ferocity when their children are threatened. Need we "save our children" from Kollwitz's vision? asks the self-consciously aware gyno-centric critic.

A different and less political response to motherhood is that of English sculptress Barbara Hepworth. Her perception of maternity, unlike that of her male contemporary Henry Moore, deals directly with her physiological and psychological awareness of it. Her vital abstracting images suggest an identification worth a timeless idea, the relationship between mother and child, which Hepworth characterized as springing from the inside of her own body.[27] Thus as a woman and artist she perceives the crucial difference between man's experience of motherhood and woman's.

Lest we assume that all women artists react to maternity positively let us turn to the work of surrealist painter Dorethea Tanning, whose identity in art has been subsumed by the fame accorded her husband Max Ernst. *Maternity 1* (1946) gives an alarming vision of motherhood. Tanning shows a mother and infant dressed in identical clothing standing in a large yellow desert expanse, their bodies glued together. The mother's long white gown is torn in the abdominal area, a device often used by the artist to indicate ambivalence concerning sexual sensations and erotic emotions. Near the woman's feet and sharing the blanket on which she stands is a Pekingese, often identified with Max Ernst in her other work. This time the dog is white and has the same face as the rosy-cheeked baby. We see an open door to the mother's left and another in the distance from which appears a biomorphic apparition constructed of tiny swollen sails. Despite the obvious power of Tanning's work, she, like the majority of surrealist women, has been ignored by the art historical establishment. Commenting on this treatment she said, "The place of women among Surrealists was no different from that which they occupied among the population in general."[28] On the basis of such analysis as the foregoing we ought to question the claim of traditional art history to represent the whole of human culture.

A careful examination of the "woman question" in the context of two traditional themes in art — eroticism and maternity — reveals the cultural imperialism of the discipline itself. Given the facts I have briefly outlined, the question still remains: What is to be done?

In an attempt to carry feminist theory into the realm of a working gynergenic critique of the discipline of art history I have tried to give a fresh perspective in terms of meaningful interpretation. This effort has required making an active commitment to redefining my critical language in terms of a gynocentric perspective, one that does not continue to serve the purposes of patriarchal art history. In this context I should like to clarify a few points of difficulty inherent in formulating and practicing such a working feminist criticism. Primary is comprehending the larger sociopolitical and economic dimensions of the problem. Second, one must consider finding a working definition for feminist criticism. Finally, one must deal with the implications of such a critique and what it tells us about culture and society. A gynergenic analysis not only may reveal the biases and inadequacies of traditional art history in regard to women artists but also suggest further critical questions that challenge not only the discipline but society as a whole.

In essence all of the feminist artists I chose as examples are dealing with subject matter that is in some way threatening to established patriarchal ideas of what constitutes proper conduct for women in our society. Doubtless, what is most disturbing to a sexist culture is that these undermine the "lady-like" approach to the arts. Indeed, such women don't even aspire to make art that apes "masculine" tastes and values. The vehement attacks on women-identified art and gynergenic criticism raise serious critical questions for us all. Such considerations as "Is it art?" or "Does it belong in a museum?" bring us to the more profound issue of "Who makes these decisions and on what grounds?" Immediately we are confronted with the sociopolitical nature of the art system itself and its power when it comes to controlling what is seen by the public. Those among us willing to risk addressing such problems as "high art," "quality," and a host of others find that we are dealing with language as a tool of exclusion. The object of such definitions and values is to keep outsiders where they belong, safely on the marginal fringes of the establishment culture. Thus, the feminist perspective would appear to be a cutting edge not only of revisionist practice but revolutionary social consciousness as well. A gynergenic criticism facilitates a greater consciousness of inequities, not only in the art world but in the lived-in world as well. What we are forced to recognize is that ours is a shared and complementary experience. It seems to me that there are compelling reasons to give that "other" experience, the women's experience, the same respect and representation that "male modes" of seeing have always received in our society.

Chapter 9

The Fallen Woman in Fiction

JANE FLANDERS

For every strong, creative, affirmative heroine in novels focusing on woman's position in society, there are a dozen pathetic, often destroyed women. Clarissa Harlowe, Emma Bovary, Anna Karenina, Hester Prynne, Tess Durbeyfield, Edna Pontellier, Nana, and Maggie "girl of the streets" are only a few of the deflowered virgins, adultresses, courtesans, prostitutes, and suicides who fill the pages of novels.[1] Even those women who somehow survive, who rise above their entrapment and (in rare cases) even triumph, must purchase their survival at the price of respectability and "virtue." And, in addition, the story of the cliché "whore with a heart of gold," the kindly madam, the "happy hooker" or cheerful courtesan, such as Daniel Defoe's Moll Flanders, John Cleland's Fanny Hill, and Anita Loos's Lorelei Lee, often involves a fanciful, comic, or sentimental account of a woman's transcendence of sexual taboos. If Georg Lukacs's theory holds true, that the typical fictional male protagonist (the "problematic hero") is a lone searcher forced to find or "create" himself in an absurd world of empty and repressive social forms offering no stable means for self-realization, what added threats or obstacles confront the female protagonist?[2] One recalls Virginia Woolf's speculation as to what would have happened to Shakespeare's imaginary sister if she had run away to London to follow her art.[3] Novels centering on the experience of women paint a bleak picture of the prospects for self-actualization and personal intergrity for women within the confines of patriarchal capitalist society.

The overwhelming popularity of the "fallen" woman as a subject for fiction testifies to the novel's function as a critical commentary on middle-class society both as a mirror of ordinary experience and as a means of shaping consciousness. The obsessive concern with chastity, typically identified with spiritual purity, honor, and virtue, and the terrors of deviating from this ideal tell us much about the social, sexual, and psychological experience of women in recent centuries and show the persistence of ancient attitudes and fears regarding woman's sexual nature even into modern times. (Only in the twentieth century is there evidence of toleration of female sexuality outside marriage, though at the same time one can observe that the overriding interest in the sexual aspects of

woman's "liberation," at the expense of other kinds of freedom, barely conceals
the attitudes of an earlier period. Pervasive in the pulp novel, this emphasis on
female sexual license is well illustrated in Judith Rossner's *Looking for Mr.
Goodbar,* a best-seller of the mid-1970s.)[4] While of course many — perhaps
most — novels reinforce prevailing norms, albeit in disguised ways, and while
even the most radical critique of the status quo may betray the novelist's awe and
revulsion for the challenge to patriarchal authority manifested in a woman's
sexual disobedience, the great appeal of the "fallen" woman theme for novelists
indicates an awareness of the injustice of the fate befalling a woman who has
been victimized by a repressive and intolerant code of sexual behavior. Major
works on this subject call for a more humane conception of womanhood and the
woman's role in society.

I am here following the approach of feminist criticism, which entails a basic
interest in subject matter — events, evidence of customs and behavior illustrating
the situation of women within a specific patriarchal culture — and also attention
to narrative form, diction, and rhetoric — what language and literary structure
reveal about how women have been perceived and how they have understood
themselves.[5] Finally, feminist criticism encourages the application of the insights
gained through such critical scrutiny as a way of developing a fresh consciousness of women's position today.

Although in the eighteenth century a number of female novelists wrote about
the sexually deviant woman, the theme has been addressed primarily by men;
therefore works by authors of both sexes are relevant to an examination of this
theme in fiction. To suggest that only women can write sympathetically about
women, that men are incapable of authentic representation of female experience,
is to restrict the novelist, ultimately, to autobiography. Men more than women
have chosen the "fallen" women theme partly because the intensification of the
mystique of gentility strictly limited the subjects a woman was permitted to write
about — and in fact the supposedly dangerous and shocking nature of the subjects
of much eighteenth- and nineteenth-century fiction accounts for the novel's
dubious reputation until recently. By the nineteenth century, and into the twentieth, only men were able to write sympathetically about such taboo themes as
adultery, prostitution, or rape — and even then against violent public disapproval.
Gustave Flaubert's *Madame Bovary* gained notoriety through the government's
prosecution of the novel for "immorality" in 1857, and the first edition of
Theodore Dreiser's *Sister Carrie* (1900) was suppressed because of its scandalous theme. It is often noted that no woman in George Eliot's novels defies
convention to the extent that the author did in real life, and the savage reception
of Kate Chopin's *The Awakening* (1899) was owing in part to the fact that this
story of adultery was written by a woman.

Writers have been attracted to the "fallen" heroine for many reasons. Primary
among them are what could be called a "feminist" sympathy and compassion

with her plight. Many have recognized the injustice to women in popular attitudes about sexuality and marriage, in middle-class moral hypocrisy, particularly the double standard, and in the impossible expectations held for women. Further, in the hands of many male novelists, the "fallen" woman motif seems to suggest a desire to achieve an androgynous vision through internalizing and giving aesthetic form to the story of the female outcast; the woman's "fall" provides a metaphor for all experience. (Thus ironically woman is once again objectified, seen as representing something else rather than as herself.) Men have seen in the feminine scapegoat a "type" of general human culpability and a recognition that in many ways modern life demands "prostitution" and "dishonor" of all people. Therefore, in addition to illustrating specific social wrongs and moral absurdities inflicted on women, the story of the woman's "fall" is united, perhaps for purposes of legitimation, with the older biblical concept of the fall of humanity from original perfection. The story of the "fallen" woman has been used to convey the spiritual alienation, the sense of homelessness, isolation, and despair, which for so many writers characterizes modern life. It expresses the condition of all those trapped in a rigid and dehumanizing social order, a civilization rife with "discontents" and "abandoned by God."[6]

As a genre, the novel has lent itself, both in form and content, to the presentation of woman's social position and associated problems. As a proving ground for the development of literary realism, the early novel — born in the "post-Lockean" eighteenth century — reveals a search for new forms and modes of expression, a concern for the individual, and an apprehension of new perceptions of experience that elude conventional interpretation.[7] The novel represents a radical challenge to tradition both in theme and narrative structure — hence the loose, plastic, sprawling quality of so many novels, modeled on a variety of narrative patterns. Only such a "novel" medium, it seemed, was capable of the psychological intimacy and reconstruction of immediacy that could redefine experience accurately. Also, the novel served a critical function as a diagnosis of social ills and hypocrisies, as a revelation of the true dynamics of behavior. According to Everett Knight, the greatness of a thinker, writer, or artist in recent centuries "has been directly proportional to the ferocity of his [*sic*] opposition to what is, after all, his *own society*. The importance of any cultural product has depended upon the degree of outrage or incomprehension with which it is greeted."[8]

The story of the sexually deviant woman has provided a naturally problematic and demanding subject of fiction. Few novels about the "fallen" woman have unthinkingly endorsed conventional behavioral norms; even the typical cautionary tale about the foolish fair one "deceived" by a "vile seducer" — such as Susanna Rowson's *Charlotte Temple* (1792) — betrays sympathy for the victim, no matter how much she is chastised for her disobedience to parents or her indifference to the rules of propriety that brought on her ruin. And beyond the stereotyped version of the theme, the great majority of novels about the female deviant have issued a protest — explicitly or covertly, with varying degrees of pity, exculpation, or blame for the victim — against the inhumanity and absurdity of the narrow code by which woman's behavior is regulated. Not condemnation, but rather pity and grief have been the expected responses to the story of the woman who has suffered from her transgression of the limits assigned her by society. The accelerating pace of social change has made readers and writers aware that women, more than men, have been victimized by the injustice and moral hypocrisy characterizing attitudes of the period about sexual behavior.

Economic Changes that Intensified the Cult of Chastity

The development of the novel coincided with the ascendance of the middle class, given new power and leisure through the massive economic and social changes transforming the Western world.[9] The novel grew in popularity through the spread of literacy, especially among the middle class. Hence as *the* bourgeois literary form, the novel echoed the major preoccupations of the bourgeoisie — money, marriage, and the transfer of property. Although a woman's "fall" could be interpreted in the biblical sense, the "fall" that became a dominant fictional theme brings the larger metaphor into a specific focus: the loss of female chastity as it affects the marriageability of the maiden and the respectability of the wife.

Marriage and its abuses long have been subjects of fiction because in bourgeois marriage can be seen a crucial convergence of sexual, emotional, social, and economic restrictions on a woman's freedom. Under capitalism and a liberal economy (which meant the removal of work from the home, a shift to wage labor, a demand for capital, and the definition of private property as the basis of political power and influence), relations between the sexes also changed.[10] Despite the growing influence of Protestant and rationalist ideas that gave women greater spiritual and domestic authority, economic realities meant intensified oppression for women.[11] Bourgeois marriage became blatantly a means of protecting men's property and assuring the legitimacy of heirs; meanwhile, it became virtually the sole means of survival for most women, whose primary value as wives depended upon their absolute chastity.

The novel typically presents a woman's situation in terms of her control of property — that is, her relation to the man controlling the money on which she depends. Whether she is poor, and requires a husband's support, or whether she brings with her a large dowry or inheritance, thus potentially the prey of fortune hunters or unscrupulous relations, the question turns on whom she will marry and whether she will preserve her virginity until her wedding day. Just as Clarissa Harlowe is a central example of so many other elements in the "fallen" woman's fate, she illustrates the victimization of the heiress. Such persecution could continue after marriage: Mary Wollstonecraft's Maria, whose profligate husband married her for her wealth, is forced by him to beg for loans from her relations; he then tries to prostitute her to one of his friends in payment of a debt. Emma Bovary's helplessness in the hands of Lheureux the merchant, to whom she became indebted without her husband's knowledge, is another variant on the theme. The wife or the widow is subject to a husband's financial control and is free only insofar as she has access to his money. Only in exceptional cases does a woman find ways of acquiring wealth without submitting to marriage — always at the cost of her reputation. The almost invariable rule is that the girl who loses reputation before securing herself through marriage is doomed. The perversion of parental (or fraternal), sexual, marital, and other relationships because of women's economic dependence on men is a major theme in fiction — as is the threat of economic deprivation for women who defy patriarchal authority.

These novelistic themes have their foundation in social realities. The subjugation of women through their inability to hold property is of ancient origin.[12] "Woman was dethroned by the advent of private property," writes Simone de Beauvoir.[13] With the beginning of monogamous marriage and the accumulation of wealth in male hands, the woman who provided a man with a legitimate heir became herself property, and her chastity took on economic value. In ancient times, transgression of the rules binding a wife to her husband could mean punishment by death — as is true in some cultures even today. Adultery in a woman is generally considered (sometimes legally) a crime far worse than adultery in a man; and in fiction, no matter what the extenuating circumstances or the author's sympathy toward the adulteress (such as Emma Bovary, Anna Karenina, or Edna Pontellier), the enormity of the wrongdoing of abandoning husband and children is given full play. Edith Wharton condemns her "lost lady," no matter how trapped she is in marriage, because her adultery constitutes ingratitude toward a rich man's generosity. It is noticeably more difficult for a novelist to condone adultery than to evoke sympathy for the ruined maiden. Defoe's Roxana and Moll Flanders are exceptional cases in being sympathetic heroines whose sexual independence forces them to cast off one child after another. However, there is a distinction between legitimate children and bastards; Roxana's unconcern for her illegitimate offspring is of minor importance, whereas having abandoned her five legitimate children, even under the most pressing need, assumes terrible significance at the novel's end, when one of them returns to haunt her mother.

Just as a man "owned" a wife, from ancient times the virgin daughter was also regarded as a father's property to be disposed of at his will.[14] By the eighteenth century women enjoyed somewhat more liberty within the family, and the choice of marriage partners gradually was being left to the young. Kitty's parents in *Anna Karenina* comment at length on the modern practice of allowing children to select their own mates, a freedom that was not permitted them in the mid-nineteenth century. The attitude persisted, however, that the normal pattern of a girl's life was to remain under parental control until being transferred to the authority of a husband. Proving that the rule is the exception is the spinster who, although not "fallen," is also held up to criticism or mockery because of anomalous sexual role. A recurrent plot motif in fiction is the maiden who casts off paternal protection, or is forcibly deprived of it, and thereby loses her "virtue" and "worth." Quite literally, the deflowered virgin loses her economic value: as damaged goods, she is no longer respectably marriageable. Because this status threatens her economic survival, in many a novel loss of virginity leads directly to death or to a precipitous descent into prostitution. Indeed, in *Fanny Hill* and *Clarissa* both victims are incarcerated in a house of prostitution before their rape; merely having left the protection of home is enough to assure sexual ruin. The more standard pattern is illustrated by William Faulkner's Temple Drake (in *Sanctuary*), who hides in a Memphis whorehouse after her shame.

To recapitulate, the "fallen" woman became an obsessively fascinating theme of fiction because of the restrictions on women stemming from their relation to property, because of the cultivation of delicacy and purity as manifestations of middle-class moral superiority, and because of the terrible economic price paid by the woman who failed to abide by an artificial and repressive code.[15] Underlying these economic and social pressures were the justifications of female subordination enshrined in myth and religion.

The Cult of Chastity

Age-old misogyny sanctioned by religion also has upheld the chastity fetish and the victimization of the sexually deviant woman. Among the earliest of civilized ideas seems to have been a belief in male supremacy, the association of the male with intellect, culture, and spirituality, and the female with nature — a theory that thus gave men a combined right and duty to dominate women.[16] At some point in antiquity, religions elevating the female principle gave way to male-centered religions (such as Judaism, Christianity, and Islam) with misogynistic tendencies. Perhaps, as Simone de Beauvoir suggests in *The Second Sex*, this change reflects movement from fear and reverence for nature to the discovery that nature could be exploited by (seemingly phallic) tools.[17] As many novels demonstrate (*Clarissa* is a central example, while the idea comes out ironically in *Madame Bovary*), religion is held up as the ostensible justification for the veneration of chastity. Taboos against women's sexual freedom, while enforced through economic and social pressures, were given an almost mystical foundation — as illustrated by the identification between the unbroken hymen and "purity" and "virtue." (This notion comes out interestingly in the novel

Dracula: Lucy and Mina, even though chaste women, become the prey of the vampire, the enemy of God, whose vampirism is a metaphor for sexual freedom.) A woman's defiance of the patriarchal code is a loss of spiritual value, analogous to disobedience of the Heavenly Father. Thus, as one observes in many novels, even the raped virgin — whose "fall" was a violation of her will — invites a retribution surpassing that invoked by any other kind of rebellion or sacrilege; female sexual activity outside marriage becomes the essence of insubordination, an intolerable breach of male authority. Like the ritual scapegoat, the rape victim must suffer — Tess is even offered up on a primitive altar before her death — whether later sanctified or not. This is the case no matter how sympathetic the author who tells her story.

By the seventeenth and eighteenth centuries, controls on female sexuality, long associated with misogyny, paradoxically began to be enforced through an opposite concept: that women, armed by their greater purity, were obliged to uphold a standard of morality, spirituality, and sanctity for society as a whole. This belief had an implicit economic rationale; clearly, the man in the marketplace or at the exchange could not be hampered by moral scruples.[18] The doctrine of economic individualism precluded the recognition of communal obligations and moral imperatives binding all members of society. It became the woman's duty to maintain moral order through her devotion to chastity, home, and family. "Morality" and "honor" could be removed from the male economic sphere and instead identified with woman's sexual restraint and conformity to conjugal and maternal roles. When she "fell" from this obligation, she assumed the guilt for the community as a whole.

As we have seen, the idealization of marriage and the elevation of the woman's role within it (which held women responsible for sustaining conjugal felicity) grew in proportion to the strains increasingly threatening the institution. Social conventions such as marriage were coming into conflict with the imperatives of economic self-promotion, upward social mobility, and the promises of fulfillment and freedom offered by modern liberal ideology. While the usual pattern for males was to leave home and to establish themselves in the public arena, to compete within a context of pragmatic moral choice, females found themselves all the more closely confined, expected to be loving, yielding, nurturing, devoted to children (whose innocence required the protection of equally inviolate beings), while at the same time making a display of liberal expenditure and conspicuous leisure. Matrimony came to be consciously regarded as proof that the libidinal, passional aspects of human personality could be reconciled with reason and social realities. In addition to regulating sexuality and providing for the rearing of the young, marriage was extolled (even by Mary Wollstonecraft, who called it "the foundation of almost every social virtue") as a microcosm of social harmony.[19] Thus the idealized roles of men and women were patterned after irreconcilable notions — competitive individual self-realization and liberty versus the ideals of charity and community.

Class Concepts of Gentility as Enforcements of Chastity

Kate Millett remarks that although physical restraints such as footbinding and keeping women sequestered and veiled have been abandoned in Western society, "the patriarchal mentality has concocted a whole series of rationales about women which accomplish this purpose tolerably well."[20] Given the massive force of economic and religious sanctions against disobedience of the code of proper sexual behavior and the sentimentalized feminine ideal, most women could be kept in line. The cult of virginity has assured male domination in various ways. Explicitly, it has limited women's opportunities — restricting where a genteel woman safely could go, with whom she could associate, what she could wear. An 1873 book of decorum included this observation about female clothing:

> Our unmarried girls are entirely overdressed. . . . The young miss, flauntingly costumed, is sure to attract a notice in the streets which should not be agreeable to, and is not safe for, virgin modesty. Overdress leads to false expectations. It has more to do than any other single cause with the fall of woman . . . as it thus takes away one of the best safeguards of virtue.[21]

The code of gentility limited what a woman could observe, learn about, and express. It kept her ill-educated, and it inhibited her aesthetic impulses. Until recent times, the middle-class woman was virtually excluded from employment outside the home and from professional life. It was generally understood that factory work or domestic service was degrading for women. Not merely class prejudice kept the bourgeois lady out of the work force; factory wages were usually so low that many women were forced to supplement their income by prostitution, and innumerable novels describe the sexual exploitation of the female domestic servant.[22]

A powerful weapon of enforcement lay embedded in the class system. Because of the distinction between "good" and "bad" women, the cult of chastity has served to set one group against another, one woman against another. By emphasizing the exemplary behavior of its women, the emerging middle class could assert its moral superiority — not only over the "sexually loose" working class but also over the "licentious" aristocracy with its open cynicism about marriage and sexuality. Thus the immodest or unchaste woman, even one tricked into seduction or rape, at once lost class status — witness the ostracism of Anna Karenina, pointed up by her humiliation at the theater. More emphatic examples are Maggie Tulliver (of *The Mill on the Floss*) and Daisy Miller who "fall" merely as the result of gossip. These last illustrations are the strongest proof of the threat of losing class status; of all the kinds of opprobrium visited on the "fallen" woman, the most ironic is the "fall" of one still physically intact — clear proof that the reality of any woman's fall resides in the estimation of others, not in herself.

Although the class basis of the chastity cult often has been overlooked, novelists such as Defoe, Wollstonecraft, Emile Zola, Thomas Hardy, Stephen Crane, Dreiser, Jean Rhys, and Faulkner have realized that chastity is a class privilege reserved for the fortunate and well-to-do, that for the swelling numbers of prostitutes whose ranks grew in proportion to the expansion of Victorian prudery among their betters, "virtue was a middle- and upper-class luxury which they quite simply could not afford," — Eva Figes's words. "The working class provided a kind of sexual sewer for the wealthy. It is important to remember just how classbound the sentimental, idealized image of womanhood actually was."[23]

The close connection between a woman's respectability and her social status is clearly recognized in many novels. A recurrent motif is the calculated entrapment and sexual ruin of the poor country maiden like Tess Durbeyfield or Fanny Hill by a representative of urban sophistication. Like her male equivalent — but unlike him in the specifically sexual nature of her vulnerability (parodied in *Joseph Andrews*) — she is typically undone in the immoral jungle of the city. As an example, Cleland's Fanny Hill is tricked into going to London, abandoned without money, promptly hired by a bawd as a "domestic," then broken in as a prostitute. Dreiser's Carrie Meeber repeats the pattern in nineteenth-century Chicago: wearying of ill-paid factory work, Carrie readily accepts the support of a man who makes her his mistress. The heroine of Rhys's *Voyage in the Dark*, realizing that she cannot survive as an actress, exchanges her virginity for a man's protection with scarcely a qualm. In all instances, the commercial nature of the maiden's "fall" is explicit. And not merely the lower-class or rural maiden was thus exploited; as Wollstonecraft noted, a girl of wealthy, genteel upbringing was equally vulnerable in having been shielded from any knowledge that might help her to defend herself. In Faulkner's *Sanctuary* there is an element of class antagonism in Temple's rape; her hysterical behavior and her assumption that her patrician status ought to protect her were elements in her undoing; she repeatedly alluded to her four brothers, and instead of praying to God for help, all she could think to say was, "My father's a judge." Thus ironically a woman's elevated class status could itself contribute to her loss of position.

Expulsion from the safety of a respectable social milieu usually was enough to guarantee the total degradation of the deflowered virgin. Once "ruined" she was shunned not only because of what had befallen her but also because she posed a threat to the good name of other women. (After her "fall," the pathetic Charlotte Temple was fair game for a tongue lashing from her crude, low-class landlady, and even the benevolent Mrs. Beauchamp required her husband's permission before befriending Charlotte.) There was no restitution, no turning back. Charlotte, Clarissa, Tess, and Temple all realized that even before being sexually abused they had taken a fatal risk in entrusting themselves to men to whom they were not married. One slip could send a girl into a lifetime of infamy; as Wollstonecraft observed, "A woman who has lost her honour, imagines that she cannot fall lower, and as for recovering her former station, it is impossible; no exertion can wash this stain away. Losing thus every spur, and having no other means of support, prostitution becomes her only refuge." No insult to womanhood, in Wollstonecraft's view, is greater than the denial of a woman's moral capacity implied by the idea that she could be "polluted" against her will: "For miserable beyond all names of misery is the condition of a being, who could be degraded without its own consent!"[24]

A female character in Robert Bage's *Mount Henneth* (1782) ironically notes the novel's obsession with a woman's irremediable ruin.

> In all those English books your goodness had procured for me . . . women who have suffered [dishonor] must die, or be immured for ever; ever after they are totally useless to all the purposes of society; it is the foundation of a hundred fabulous things called novels, which are said to paint exactly the reigning manners and opinions: all crimes but this may be extirpated; no author has yet been so bold as to permit a lady to live and marry, and be a woman after this strain.[25]

Only a few "radical" writers of the late eighteenth century (of whom Bage was one) suggested that a "ruined girl" could be restored to society. Charles Brockden Brown makes such an argument in *Arthur Mervyn* (1798): the hero asks a respectable widow to adopt and rehabilitate a maiden who had been seduced by a villain: "Restore her to that purity which her desolate condition . . . and the artifices of a skillful dissembler, have destroyed, *if it be destroyed*."[26] But such tolerance is unusual. Even the brittle Temple Drake, in remaining with Popeye, exhibits the transformation and mandatory obedience to her ravisher that follows the "fallen" woman's shame. Once Clarissa had left her parents' house, ironically in an attempt to defend her own integrity, her loyal friend Miss Howe urges her to marry her abductor.[27] And George Eliot makes it clear that Maggie Tulliver might have suffered less to have married Stephen after their brief flight than to have returned for reasons of conscience.

Emotional Conditioning as Enforcement of Chastity

The psychological indoctrination necessitated by the insistence on female delicacy and chaste behavior frequently has surfaced in the novel. In fact, the "fallen" woman theme itself—no matter how sympathetically a heroine is portrayed, no matter how radical the novel's attack on contemporary mores and social hypocrisies—can itself be regarded as a mechanism for the enforcement of the cult of chastity. The repression of natural impulses in a society increasingly committed to freedom has had bitterly ironic results. Many observers have realized that the inevitable result of teaching girls from infancy to be modest and to guard their "innocence" is to make them anxious because of their sense of vulnerability, thus passive and dependent. Wollstonecraft explicitly noted the contradiction in female education: that it was the very susceptibility to feeling and the underdevelopment of the intellect encouraged in young girls that led to their downfall. She also observed that it was a wife's disappointment, after a romantic courtship, in discovering that marriage was not one long ecstasy, that caused her to seek erotic and emotional satisfaction in adultery: "For she cannot contentedly become merely an upper servant after having been treated like a goddess."[28] In *A Room of One's Own*, Virginia Woolf points to the repression of woman's creativity, aggressiveness, and risk taking caused by the fear of loss of chastity. Speaking of Shakespeare's imaginary "sister," she speculates that the courage required of a young girl to defy the conventions of virginal modesty would have meant

> doing herself a violence and suffering an anguish which may have been irrational — for chastity may be a fetish invented by certain societies for unknown reasons — but were none the less inevitable. Chastity had then, it has even now, a religious importance in a woman's life, and has so wrapped itself round with nerves and instincts that to cut it free and bring it to the light of day demands courage of the rarest.[29]

In 1929 the feminist Woolf still acknowledged the "inevitable" anguish attendant upon a threat to chastity, and its continuing religious importance.

Because in modern cultures one cannot keep females supervised and confined at all times,[30] because the preservation of respectability requires behavioral conditioning, a major novelistic theme is the internalization of social taboos enforcing the chastity fetish. Many novels unwittingly delineate the psychological effects of the sexual repression of women and the emotional damage and deterioration following disobedience of the sexual code. Central examples are Emma Bovary and Anna Karenina, who suffer breakdowns and commit suicide, and Clarissa Harlowe, who exhibits a character transformation that can only be termed suicidal in her resolution not to be broken in will. From *Les Liaisons Dangereuses* (especially in Madame de Tourvel) to Sylvia Plath's *The Bell Jar*, the heroine's psychological suffering is closely tied to the ambiguities of her sexual role. In *Clarissa, Tess of the d'Urbervilles*, and *The Scarlet Letter*, the heroine becomes morally exemplary; her emotional travail assumes strong moral

and spiritual meaning. She is "purified" as victim and scapegoat, taking on the
evils of the community and clarifying and restoring order.[31] The plight of the
sexually abused female, no matter what her circumstances, becomes in fiction a
metaphor for the endangered integrity of the individual. In other cases, such as
Charlotte Temple, Cather's "lost lady," Rhys's Anna Morgan, loss of chastity
precipitates personality disintegration — a pattern returned to ironically in *The
Bell Jar*. Faulkner presents Temple Drake's "fall" as confirmation of her preex-
isting moral degeneracy.

Apparent exceptions are stories of the female deviant who breaks the code of
decorum with impunity and even achieves happiness, wealth, and success.
Significantly, such stories are notably fantastic, sometimes farcical, and often
suited to the purposes of pornography, and thus they only prove the rule that
there is no escaping the prevailing forces of subjection. Clichés include the
"whore with the heart of gold," the "happy hooker," the "game girl" of casual
sexual morality, the kindly madam, and the "fortunate mistress." Anita Loos's
Lorelei Lee (of *Gentlemen Prefer Blondes* [1925]) exemplifies the fantasy-image
of the enterprising female who understands the ways of the world well enough to
become rich and secure through her power to manipulate men; the author, with
comic euphemisms, avoids mentioning that Lorelei's metier is high-class prostitution. As *Fanny Hill* illustrates, a favorite motif of pornography is the sexually
insatiable female, free of moral inhibitions, with the corresponding assumption
that casting off restraints for total abandon is the key to happiness. More complex
versions of the story are *Les Liaisons Dangereuses* (bordering on the porno-
graphic), which centers on the brilliant, cynical, and wicked Marquise de
Merteuil, and Defoe's *Roxana*, which presents a highly ambiguous picture of the
unconventional woman. Roxana, a wife and mother of five children, is abandoned by her husband and forced by starvation to capitulate to her landlord's lust;
once launched on her new way of life, she becomes a free-wheeling sexual
entrepreneur and grows enormously wealthy through shrewd management of her
sexual favors. But the author's vicarious enjoyment of her pragmatism, intelligence, and success is tempered by his recognition of the socially dangerous
character of her behavior. The novel ends inconclusively, as though Defoe the
realist could not sustain the premise with which he had begun — that woman's
chastity is no more than her stock in trade, and that under certain circumstances
it is as subject as anything else to the pressures of moral compromise.

Summary

In addition to making specific attacks against the social injustices that have
persecuted the "fallen" woman, novels centering on female deviancy treat of
paradoxes and strains in modern social experience that affect both sexes. The

"fallen" woman theme has served to express a sense of a pervasive spiritual malaise, already evident in the eighteenth century, which remains with us.[32] The pilloried and ostracized woman is symptomatic of the alienation of all people in modern life, the corruption of all human relationships, and the inadequacy of theoretically sacred institutions. Novelists have attacked the hypocrisy of venerating the maidenhead or the marriage ceremony as signs of sanctity in lieu of more fundamental definitions of moral and spiritual value. Although some have seen woman's sexual deviancy as a manifestation of inner corruption, most have noted the irony of castigating a woman for sexual license while condoning not only male promiscuity but also widespread immorality of all kinds.

Just as Freud observed a conflict between "civilization" and its "discontents" — that is, the necessary repression of instinct in organized society in conflict with the constant eruption of instinctual drives into the orderliness of everyday life — the recurrent theme of the victimized female expresses the difficulty that all people experience in trying to survive in a cruel and competitive society, and the injustice of making a woman a scapegoat for everyone who struggles to walk the razor's edge between the demands of freedom and conformity.

The "fallen" woman shows the hollowness of the promises of widening opportunity and personal self-actualization held out by modern liberal ideology. When pursued by women, the goals of individual self-assertion, rebellion, and exploration of the unknown became crimes punishable by universal censure, lifelong shame, or death. According to Georg Lukacs, the novel expresses the central problem of modern experience, which is "the inadequacy that is due to the soul's being wider and larger than the destinies which life has to offer it."[33] This theme is exceptionally well dramatized in the story of the "fallen" woman, which exhibits the incompatibility between the self and the cultural framework in which it must strive to come into full being. By the eighteenth and nineteenth centuries, social patterns such as marriage and family were becoming increasingly perceived as absurd conventions within which acceptable behavior is mere "conventionality," having no correlation with the inner being of those involved in them. In Lukacs's words, "Nature is alive inside man but, when it is lived as culture, it reduces man to the lowest, most mindless, most idea-forsaken conventionality."[34] The woman victimized by hollow social forms is all the more clearly the victim of arbitrary tyranny, hypocrisy, and the hidden cruelty dominating social relationships. Her story shows the subjection of all people to unnatural and meaningless definitions of virtue. It is ironic proof that the victims of arbitrary power have been made to carry the blame for their own suffering. The female scapegoat is a representative of all who are trapped, stereotyped, violated, and unjustly blamed by a degraded social order under the command of unworthy authority.

Chapter 10

Redefining the Family and

Women's Status within the Family:

The Case of Southern Appalachia

MARY ANGLIN

The question of what the family means, or what it has become, is a topic that has received a lot of recent attention. Liberals and conservatives alike have pointed to the impending demise of the nuclear family and have sometimes even agreed in their assessment of the factors behind its dissolution. For example, the noted liberal Christopher Lasch points to the declining strength of patriarchal authority as one of the problems facing the nuclear family.[1] The danger behind this argument centers not around the issue of its correctness but in the assumption that either we are tied to the will of the patriarch or we become a society of self-absorbed individuals who feel no connection to each other. The implications of such a position are very serious. In terms of scholarship, it suggests that we continue to bury our concern about women and the dynamics of their participation in the family in order to maintain a semblance of security in this chaotic world. In terms of public policy, it suggests that we trade off autonomy, particularly as it pertains to women's rights, for programs and laws that will bolster the strength of the family.

As might be predicted, this argument has drawn a strong response, particularly from the feminist community. Some feminists have accepted the idea that the nuclear family and patriarchy are intrinsically connected but have turned the argument around to use the tensions of the nuclear family as one more indictment against patriarchal exploitation.[2] Others, however, have done historical research, showing that the nuclear family is not the only physical form the family has taken in past epochs and questioning the idea that it is through the nuclear family that we are fitted to the dictates of (patriarchal) society.[3] In other words, what is being questioned is not only the universality of the nuclear family but the necessity of its existence for the preservation of social order.

Arguing in this vein, anthropologists and sociologists have demonstrated that different family forms are not only historical possibilities but present realities that constitute viable responses to the complexities of particular social settings. For example, due to the work of Carol Stack and others, it is no longer possible to dismiss families with female heads of household as deficient, if not pathological, arrangements.[4] As Stack has shown, this family form represents not a social aberration but rather a flexible solution to the dilemma posed by Aid to Families with Dependent Children regulations: that, in order to receive welfare payments, a family must prove there are no males residing in the household. Moreover, this kind of arrangement is not simply a last resort for families on welfare but an alternative taken by middle- and upper-class families as well. Single-parent families seem to be on the increase and certainly are becoming more visible at all levels of society.

In effect, feminists have challenged the great lament over the nuclear family by posing a different question. Instead of asking, What is happening to the family? we now ask, What do we mean by "the family"? It is no longer sufficient to assume that the institution of the family is self-evident, nor is it safe to claim that "the family" means the same thing to all its participants.

Thus, Rayna Rapp proposes we look upon the family as a form of ideology, the normative explanation we give for entering into particular social arrangements.[5] From this standpoint it is useful to contrast "family," as the ideological interpretation, with "household," as the physical structure of the arrangement. We then can talk about different kinds of household arrangements and the historical material conditions that have given rise to them while at the same time acknowledging our tendency to define "the family" as if it were invariant over time and across social class. In addition, we can talk about the dynamics of the household, both in terms of its connection with society at large and from the perspectives of its various members.

This premise does not mean that we dismiss the concept of the family as mere ideology but instead that we examine our understanding of this concept for its ideological implications. It suggests that we look at the role the state has played in formulating this conception through the programs and rhetoric of politicians and administrators. It also prompts us to watch those who style themselves experts on the family — whether they are educators, physicians, or adminstrators — for the impact they may have at the level of popular understanding as well as policy making.[6]

With respect to research on women's issues, such a position would locate an analysis of women in the nexus of pressures and constraints that shape the family as we know it. However, taking this approach is not to argue that women are mere extensions of their families or that our understanding is complete once we have studied women in light of their families. On the contrary, it is simply the starting point for an inquiry that is presumably much broader, but as such it is significant in that it forces us to examine women's lives from the vantage point of the socioeconomic conditions that frame their lives as members of particular households. Furthermore, by looking at women in the context of their families, we gain a sense of how their roles and their sense of themselves are shaped by this powerful source of ideology.

My research on women in southern Appalachia may be seen as an application of this perspective to an area that is experiencing rapid social and economic change. Since the early 1960s, the development process has intensified in Appalachia, which has meant, among other things, a host of social programs aimed at integrating the region into American society. As might be expected, a large number of these programs are geared toward the family and toward women as pivotal members of their families.

The other side of development is the economic pressure it generates: the creation of a cash economy and the need for jobs in an area that previously was oriented around subsistence farming. The fact of having and/or needing jobs outside the home creates a different set of dynamics within the household, particularly when some members are drawing wages and others are not. In the region I am studying, women are entering the labor force in increasing numbers while their husbands are not necessarily formally employed, often working odd jobs so that they can devote the majority of their time to farming. My speculation is that this state of affairs has offset some of the power traditionally vested in the male heads of household.

These two sets of pressures, then, are visited upon families in southern Appalachia, an area in which family ties have continued to exercise a great deal of power and where the extended family is still a viable social form. It seems that women, in particular, are caught in the middle of this situation. On the one hand, they have gained some autonomy from the power of the family and the kind of exploitation it represents. However, it would appear that they have paid for this measure of freedom by submitting to the authority of the state as represented by the social policies and economic programs it has instituted in the region. And, in the process, their understanding of the family and women's place within it is being changed.

In my research I have been more interested in the social policies and programs brought into the region than the economic changes and industrial development it is experiencing. I regard the latter as extremely important, but I am more interested in the subtle changes wrought by the advent of social services, not to mention the influence of the school system. The effect of these agencies, is, in Jacques Donzelot's terms, to create a system of flotation whereby family values are reoriented in relation to social norms, the better to serve the needs of the state. As Donzelot explains, this process is complicated, involving a transformation in understanding rather than a simple application of regulations and principles.

Moreover, as I see it, it is a process born amid changing material conditions and thus has no certain end to it. For example, given the recent changes in administration and the proposed budget cuts, the fate of social programs in Appalachia is unclear. Consequently, while I may safely refer to southern Appalachia as being in a state of social upheaval, I cannot predict where this turmoil will lead, except in the most general terms.

Before elaborating on these themes, however, I would like to address the issue of methodology: the problems and considerations involved in doing this kind of research. In my own work, I am finding it very difficult, often frustrating, to get the information I need. First, there is the problem of one's presence in the community, and, second, there is the way this problem affects the kind of interactions and perceptions one has in that setting. In my area there is a sharp distinction drawn between insiders and outsiders, the latter being anyone whose family has not lived there for generations. To be an outsider puts one on the fringes of the local community to begin with, and the situation becomes further strained if one does not fit the conventional image — for example, if one is an unmarried female. Add to that the complications introduced by differences in education and vocation, and the potential for misunderstanding increases still further. This problem does not mean that it is impossible to communicate, but it does make for a delicate situation, of which the well-intentioned outsider often is not aware. In sum, interviewing seems to be a subjective process that requires all the sensitivity and awareness the interviewer can muster.

My response to this problem besides the inevitable blundering, has been to seek out people with whom I already have an entrée, either because I visit them with someone they know well or because there is a clear, understandable purpose behind the conversation. Then too, I try to develop relationships with these people before asking some of the questions pertaining to more confidential information. I have held off on some of the questions I am interested in asking because they would seem inappropriate at this point. To date, I have conducted mostly informal interviews, letting people talk to me about what they feel is important and, I hope, building up a sense of trust. But in so doing I learn a great deal about daily life and family matters, much of which I would not know how to ask about. I have been able to be more direct with health care and social service providers I have interviewed because many of them are outsiders who not only are willing but, indeed, need to talk about their work with local people. But there again it is important for me to let them tell their stories in their own way, and this approach is, in some ways, more difficult than listening to the concerns of people whose lives are so clearly different from my own.

If interviewing is as subjective a process as I claim, then an obvious problem to confront is the reliability of one's findings. How can we know that the observations I report are valid representations of that person's point of view, much less of other people in the region? This problem is further complicated in my work by the fact that the area differs greatly from one community to another, not to mention from one county to another. For example, the kind of perspective entertained by people living near the county seat or closer to the highway, who have had more exposure to modernizing influences, does not come close to the views expressed by people back in the hollows. Indeed, because of the physical isolation of many people living in the area, it is hard to have a realistic sense of population, much less access to those who live in more remote spots.

My response to this dilemma has been to extend my study to include other counties besides the one in which I am centered. Within the main county I am trying to visit all the different settlements and communities to get at least a feel for the variation that exists. Even so I am forced to assume that my interpretation is slanted in the direction of those people with whom I have the most contact.

To compensate for the bias of my sample, I am trying to cross-check my findings as much as possible by talking to other researchers in the region and using the statistical information that is available. The latter consists of limited amounts of economic information, surveys compiled by the state governments, and the recent United States census. While these accounts are somewhat schematic in the type and quantity of information they offer, they are nonetheless helpful in rounding out a portrait of the region. Finally, I am relying on historical material to give me a sense of the changes the area has experienced in the last hundred years, lest I overestimate the significance of recent change.

From this brief description of methodology, two things should be clear. First, it should be evident that I am reporting from research that is still in process and thus incomplete in its findings. Second, irrespective of the question of completeness, I do not wish to extrapolate too broadly from my research. I choose instead to view it as a case study based on specific and therefore limited socioeconomic conditions. Within this context I hope to add another facet to the discussion on the family.

One of the first things I learned in fieldwork was that it was all too easy to romanticize the Appalachian family. The image painted by the folklorists is that of a self-sufficient unit, bravely struggling in the mountains. For the social worker or the health care provider, however, the Appalachian family often conjures up images of malnutrition, ignorance, incest. Both are stereotypes with limited validity except insofar as they influence our perception of the families in Appalachia. And, sadly enough, not only outsiders but Appalachian people as well have been so persuaded, to the point that many disavow their connection to that way of life. The question of normalcy, of fitting in with the rest of the world, has become important to them.

The question of normalcy arises not simply as a result of contact with the outside world, or lack thereof, for Appalachia has been trafficked since the early 1800s. Nor can one attribute the issue to the influence of the media, although the media certainly have had an effect. It is more than that, more than the effect of two world wars, more than the need to leave to find a job, more than these factors combined. Somewhere along the line the idea of what it means to be a part of

American society has filtered in with the other changes introduced to Appalachia.

It is important, I think, to view these changes as not simply imposed from the outside but *accepted* by people in the community. One of the great paradoxes in my area is the fact that local people are the greatest advocates of change and often are prejudiced against "traditional" Appalachia; recent immigrants are generally people who have moved away from (sub) urban areas and thus have strong feelings about "progress," while local people are more aware of the needs of their communities than the trade-offs that progress brings.

Moreoever, local people are not only advocates of change but agents of change: staffing social programs, teaching in the schools, providing health care and so on. But it is easy to overstate the case here, for the local people staffing social programs tend not to be the directors or formulators of policy, nor are they always wholeheartedly in favor of the policies implemented in their programs. The point is that local people are caught in the middle, desiring some changes and resisting others.

Nevertheless, things are changing rapidly in southern Appalachia, and with changes in socioeconomic conditions have come changes in the relations and beliefs that make up the family. For example, the last ten years have brought my county a new health care system, school consolidation, a new highway, and a host of social programs. These changes have taken concerns and needs that traditionally have been met within the community and put them in the hands of experts outside. School consolidation, in particular, has had a strong impact, taking the curriculum out of the hands of the parents and busing children away from their homes to the county seat. The transition has been especially hard for those who live on farms back in the mountains, given the length of the ride to school and the problem of fitting in with those who come from more urban backgrounds. For those who make the transition, life in the community becomes confusing.

The new highway has, of course, facilitated the process of reaching people in the back parts of the county, making it easier to bus children and enabling people to get work outside their communities. Fewer than 25 percent of the residents in the county now work as full-time farmers and at least 30 percent commute to a nearby city for work.[7] Between wage labor and school consolidation, people are spending more time away from their communities than at home. As a result, while farm life still absorbs a lot of energy and concern, it is no longer the driving force that it once was. Not everyone farms, even in a part-time capacity, and those who do are not as eager to work collectively on various efforts, whether involving the immediate family or the support of one's neighbors as well. Time and energy have become precious resources that are not parted with easily.

Thus farming no longer provides the pragmatic basis for family and community solidarity that it once did. Family members no longer *have* to work together, and often they cannot, even if they so desire, because of other pressures in their lives. Husbands and wives may work split shifts or have jobs that leave them with no energy once they have returned home. Children learn to be beauticians and mechanics or want to go to college rather than farm.

Put another way, members of the households no longer function as units of production but instead are tied to productive forces that stand apart from their community. The effect of this change in production relations is that family ties are beginning to erode as people develop bonds with peers at work, which, to some extent, replace connections with kinspeople.

It would seem that women are particularly affected by these changes because they are pivotal members of kin networks as well as real or potential laborers. To the degree that the roles of family and community are compressed into maintenance functions, women experience a loss in value and/or power although they do a great deal of work.[8] What has changed is not the significance of their work but its social definition: work within the home is regarded as less productive because it is not performed for a wage. As domestic work becomes socially invisible, those who are responsible for these tasks likewise decline in significance. Although some of the work that women do at home is geared toward the market — as in the raising of livestock or the tending of cash crops — invariably it is the men who get credit for the produce because they are the ones who take it to market. In my area, cows and tobacco are the principal concerns of farmers, and they are regarded as men's property regardless of the care women may have given them.

With respect to work outside the home, there are two kinds of jobs available to women: the first and more likely choice is unskilled work in the factories; the second is some kind of (semi)professional work. The latter is difficult to find because the region is quite poor and cannot support many different enterprises beyond those funded by outside sources. As the funding gets more tenuous, so does the prospect of this kind of work. Nevertheless, many local women go to school to be trained for professional careers and compete for the few jobs that exist, generally in social services or education. For those with strong aspirations toward a career, the lack of job opportunities within the area proves frustrating and sometimes impels them to move away, at least temporarily.

Unskilled jobs are not abundant but are certainly more accessible than professional or semiprofessional work. Although electronics firms are beginning to move into the area, most of the factory jobs now available are related to some aspect of textile production and thus offer minimum wages for difficult, often hazardous work. But it is work, nonetheless, and local women will travel great distances in order to be so employed.

In other words, while the job prospects are not appealing, the pressure of economic necessity is drawing women into the labor force in large numbers. Moreover, it is clear that the fact of working is having a substantial impact on their lives and on their families. But, because local women are being drawn into the labor force in different capacities, the changes experienced as a result of working have different effects. To state the point another way, local women are becoming members of different social classes and thus are developing divergent perspectives on who they are and what they want. Those who are not participating in wage labor directly are nonetheless feeling the effects of this process.

If this analysis is correct—that women are caught in the midst of the process of class formation—then the function of the social services may be seen as helping them to integrate the changes attendant with this process. It is not a simple question of adjustment but instead involves a transformation in one's sense of values, responsibilities, and family ties. Thus social workers and therapists offer people guidance in redefining their lives and, in so doing, inform them from a middle-class perspective.

Furthermore, because many of the programs offered through social service agencies are geared toward poor and unemployed women (and their children), they also incorporate families on the periphery into the process of social change. They teach women the basics of nutrition and health care, tell them how to cope with family problems, and, if necessary, intervene directly in the affairs of the family.

In my county, because certain families still wield a great deal of influence, the carrying out of these duties has to be handled deftly by service providers, particularly if the workers are outsiders. More than one person has been forced to leave the county because of a failure to understand how local politics and the agendas of health and social welfare intermingle. Nor is this issue easy to fathom, for local politicians are in favor of change but only insofar as they can maintain their control of county affairs. It is not always clear where certain policies or ideas will collide with the plans of those in charge. This point is precisely where having local staff workers is effective, as program directors well know. Local people can act as liaison persons between the agencies and the communities. Moreover, they know enough about the channels of power within the area to know which policies might be regarded adversely and how to soften their effects. If their advice conflicts too strongly with the rationale of the program, however, it may go unheeded or be misunderstood.

It is revealing to look at the people who most readily avail themselves of the services offered by the various programs in the county. For the most part, the people who go to the mental health agencies or the Department of Social Services are marginal members of their communities, either because of some type of disability or because they cannot abide by the conventions of the area, which leans heavily towards the teachings of the Baptist church. Because of their questionable status within their communities, they are perhaps more susceptible to the influence of the agencies, and they are certainly more dependent upon the services offered there.

Local people who are more actively a part of their communities, even women who work outside the county, are somewhat reluctant to seek out the services offered them by these agencies. They are well aware of the impact of their decision to ask for outside help in family problems and will forestall this request as long as they can. Above all, they know that they will continue to live in their communities, while the experts whose advice they are consulting may well move on.

The situation is more complicated than the simple matter of professionals coming in and setting the wheels of change into motion. There are some ideas local people are not ready to accept and may not be for quite some time. The question of what the family has come to mean is one such point of equivocation. On the one hand, it is obvious that the family has changed, both in meaning and structure: kin ties are no longer as important as they once were, and members of families relate to each other differently. Yet, because the family still has a great deal of significance vested in it, these changes are being resisted all the more strongly.

Local people will insist upon the durability of the family, continue to frown upon divorce. They will refuse to see wife beating and incest as social problems that need to be addressed directly—but not because they are unaware or unconcerned. Resistance occurs because the implications of confronting problems in family life are too overwhelming to be entertained; thus, for the time being, local people try as much as possible to avoid dealing with social workers who contradict their notions of the family.

Yet the agencies have had an impact as have the pressures of changing socioeconomic conditions. The traditions of Appalachia are dying out with the old sense of individuation, in contrast to the sense of family and community that formed the basis of the traditional ideology. In place of family solidarity, people in Appalachia are beginning to talk in terms of *personal* priorities and the need for independence. It remains to be seen where this change in perspective will lead, except toward the steady erosion of family ties. Nor is it clear whether the change will bring Appalachian women new freedoms or simply exploitation in different form.

Chapter 11

Sexism and Racism:

Obstacles to the Development of

Black Women in South Africa

MAMIE LOCKE

> Women carry a double burden of disabilities. . . . They are discriminated against on the grounds of both sex and race. The two kinds of discrimination interact and reinforce each other.[1]

Most writers on what has been called "the woman question" often have attempted to mold all women, including African women, within the framework of Western societies. Thus they are guilty of bringing their own prejudices and experiences into any observation of women in other cultures.[2] The status of black women in Africa in general and South Africa in particular cannot be measured within the context of Western society.

People are a composite of the influential factors in their environment. The evolution of black women in South Africa has been shaped by their experiences, tradition, colonialism, and the country's racist system of apartheid. Discrimination on the basis of sex and race is not, by any means, unique to South Africa. The latter merely compounds the problem through apartheid. It is because of that racial system that black women in South Africa find themselves at the lowest possible position in the society. It is the purpose of this essay to present an analysis of the special problems that black women in South Africa face.

Two theoretical assumptions are put forth here: (1) black women in South Africa are discriminated against because they are black; and (2) black women in South Africa are discriminated against because they are women. As a result of discrimination based on these two premises, a black woman's development as a full-fledged citizen with rights equivalent to all others in the society is kept at a minimal level. The underlying assumption is that a primary perpetrator of racism and sexism is the colonial legacy. Colonialism, followed by apartheid, has perpetuated both racist and sexist notions, not only to divide blacks and whites, but also to divide blacks into groups and to divide black men and black women. This is not to overlook the role of historical and traditional influences. Historically, factors influencing distinctions based upon sex include economic necessities of a subsistence economy, cultural and religious traditions, and the practices, beliefs, and attitudes of the early European traders, missionaries, and colonial administrators. The combination of these factors has molded the attitudes of men toward women and the attitudes of women toward their own role.[3]

Shelby Lewis puts forth several basic assumptions in the literature regarding the status of women in African society. One of these assumptions is the degradation thesis, which has three subtheses: (1) the anti-traditionalist perspective, (2) the anti-Western perspective, and (3) the socialist perspective. The anti-traditionalists argue that African culture and traditions are negative and primitive. This situation, they claim, is the cause of the oppressed and marginal status of women. The Western influence improved the status of African women. On the other hand, the anti-Westerners believe that the infiltration of the colonialists onto the continent had direct repercussions for women. Westerners with their capitalist system made African women dependent on men, thereby reinforcing the emerging patriarchal system. The woman's role was no longer economic but social and domestic.[4]

The third subthesis, the socialist perspective, attributes the oppression of women in African societies to both traditional and capitalist influences. The socialists argue that religion and customary traditions exploited women, while colonialism and capitalism combined to perpetuate this exploitation.[5] This degradation thesis supports the earlier statement that people are a composite of the varying factors in their environment. The lives of African women have been shaped by their history, culture, and tradition, by colonialism and capitalism, and, in South Africa, by apartheid.

The omission of a discussion on class discrimination does not in any way dismiss it as an unimportant aspect in the obstacles with which black women are confronted in South Africa. Sex, race, and class are intricately intertwined, and a discussion of sex and race discrimination cannot exclude class discrimination. However, for purposes here the discussion will deal primarily with race and sex.

Sexism and racism as they affect black women in South Africa will be discussed from three perspectives: (1) the historical and traditional roles of women, (2) the role played by colonialism in the undermining of women's rights, and (3) women under apartheid. The conclusion will focus on struggles undertaken by women to elevate their status, the struggles of women in other African countries, namely Angola and Mozambique, and what action must occur before black women will be treated as productive and useful components of the society.

For clarification, operational definitions are in order. Sexism may be defined as those practices and beliefs that deny opportunities to certain individuals or a group based upon sex; sex becomes the determining factor in whether one will be rejected or accepted.[6] In male-dominated societies acceptance is based upon the values, goals, and means that men deem important. One either accepts their paradigm or faces rejection. Racism will be defined within the context of South Africa's apartheid system. Hilda Bernstein views apartheid as a "totally divisive society, one in which the emphasis is always on the differences between people . . . superficial differences, such as the amount of pigment in the skin . . . a policy of privilege based on the desire of the politically dominant white minority to maintain a system of extensive exploitation, racially based."[7] In short, apartheid is a system of racial separation based on the presumption that blacks are subservient and inferior to whites. Apartheid segregates African women because they are black and because they are women. Besides, black women are capable of building a stable family structure, something the white government does not want to happen. The idea of apartheid is separation and the separation of women is based on race and sex.

Apartheid also is based on the exploitation of black land and labor. South Africa's population is 70 percent black and less than 20 percent white (the remaining percentage being coloreds and Asians). The government has allocated nine homelands for the black population. These isolated areas, 13 percent of the total land surface, are overfarmed and eroded and lack urban areas, industries, seaports, and mineral deposits. These homelands are seriously depleted, and their black occupants find it most difficult to eke out a bare living. On the other hand, the white minority occupies 87 percent of the land, which contains the cities, mines, industries, roads, and ports.[8] The whites exploit blacks by using them solely as a labor force to fill subordinate positions.

Lewis states that development plans have a tendency to overlook the rural areas in Africa. This neglect is unfortunate in that most women are found in these areas. She adds:

> In the absence of a conscious rural-agricultural development policy, the female majority is relegated to a position of relative unimportance. Even in cases where agriculture is consciously designed, those selected for participation in the development effort are largely men . . . women are neglected in development plans, and the conceptualization of "development" leads to the exclusion of women's activities in development programs.[9]

For purposes of this essay, "development" will be defined as the general progression and elevation of the status of black women in South African society politically, socially, and economically. They, too, must be beneficiaries of national programs, and their contributions to society must be recognized.

Historical and Traditional Roles of Women

Although cultural, ethnic, and regional differences exist in Africa, the traditional African family had certain general characteristics. Families were extended, mostly rural, self-contained, and polygamous. The society was divided into two spheres, male and female. The rigidity of this division was dependent on the particular African society. Often men and women lived in different homes, ate separately, owned separate property, performed different tasks, and kept their own earnings. Under these conditions, the woman was economically independent. She owned as personal property the fruits of her labor.[10] On the role of women, Senegal President Leopold Senghor has said that the woman was not considered inferior in traditional black African society. She is a person and has the right to own and sell or trade property just as a man does.[11] However, women were discriminated against on the basis of sex in traditional societies. They were excluded from many phases of the society depending on religious and cultural backgrounds.

With the advent of colonial rule, the exclusion was intensified. The African woman's traditional role in economic development is not evidenced or acknowledged in the modern sectors of industry, government, commerce, and agriculture. The rapidity with which industrialization and urbanization were introduced to the continent produced far greater psychological and social shocks on Africa than they did in Europe.[12]

Under the guise of customary laws, as interpreted and applied by alien courts, black women have no legal capacity in African laws. They do not have the right to own or inherit property and they cannot act as guardians of their children. Further, they cannot enter into contracts or sue or be sued without the aid of male guardians. Despite their age or marital status, women are subjected to the authority of men at all times. H. J. Simons stressed the point that this interpretation and application of "African law" is erroneous. In traditional African law women had more rights. The family, not individuals, had full legal capacity. A woman was equal to her father and her husband in many aspects of traditional life. Women were not so much in contention with men for power because their roles were incompatible, not competitive.[13]

In traditional African society a woman had some control over her life, especially within the economic sphere. Although her economic role did not give her political dominance, she did have the power to allocate resources.[14] She had to deal with sexist discrimination in the traditional patriarchal society that was also polygamous. With the advent of colonialism, her burden was doubled with the additional problem of racial discrimination.

The Legacy of Colonialism and the Rights of African Women

Leith Mullings places part of the blame of the deteriorated status of women on colonialism.

> It might be more useful to understand the deterioration of the status of African women as bound to the disruption of African society as a whole through colonialism's imposition of a social structure based on stratification by class and sex. Colonialism often resulted in the differentiation of social and domestic labor, the introduction of large scale production for exchange, and the transformation of productive resources into private property — processes that significantly altered the status of women.[15]

First to suffer from the industrialization and urbanization brought on by colonialism was the African family. Men migrated to the plantations, mines, and cities where new skills were needed. The colonial administration and commercial enterprises needed Africans to fill the subordinate positions and, in line with their prejudices, offered education primarily to males. As a result, the traditional division of labor between African men and women was severely altered. The family was no longer one production and consumption unit. Of course, women bore the brunt of this disintegration of the traditional family unit. For example, money economy completely changed "brideprice" from a symbolic pact between two clans to a commercial operation. A daughter became a source of profit if sold by her family at auction.[16]

Colonialism completely upset the balance of labor. Men previously had performed heavy tasks only during certain agricultural seasons. Under colonialism they had to cultivate crops for export. Therefore, sex roles in African agriculture were reversed: the men concentrated on cash crops while all tasks connected with food production fell to women. Women were ignored by both colonial and postcolonial extension services. Education in better techniques failed to make headway because the newer methods were taught to men. Thus the women, the actual cultivators, continued to perform their tasks in the old ways. As a result the gap between the productivity of men and women continued to widen. This method of development enhanced the prestige of men and lowered the status of women.[17]

Few of the development changes have been of real benefit to women. Technological changes merely aided in the perpetuation of the dominance of men. The bulk of technological advancements was transferred to the modern sector.

Women were a part of the traditional sector and therefore not considered a vital part of the development scheme.[18]

Colonial officials not only disrupted the traditional African agricultural setup but also gave preference to men in the recruitment for clerical and administrative positions. Consequently, economic progress benefited men rather than women as wage earners. As the growing modern sector began to eliminate traditional jobs handled by women, their position in society began to deteriorate. When hired at all in the modern sector, women were placed in unskilled low-wage jobs. Colonial interlopers from the Western world used their own definitions regarding the roles of women. These definitions had a profound impact on the state of women in the society. Because of colonial influence, women often found themselves speaking of their traditional roles as if they were only domestic and social rather than economic as well.[19]

As their men migrated to the towns, women became heads of households. The ideology of the dominant colonial white society excluded women from so-called productive economic enterprises by depriving them of access to training in modern skills. By teaching modern farming methods to men rather than women, the dominant subsistence producers, the most significant labor force was neglected. The "betterment schemes" incorporated by the colonial governments included model farms on which agricultural demonstrations were carried out with exclusive use of male labor. These farms existed side by side with the poor unproductive fields cultivated by women. This concept, coupled with the traditional patriarchal system to form a Western legal system, reinforced the subordination and oppression of women. It increased their dependency on the new system.[20]

Ester Boserup documents cases in South Africa where European attempts at reform resulted in the actual transfer of women's land to men. She further states that products sold by women are basically agricultural and that market women have few opportunities to enter other sectors. Additionally, the participation of women in the modern sector is held down by a low level of literacy and by the general tendency to give priority to men in both employment and recruitment.[21]

Walter Rodney also blames colonialism for the deterioration of the status of women in Africa. He asserts that colonialism was the cause of the disappearance of social, religious, constitutional, and political privileges and rights. As economic exploitation continued and intensified, the division of labor according to sex was disrupted. When men left the farms seeking work, women were left with the handling of their traditional roles as well as those of men. Men could enter the money sector more easily and in greater numbers than women. As a result, women's work became greatly inferior to that of men within the new colonialist value system. Men's work was considered modern whereas women's was traditional and backward. Moreover, Rodney states, "the deterioration of the status of African women was bound up with the loss of political power by African society as a whole and with the consequent loss of the right to set indigenous standards of what work had merit and what did not.[22]

On the role of colonialism as a detrimental factor to the status of African women, Hilda Bernstein says:

A crucial factor in the position of the women of South Africa has been that of the impact of imperial power on an indigenous culture. Inferiority was imposed on African people by the nature of colonialism in Africa. But the woman has the burden doubled: the black consciousness of "inferiority" ingrained by the colonists, the destruction of tribal structures that gave status to both sexes and the denigration of any culture other than that of the colonists themselves is the first imposition; the second is the inferior status imposed by the relationship of the women and men.[23]

Colonialism contributed greatly to the demise of the status of women. As Audrey Wipper asserts, "In their struggle for equality, African women have had to contend with a kind of coalition between Western and African men about what their roles should be."[24] Thus tradition and colonialism combined to relegate women to a subordinate status in the society.

African Women under Apartheid

Hilda Bernstein states that African women suffer first and foremost from the disabilities imposed by apartheid. Within this racist system black women are at the bottom rung of the ladder. They have been stripped of most of their rights and of opportunities to improve their position. Because of apartheid women are cast in a subservient, demeaned role, and it is almost impossible for them to develop beyond the function of domestic work and reproduction. Bernstein adds, "In the special language of apartheid, Blacks are not ordinary human beings. They are labour units, who are productive or non-productive . . . wives and children are superfluous appendages—non-productive, the women being nothing more than adjuncts to the procreative capacity of the black male labour unit."[25]

African women living in the reserves are bound by the complexities of tribal and common law. Unlike the men, they are unable to escape to the cities. Their movement to cities and towns is restricted by the pass laws and influx control. They are denied the right to own land in the cities and are further hampered by a lack of job opportunities. In regard to land in the reserves, women property owners have the same proprietary rights as men, but if a woman marries she must secure her husband's consent for disposal of land. Women cannot acquire quitrent land either through purchase or inheritance. Land descends according to the rules of male primogeniture.[26]

H. J. Simons points out that when land is being allocated preference is given to men. Although women do most of the work in the fields the government claims that they are less productive. Unmarried women have little hope of acquiring land allotments. Widows are allowed only half the area allotted to men. The explanation given by the government for this discrepancy is that widows do not have the means to cultivate a full-sized plot and that all farms should be *properly managed* (italics mine) because of the need to increase the production of foodstuffs.[27] The implication here is that women are incapable of properly managing farms. Of course, the government has refused to provide them with the means or the land to prove themselves capable.

As stated earlier, fewer women than men qualify to live in towns and cities. Women are denied permits to work on a variety of grounds and are hampered by the various apartheid laws regarding housing, marriage and children (wives and children are "superfluous appendages"), and idleness. Under South African law women are prohibited from being legally registered tenants in urban areas. Should a woman become widowed, divorced, or separated after having been allowed to live in the city with her husband, she is subject to eviction. Women (wives and daughters) formerly were given special right of admission to cities until the law was repealed in 1964. The official view was that Bantu women were not wanted in the towns as an adjunct to the procreative capacity of the Bantu population. A Bantu woman was needed only on the labor market. Thus, she had to stay on the reserve with occasional visits from her husband. The husband could accept this rule or give up his job and discontinue being a migrant worker.[28]

Those women who are urban dwellers are separated culturally from those on the reserves. Their separation from husbands and fathers is less significant than that of women living in rural areas. The latter are separated from their men geographically. Urban women live in an environment where they can make any adaptations necessary to survive in a nontribal world. Nevertheless, urban women still are subject to the laws of apartheid and are hampered by many of the same disabilities imposed on women on the reserves.[29]

In employment women are restricted to jobs no one else wants and those that pay less than others. Many jobs are reserved for men. Because the women are far less mobile than men, they cannot leave household responsibilities. This immobility is especially true of widows who may lose their right to cultivate family land should they seek employment apart from the homestead. Even when African men and women hold the same kinds of jobs, there is discrimination against women in both working conditions and pay. Most fields of employment for which women are suited are occupied by African men, colored women, or white women.[30]

As previously stated, racist and sexist discrimination is largely to blame for the exclusion of African women from most professions. There are agencies that hire many women (public services, banks, insurance companies), but all those women are white. Africans are not apprenticed in the skilled trades. African men, however, can qualify as building artisans, electric wiremen, woodworkers, and surveyor assistants. Women are not admitted to the few technical and vocational schools open to Africans to learn these or any other skills.[31]

Apartheid not only hampers women economically and culturally but politically as well. The incorporation of women into decision-making roles and political power in South Africa is extremely poor. The lack of prominence in the national political arena has resulted in women not receiving the attention they duly deserve. Their exclusion from political involvement merely reinforces the structure of oppression and inequality.[32]

Women actively have opposed the racist policies of the South African government. In cases where they directly feel the oppressiveness of apartheid, women have initiated political resistance. Consequently, they have been identified as political revolutionaries. They have worked for the repeal of pass laws as well as laws on land segregation, discriminatory education, and job reservation. They have sought to obtain the vote and to participate actively in the government of the whole country.[33] In an interview with *Africa Report*, Miriam Makeba, a South African woman banned from the country, argues that women always have been involved in political struggle. Despite the fact that many have been imprisoned or detained under house arrest laws, they are determined to remain a part of the vanguard in the struggle.[34]

The peasant revolts of 1957–1962 were a reaction to poverty, deprivation, and the extension of the Bantu Authorities Act. This protest was initiated by women. The demonstrations spread rapidly, and women faced flagrant brutality levied against them by the government forces. The movement spread to include other demands, such as improved wages and removal of influx control.[35]

Initially, men were excluded from the movement but became a part of it as it spread. Women were excluded from participating in the decision-making process on issues they had brought to the surface through their protests. For example, in 1959, when women presented their complaints to a government commissioner in Ixopo, they were told to submit grievances through their men and chiefs. Hence, their dependency and inferiority were reinforced.[36]

Women faced not only sexist and racist discrimination from the government but also sexist discrimination within their African organizations. Women were not admitted to the highest offices of such organizations as the African National Congress and the Pan-African Congress before they were banned in 1960.[37] However, the chief culprit in perpetuating the subordinate status of African women was the apartheid system. The apartheid system reinforces the disabilities and sub-African status of women. It makes discrimination inevitable and the attempts to end women's disabilities virtually impossible.[38]

Conclusion

The foregoing has been an overview of the problems of black women in Africa in general and black women in South Africa in particular. Martha Mueller feels that in southern Africa race is a more powerful factor than sex in the determination of social relations.[39] I agree but add that race, sex, and class reinforce each other in the denigration of the status of women in South Africa. The South African system of apartheid creates levels in the country with white men at the top and black women at the very bottom. White women, Asians, coloreds (men and women), and black men precede black women in the hierarchical structure.

Yet black women have not been complacent and have not accepted the roles assigned to them by the white-controlled government. As stated earlier, they have been politically active and vocal in their opposition to apartheid laws, which not only relegate them to a subordinate status but prevent the race as a whole from advancing. In 1959 more than twelve hundred black women armed themselves with sticks and clubs to protest poll taxes and influx regulations. The movement was considered quite remarkable for the traditionally subordinate Zulu women. This militancy showed the government that both urban and rural women were capable of such action "however uncompromising the circumstances."[40] Hilda Bernstein's extensive list of those women who have been imprisoned, banned, detained without trial, held under house arrest, or banished for their opposition to apartheid is indicative of African women's protest to the system.[41]

South African women also can look to their sisters in Guinea-Bissau and, even closer to home, Angola and Mozambique, for role models. During the struggle in Mozambique the army revolutionized by accepting women into their forces. Women played an active role in running militias, and many of the guerrilla units were composed of women. They played a key role in the mobilization and political education of the people as well as the soldiers themselves.[42] The Mozambique Liberation Front (FRELIMO) declared the emancipation of women as one of its primary goals. Samora Machel, president of the People's Republic of Mozambique, stated in 1975: "The emancipation of women is not an act of charity, it does not result from a humanitarian position or act of compassion. The liberation of women is a fundamental necessity of the Revolution, a guaranty of its continuity, a condition for its triumph."[43]

According to Ruth Neto the traditional role of Angolan women was that of mother, educator, and adviser. They were exploited because of sex discrimination, principally after colonial penetration. Colonialism condemned them to a life of poverty and ignorance because they had to suffer from racial and wage discrimination as well. However, after the revolution, women were no longer bound to their traditional role. They participate in all the work that must be done for the progress of the country, including combat, teaching, medical aid, and agriculture.[44]

Miriam Makeba dismissed the arguments that claim that the black people in South Africa are not fighting. Black people in South Africa always have fought against the imposition of colonialism. Although this struggle takes various forms, it will continue until the country has been freed from white domination.[45]

African societies, South Africa in particular, must recognize the worth of women in society. Florence Mahoney and Shelby Lewis illustrate this point effectively. According to Mahoney the contributions of women to development have been and will continue to be vital. If society is to advance, it must include women and prevent further oppression. Lewis states that women, too, must work together to achieve changes. Likewise, leadership always should acknowledge the achievements of women and include them in development plans and efforts to transform society. Change cannot take place without the participation of women.[46]

A United Nations seminar on the participation of women in economic life recommended that all public and private bodies take vigorous measures to integrate women into all sectors of economic life and to ensure their participation on equal footing within the framework of national development plans and programs. There should be emphasis on the important role of women in agricultural development. There is also a need to provide women with suitable education and training to improve their skills and efficiency as well as acquaint them with better methods of conserving and marketing agricultural produce and cooperative organization.[47] It is also important for men to realize that it is beneficial to them to integrate women into all levels of the developmental process. If this integration is not achieved, the only option left for women is to exert pressure through their collectivity as a social force.[48]

As far as the government of South Africa is concerned these suggestions are mere rhetoric. Apartheid is a law unto itself. The government does not want to elevate the status of black women or men. They are viewed simply as a labor source to be used and discarded at the will of the government. As long as the apartheid system exists, black women will continue to occupy the most subordinate status in the country.

With the recent downfall of Rhodesia, South Africa is in the position of being the only white-dominated country left on the continent. The country thus is in a vulnerable position despite its advanced development. It is hoped that the struggle that women have undertaken in the past will continue in the country until it is in the control of those who own it — the Africans.

Chapter 12

Of Paradigm and Paradox:

The Case of Mary Boykin Chesnut

ELISABETH S. MUHLENFELD

Labels that traditionally have applied to southern women — southern belles, for example, or southern ladies — are little more than catchwords, misused so frequently that their original meanings have become somewhat murky. One of our tasks, then, as southern scholars concerned about women must be to examine images of southern women to discover their real meanings. We want, above all, to understand our heritage, our culture, and where necessary to correct false impressions and question inappropriate labels. To do so, we have begun in the last fifteen years or so to turn to evidence supplied by women themselves, particularly to the writings, both published and unpublished, of nineteenth-century women.

Among nineteenth-century women certainly the most widely quoted southerner is Mary Boykin Chesnut, author of a justly famous firsthand account of the Confederacy known to most of us as *A Diary from Dixie*. Since the first publication of *A Diary from Dixie*, a heavily edited and severely cut version published in 1905, Mrs. Chesnut has been a valuable resource for historians and sociologists as well as for writers and journalists interested in the pre-Reconstruction South.[1] Few historians of the Confederacy, for example, have dared to ignore Mrs. Chesnut. Popular novelists have drawn heavily on the events, people, and settings she describes, and at least one novelist based a central character on her. Ground-breaking studies concerned with nineteenth-century women by such scholars as Mary Elizabeth Massey, Anne Firor Scott, and Carl N. Degler refer frequently to Mary Boykin Chesnut. Edmund Wilson in *Patriotic Gore* calls Chesnut's book "an extraordinary document — in its informal department, a masterpiece," and historian Lyman Butterfield, editor of the Adams Papers, has called the Chesnut journal "the best written by a woman in the whole range of our history . . . in the same top bracket with that of Sewall, Byrd, Cotton Mather, John and John Quincy Adams."[2]

Perhaps most symbolic of her importance among nineteenth-century southern women is the fact that in the redoubtable National Portrait Gallery of the

Smithsonian Institution, in the gallery room devoted to the Civil War, Mary Boykin Chesnut holds a place of honor, surrounded by Stonewall Jackson, Jefferson Davis, and Robert E. Lee. No portrait of Varina Davis hangs in the room, nor do those of Sally Tompkins, Louisa McCord, or Rose Greenhow — all women Mary Chesnut knew well. Looking her best, with her wide, intelligent brow and charming smile, Chesnut stands alone among all those powerful men — just the sort of situation she thoroughly enjoyed in life and recorded so happily in her journal. She is preserved there as the very paradigm of the southern lady.

As the pages of her book reveal, however, Mary Boykin Chesnut was also a woman of startling paradoxes. C. Vann Woodward, editor of a new, scholarly edition of her journal, has characterized her thus:

> Mary Chesnut was a complex and paradoxical personality, and her book often does more to multiply than to answer the questions that it raises about the author. Among them are the puzzles of how such strong antislavery sentiment was bred in the very heart of a slave society and how such vehement feminism burst out of a thoroughly patriarchal order. Here was an essentially secular-minded intellect in the midst of a deeply religious community, an independent-minded intellectual planted in the elite of a traditionalist social system. She loved city life and lived a rural life. Her interests were cosmopolitan and her existence parochial. She could at times be as arrogant and ambitious as the males she scorned, yet she always had an eye for appealing men and the capacity to charm when she chose.[3]

By reading Chesnut carefully, we can learn a great deal about southern women; but because she is in some respects atypical we must be careful about generalizations. In fact, the life and work of Mary Boykin Chesnut provide us with an excellent example of a body of material that can be, for the feminist scholar, a gold mine — but a mine we must explore very carefully, very responsibly, taking every precaution to avoid bringing to it our own preconceptions and prejudices.

It has become a truism of southern studies that the ideals shared by most southerners — those ideals based on the gentleman of honor and the gentle lady — tended to work their way down into the middle and lower classes from the planter aristocracy. One reason, then, for our continuing fascination with and trust in the views of Mary Chesnut is that she was a product of that aristocracy: an intelligent representative of the establishment. Until recently, very little has been known about her life before 1861 or after 1865. In fact, that life accords beautifully, at least in outline, with stereotyped notions of the prewar belle, pampered by her mammy and living in the lap of luxury, and the postwar woman, carefully preserving her threadbare antebellum dresses and engaged in a dignified struggle to make ends meet in a ruined world.

Mary Boykin Miller Chesnut was born in 1823, to a mother of an old and respected South Carolina family and to a father, Stephen Decatur Miller, who already had served a term in the United States Congress. Before she was ten years old, her father also would serve terms as governor of South Carolina and United States senator. Thus, throughout her childhood, politics — in particular, the states' rights and nullification controversies of the late 1820s and early 1830s — were in the very air she breathed, and her circles included most of the politically and socially prominent families of South Carolina.[4]

Mary was educated in a manner commensurate with the economic and social standing of her family. Her earliest memories were of being instructed by her maternal grandmother in the art and duties of running a large plantation.[5] She was educated first at home and then attended, from 1833 to 1835, a school for girls run by Stella Phelps in Camden.[6] At age twelve she was enrolled by her father in a fine French boarding school in Charleston, run by an indomitable Frenchwoman, Ann Marson Talvande, where she spoke only French or German during school hours. At Madame Talvande's she received formal education in languages, literature, history, rhetoric, astronomy, botany, and chemistry, as well as in the "accomplishments," such as music, drawing, and dancing, so necessary to a young lady of good breeding.[7]

Madame Talvande, who possessed what Mary later described as "the fiercest eye I have ever seen in a mortal head," was a strict taskmaster and kept a close watch on her young charges, but Mary managed now and then to escape her watchful eye and to explore the pleasure of Charleston society. A frequent companion was James Chesnut, Jr., a recent graduate of Princeton and son of one of the wealthiest and largest planters in the state. When Governor Miller discovered that his thirteen-year-old daughter had been seen walking on the Charleston Battery in the moonlight with a gentleman, he determined less than a year later to remove Mary from gossip. He took her for several months to his cotton plantation in rural Mississippi, a state just emerging from frontier status. In 1837, at fourteen, she returned to Madame Talvande's school for an additional year or so of formal schooling, which ended abruptly by the death of her father in 1838. Mary returned to Camden, made one trip with her mother to Mississippi to settle the estate, and then became formally engaged to James Chesnut, Jr. In 1840, three weeks after her seventeenth birthday, she married and went to live with James at Mulberry, his family's plantation three miles south of Camden.[8]

The new Mrs. Chesnut came to Mulberry expecting, in due course, to assume her prescribed role as wife, mother, and mistress of the household — a position for which she had been carefully trained. James Chesnut, Jr., was heir to an immense fortune, and his parents were both in their mid-sixties. But Mary Boykin Chesnut gradually realized that her very natural expectations were destined to go unfulfilled. Her in-laws, James Chesnut, Sr., and Mary Cox Chesnut, retained vigorous control of lands and household for twenty-five more years. Neither died until the 1860s. Far more devastating for Mary was her failure to have any children. Thus, the first twenty years of her marriage provided her with few outlets for her creativity and fewer still for her emotional, passionate nature. She suffered from periodic illness; the nature of her sicknesses is unknown, but they may have been at least partially psychosomatic. Occasional bouts of depression plagued her throughout her twenties, thirties, and forties.

Her relationship with her in-laws and even her husband was often tense. After outbursts of temper, she developed the habit of retreating to her third-floor library to read religious works for penitence, French, English, and German classics for intellectual stimulation, and novels for pure pleasure. "How much of the pleasure of my life," she later wrote, "I owe those much reviled writers of fiction."[9] Many aspects of life at Mulberry seemed precious to her: the beauty of the grounds, the ease of an existence smoothed by well-trained servants. But hers was a restless, gregarious personality. In later years, she would say of life at Mulberry: "A pleasant, empty, easy going life. If one's heart is at ease. But people are not like pigs; they cannot be put up and fattened. So here I pine and fret."[10]

James Chesnut, Jr., a lawyer by training, spent the years between 1840 and 1860 in public service, serving the state legislature and eventually becoming a leading statesman. Not surprisingly, Mary involved herself in his work, serving as his hostess, secretary, and amanuensis, and keeping herself well abreast of the political realities of the day. When in 1858 Chesnut went to the United States Senate, his wife accompanied him to Washington and quickly found herself in her element. Hers was, of necessity, a social role, and yet she was a far more astute politician than her husband. During her years in Washington she came to know most of the prominent politicians of the day and formed fast friendships with numerous southern legislators who would soon become the military and political elite of the Confederacy. Her intelligence, her wit, her reputation as a "literary" lady, her facility for languages, and her skill as a conversationalist all worked together to make her sought after in social circles. More important, by all accounts she possessed what we can only call charm. Women were occasionally uneasy in her presence, but men—some of the most powerful men of her time— were drawn to her.

As hostility between North and South grew in the fall of 1860, James Chesnut, Jr., resigned his seat in the Senate and returned to South Carolina to help draft an ordinance of secession. His wife's comment was succinct: "I am not at all resigned."[11] In spite of her love for Washington, she quickly cast her lot with her state and became an ardent supporter of the South and of Jefferson Davis, whose wife Varina had become a friend when both husbands served in the Senate.

As war became a certainty, Mary Boykin Chesnut began to keep a journal of her day-to-day routine and of the rumors and news she heard. At first she wrote in an elegant, red, leather-bound diary with gilt edges and a brass lock, but as the privations of wartime cut off supplies she continued her journal in anything she could find, at last recording the bleak aftermath of civil war in the blank pages of an old recipe book. The journal she kept was a private one. Portions of it that survive today contain notes hurriedly jotted down, designed to remind her later of people, events, opinions, conversations, and impressions of the moment. Many of her entries are almost cryptic; all are utterly candid. By keeping her diary under lock and key, she could record exactly what occurred to her. After meeting South Carolina's Governor Francis Pickens, she could write, "old Pick was there with a better wig — & his silly & affected wife." After dining at someone else's house, she could write, "I can give a better dinner than that!"[12] Blisters, bug bites, and other unmentionable miseries of the body and spirit all were recorded in this original diary.

Mary Chesnut was in an excellent position to "cover" the war. She was in Charleston with her husband at Christmas 1860 when Major Robert Anderson moved into Fort Sumter. The Chesnuts then went to Montgomery, where James attended the Confederate Provisional Congress and where Mary's hotel quarters served as the first of her wartime salons in which the men engaged in forming the new government and their wives congregated to gossip, to plot and plan, or simply to relax. In Montgomery, Mary renewed her friendship with Varina Davis, a friendship that deepened throughout the war. From Montgomery the Chesnuts returned to Charleston. James, as an aide to General Pierre G. T. Beauregard, participated in negotiations with Major Anderson, and Mary recorded the first event of the Civil War. She spent most of the next several months in Richmond while her husband continued with his staff duties and his role as member of the Provisional Congress. Mary, from her vantage point in the Spottswood Hotel, temporary headquarters for the Davises and numerous other dignitaries, participated fully in the social events of a city pulsing with excitement. She waited with Varina Davis for news of the battle at Manassas and visited the first sick and wounded of the war. And always, she wrote in her journal, sometimes expressing there her fears for her country and her outrage over the antics of the men in positions of authority. "This war began a War of Secession," she wrote as early as March 1861, "and it will end a War for the Succession of Places." By August, when her husband seemed unable to decide whether to go into the army or stand for reelection to the Confederate Senate, she exploded in her journal, "Jeff Davis ill & shut up — & none but noodles have the world in charge."[13]

As a woman Mary could neither join the army nor hold office, and her frustrations frequently found their way into her journal. "Oh," she moaned in April 1861, "if I could put some of my reckless spirit into these discreet cautious lazy men." She hoped James would be appointed ambassador to France; failing that, she wanted him to be reelected senator, not least because she wanted to avoid having to go home to Mulberry. At one point, she wrote, "I wish Mr. Davis would send *me* to Paris — & so I should not *need* a South Carolina Legislature for anything else." Back in Camden, her husband's apparent indifference to the war raging in Virginia infuriated her: "*Now* when if ever man was stirred to the highest for his country & for his own future—he seems as utterly absorbed by Negro squable [*sic*], hay stealing—cotton saving. . . . If I had been a man in this great revolution—I should have either been killed at once or made a name & done some good for my country. Lord Nelson's motto would be mine—Victory or Westminster Abbey."[14]

James Chesnut finally chose to run for the Senate rather than enter the army, and, because he refused to do anything to further his own election, more aggressive politicians secured his seat. During 1862 he served as chairman of a wartime executive council in South Carolina empowered to oversee the military and defense concerns of the state. In December 1862 President Davis appointed him colonel and summoned him to Richmond as a personal aide. This appointment suited Mary Chesnut perfectly. She managed to rent quarters close to the White House of the Confederacy, and thereafter the Chesnuts and Davises visited almost daily. In Richmond, as in Charleston, Montgomery, and Columbia, Mary Boykin Chesnut's renown as a hostess assured that she had a constant round of visitors; genteel guests of any rank were certain of a hearty welcome, good food, lovely women, and interesting conversation, most of which found its way into Mary's journal.

As the South fought on to inevitable defeat, Mary Chesnut was forced into exile, tasting for the first time the devastation wrought upon her homeland. In adversity, the qualities that characterized Mary sustained her. In Lincolnton, North Carolina, for example, while Sherman burned Columbia, she experienced poverty and met that horror with strength and wry good humor. She had bought books—"Shakespeare—Moliere—Sir Thomas Browne Arabian nights in French—Pascal's letters"—but her Confederate money was worthless to buy food. "I am bodily comfortable—if somewhat dingily lodged," she wrote, "and I daily part with my raiment for food. We find no one, who will exchange eatibles for Confederate money—So we are devouring our clothes."[15]

Two months later, as word came of Robert E. Lee's surrender, she had moved again, this time to three vacant rooms in Chester, South Carolina. Again she kept open house as old friends were drawn to her. "My dining room is given up to them—and we camp on the landing—with our own table and six chairs." Lacking beds, everyone slept on the floor. "Night and day this landing and these steps are crowded with the Elite of the Confederacy—going and coming—and when night comes . . . more beds are made on the floor of the landing place. . . . The whole house is a bivouac."[16] General John Preston and his daughters came, as did General John Bell Hood, Senator and Mrs. Louis Wigfall, Mary's own nephew John Chesnut, Governor Milledge L. Bonham of South Carolina, Senator Clement Clay, and finally, utterly exhausted, Varina Davis and her four small children, fleeing arrest.

The Chesnuts returned to Camden, to a society in many respects devastated by four years of war. Family fortunes had been lost. Although the land remained, it was encumbered by huge debts that, during the Reconstruction years, the Chesnuts were unable to repay. James finally inherited Mulberry in 1866, but his inheritance included not only debt but a host of relatives and former slaves dependent upon him. The Chesnuts were by no means poor — money usually could be scraped together for trips to visit relatives; when visitors came, Mary could and did don her antebellum Paris dresses and set her tables with fine china and crystal. But her scale of living had changed dramatically, cutting her off from her friends of the war years and from the luxuries she so loved. As a realist she knew that she might hope for stability but that she would never again enjoy wealth. Despite bouts of sickness in the years immediately after the war, Mary took over the responsibilities of running the household and the cottage industries that supplied the plantation, assisted in overseeing farming affairs and keeping plantation records, and establishing a small butter-and-egg business that brought pin money into the household. Because she lacked the ready cash with which to buy the books and magazines so necessary to her existence, she formed a book cooperative with relatives and friends in which money was pooled to buy current publications that the women passed among themselves.

Reading and discussing literature thus continued to be an important outlet. Another was writing. The journals Mary had kept during the war had served as an emotional release during a turbulent time. Now she saw the possibility of earning money by some kind of literary effort. She began by translating portions of French novels but apparently never published any of her efforts. Instead, in the early 1870s she decided to try her hand at fiction and worked on two novels more or less simultaneously. One was a largely autobiographical novel she called "Two Years of My Life" that deals with a schoolgirl at Madame Talvande's French School for Young Ladies in Charleston who is taken by her father to a raw cotton plantation in Mississippi. The other was a Civil War novel, entitled "The Captain and the Colonel," Mary Boykin Chesnut's first effort to use, in palatable form, the materials of her wartime journals.[17]

Neither of these first two efforts at fiction nor the surviving fragments of a third novel are polished works. These manuscripts are heavily revised in early chapters and show signs in late chapters that the author simply tired of them. Both, however, are extremely interesting for two reasons. First, they deal with themes that Mary Boykin Chesnut later was to develop effectively in her revised Civil War journal, including women's rights, the relationships of blacks and whites, and the impact of history — public and private — on the individual life. Second, these manuscript novels show the care and deliberation with which Chesnut, now in her mid-fifties, was teaching herself to write, to handle dialogue and description, to use imagery, to parallel characters and events, to wed theme with action, and to speak with a clearly defined narrative voice.

At one point in the 1870s Chesnut began the process of revising her Civil War journals, but it was not until 1881, when her apprenticeship in fiction was complete, that she bought a supply of notebooks and began revision in earnest. For the next three and a half years she patiently carved an hour or two from each day to work on the one incomparable book for which we remember her. The task was exhaustive, for in the twenty years since she had begun the journal she had gained objectivity. She had time to sort out the significant from the trivial and to find in trivialities emblems of the whole. She had discovered that she was a writer and a historian, with something crucially important to say to the generations that would live after her. So the diary was no longer a diary, and though she preserved the diary format and took care never to alter fact or to admit an anachronism into her book, the diary had become a carefully structured and dramatic literary work.

When James Chesnut fell ill in 1884 his wife put aside her book to care for him and for her mother, who succumbed to a final illness less than three weeks later. Mother and husband died within a week of each other early in 1885, leaving Mary ill, emotionally exhausted, grief stricken, and desperately poor. Chesnut's estates reverted on his death to his nephew; Mary now had only her home, Sarsfield. For the next year and a half her time was taken by the running of her dairy business and the settlement of her husband's affairs. She died in 1886, before she could resume work on the revised journal.

Mary Boykin Chesnut's book, unfinished at her death and unpublished in any form for almost twenty years thereafter, is an enormous work. (Woodward's complete edition runs to nearly nine hundred large pages.) And, of course, it is far more than merely a detailed listing of the events that filled one woman's days for more than four years. It is also a broad picture of a society — of country and city life, of the motives and emotions that lay behind political, military, and domestic events, and of the views expressed in drawing rooms, across dining tables, in churches, railroad cars, and hospitals throughout the South from the beginning of a glorious war to the end of a way of life.

The particular triumph of this book is that, although Chesnut wrote it twenty years after the war, she never allowed herself to slip into stereotypes. Here, surrounded by belles and flirts, is a slave-owning lady of refinement, moving around in hoop skirts, knitting socks for the soldiers, soothing the brows of the wounded, and mixing mint juleps. She tells us about fire-breathing devil-may-care rebels, ruthless slave masters and kindly ones, crafty slaves and slaves proud of their loyalty, good ole boys and brave young gentlemen privates who ride hell-bent for leather and who love to dance and die with the word "mother" on their lips — and yet all of these characters really existed; they are not caricatures.

Scholars have difficulty looking at this book as a whole. Our tendency is to snip out little portions of it — rarely more than a sentence, often just a phrase — as supporting evidence for our own analyses. Most of us, in other words, have used Mary Boykin Chesnut as a source of quotations, rather like the Bible. By carefully choosing quotations and gently lifting them out of context, we can find proof of almost anything. To show that Mary Chesnut loathed slavery, we need only to quote: "I wonder if it be a sin to think slavery a curse to any land — Sumner said not one word of this hated institution which is not true — men & women are punished when their masters & mistresses are brutes & not when they do wrong. . . . God forgive *us* that ours is a monstrous system & wrong & iniquity."[18] On the other hand, we can easily prove Mary Chesnut a racist who refers to blacks as "dirty — slatternly — idle — ill smelling by nature."[19] To show her subordinate relationship to her husband (a relationship typical of nineteenth-century southern families), we can cite her comment when he ordered her to stop socializing in December 1863: "JC laid the law down last night. I felt it to be the last drop in my full cup. . . . He is the master of the house — to hear is to obey."[20] But turning to another page, we illustrate Mary Boykin Chesnut's feminism by quoting her description of the slave-owner who dallies in the quarters but demands respect at home: "From the height of his awful majesty he scolds and thunders at his wife and daughters as if he never did wrong in his life. Fancy such a man finding his daughter reading 'Don Juan' — 'You with that immoral book!' and he orders her out of his sight. You see Mrs. Stowe — did not hit the sorest spot — She makes Legare [Legree] a bachelor."[21]

The point here, of course, is that the Chesnut journal, written by a complex woman, offers us a complex picture of a complex society. We cannot use the journal properly unless we are willing to acknowledge and carefully preserve that complexity. The Chesnut journal and its author defy labels. In fact, a central purpose behind this remarkable body of material may well be to compel future generations to confront the nuances and interrelationships within every element of the society about which Mary Boykin Chesnut wrote. As scholars, we ought to avoid using the journal casually, to buttress our generalizations. Mary Chesnut did not flinch from the necessity to place conflicting rumors, opposing opinions, contradictory facts side by side. She challenges us not only to use her material but to emulate her determination to present all sides of the truth as she saw it.

Chapter 13

Careers in Landscape Architecture:

Recovering for Women

What the "Ladies" Won and Lost

CATHERINE M. HOWETT

Writers and commentators upon the discipline of landscape architecture are fond of introducing their subject with the observation that landscape design is a science and an art as old as human history — "as old as man himself" is the preferred phrase — and historical surveys usually take as their starting point those earliest civilizations that have left evidence of their manipulation of the natural landscape to serve a variety of communal needs, ranging from mere survival to myth, magic, and sensory delight. Nevertheless, as an officially recognized and classified profession in this country, "landscape architecture" is little more than a century old, having been first given this designation by the "father of landscape architecture" himself, Frederick Law Olmsted, at the time of his involvement with the design of New York City's Central Park in the 1860s. The coining of this new title — landscape architect — undoubtedly was motivated in part by the inadequacy of the earlier description, "landscape gardener," a term inherited from the English eighteenth-century landscape tradition and perhaps too effete to convey the sense of high public purpose to which the new practitioners felt themselves called. The choice of the new professional designation was probably meant to sever the identification with exclusively horticultural concerns, particularly those associated with the domestic landscape. Landscape architecture suggested an occupation more virile and pragmatic, borrowing the historic prestige of architecture as a rigorous intellectual, scientific, and aesthetic vocation. The change in title responded, moreover, to the realities of the new opportunities for work provided by the burgeoning demand in cities across America for improvements to the municipal fabric — the movement for rural cemeteries first of all, and then public parks, parkways, residential subdivisions, and finally the kind of idealized urban complex that found its consummate expression at the end of the century in the "White City" created for the Chicago World's Fair. Olmsted's firm had been part of the consortium of designers given the commission by the federal government to design the World's Columbian Exposition in 1893 and would be part, as well, of the interdisciplinary design team charged by Senator James McMillan's special commission with producing a plan for the improvement of Washington, D.C., in 1901. The fledgling profession that Olmsted had named forty years earlier clearly had come into its own by the turn of the century.

Curiously, however, the complex of associations summoned up by the older term—landscape gardening—persisted well into the new age of city building and beautifying and served to accommodate the identification of the profession, especially under its older title, as one appropriate to feminine interest and involvement. This identification had not always been the case. In 1841, when Andrew Jackson Downing published his enormously popular *Treatise on the Theory and Practice of Landscape Gardening, Adapted to North America*, the audiences for such a manual on the "tasteful" improvement of house and grounds were clearly the male landholders; all of the estates Downing illustrated were described in terms of their gentlemen owners, who very often served, Downing noted, as their own architects and landscape designers. By the end of the century, however, women had assumed a much more influential role in residential design decisions, a fact amply demonstrated by the emergence, in quite a short span of years, of a series of magazines dealing with the interior and exterior environment and addressed almost exclusively to women as homemakers. The *Ladies Home Journal*, which had begun publication in 1883 with a focus on fashions in food, clothing, and manners, by 1901 was publishing the plans of Frank Lloyd Wright for a new kind of prairie house. Some building trade magazines actually changed their titles to attract the new feminine market: The *Scientific American Building Monthly* became *American Homes and Gardens* in 1905, while *Keith's Magazine on Home Building* became *Beautiful Homes Magazine*. *House Beautiful*, begun in 1896, and *House and Garden*, founded in 1901, were perhaps the most influential of these new journals; the latter was subtitled: *An Illustrated Monthly Devoted to Practical Suggestions on Architecture, Garden Designing and Planting Decoration, Home Furnishing and Kindred Subjects*.

The laying out of house and grounds and the planning of the garden, then, were coming to be seen as natural extensions of the Victorian woman's domestic concerns. A number of women were active contributors on gardening subjects to the new homemaker magazines and to horticultural periodicals, and women predominated over men as authors of garden "biographies," a literary genre that achieved new heights of popularity in this period, the female author sharing with her readers glimpses into the world of her own garden. Celia Thaxter's *An Island Garden*, published in 1893, is typical of many such books, recording in intimate detail every aspect of the design and care of her Maine garden and the myriad pleasures it afforded.[1] Another work published in the same year, Mrs. Schuyler

Van Rennselaer's very successful *Art Out-of-Doors*, is not a garden biography but an eloquent apologia for the profession of landscape architecture, arguing that landscape design is a "fourth art" that must be ranked with architecture, sculpture, and painting inasmuch as "it demands quite as much in the way of aesthetic feeling, creative power, and executive skill." Van Rennselaer's book reveals a sophisticated understanding of the historical evolution of landscape fashion, as well as the criteria employed in current practice. She praises Frederick Law Olmsted as "the most remarkable artist yet born in America," and, although most of the book's recommendations have to do with what Van Rennselaer calls "the home grounds," she fully comprehends the new breadth of the profession's role, which the design of the Chicago World's Fair, described by her at some length, had demonstrated.[2] She puzzles over the problem of nomenclature, observing that "landscape gardener" as a description has "fallen into such disrepute that it is often replaced by 'landscape-architect'":

> French usage supports this term, and it is in many respects a good one. But its derivative, "landscape-architecture," is unsatisfactory; and so, on the other hand, is "landscape-artists," although "landscape-art" is a good general term. Perhaps the best we can do is to keep to "landscape gardener," trying to remember that it ought always to mean an artist and an artist only.[3]

A good case might be made that in holding out for the older term Van Rennselaer was intuitively defending her right, and the right of other women, to play some part in this profession she admires with such passionate intensity. It is ironic that in a chapter of her book that she devotes to explaining the exciting career possibilities in landscape-gardening ("The chances for employment are already good . . . and are growing better year by year; and surely there is no profession whatsoever . . . which suggests to the imagination so delightful an existence") she ends by expressing the hope that "many young men" will feel called to pursue such an option.[4] Nevertheless, for all that she may, out of a demure Victorian lady's respect for social custom, always refer to the landscape architect in masculine terms, it is also true that she clearly considers herself to be an authority on her subject, in all aspects.

We are describing, of course, a historical moment in which women were just beginning to consider respectable alternatives to nursing and teaching as career possibilities, with most careers being seen as appropriate only to the few years before marriage, barring the grim possibility that the woman might remain a spinster having to support herself. What the new literature seemed to suggest — the homemaker magazines and the books by women on gardening and landscape subjects — was that it was not unladylike to enjoy the landscape arts, even to pursue them. As early as the 1870s, the University of Illinois had offered formal courses in "landscape gardening" that advertised that "ladies and gentlemen alike engage in the studies and exercises of the course," and the Massachusetts Institute of Technology had a program in the 1890s that apparently graduated a number of successful women.[5] A few women practitioners actually were becoming very well known for their work and were able to serve as models for other aspirants. Gertrude Jekyll, a wealthy and aristocratic unmarried English-woman, wrote prolifically about gardening but was also an active professional in a genteel way, designing over 350 gardens in her lifetime and earning wide respect for her imaginative and painterly landscape compositions. She had studied the work of William Robinson, an important English landscape gardener and author, and she worked very closely with Edward Luychens, one of the major architects of the period. In this country, Beatrix Jones Farrand was one of the eleven founding members of the American Society of Landscape Architects in 1899. Norman T. Newton's history of the development of landscape architecture summarizes her career.

> As a young woman she lived in Brookline [Massachusetts] with the Sargents while studying under Professor Sargent at the Arnold Arboretum. From the large office that she later maintained for some years in New York, she carried on an extensive and demanding practice, mainly on private residential projects but also as consul-tant landscape gardener — a title on which she always insisted — to Princeton, Yale, the University of Chicago, Oberlin and other institutions. . . . From 1922 on, she was in full charge of all outdoor efforts at Dumbarton Oaks; these gardens and the great quadrangles at Princeton and Yale are generally regarded as her most out-standing professional work. Yale made her an honorary Master of Arts in 1926 and Smith College a Doctor of Humane Letters in 1935. She was an Honorary Member of the American Institute of Architects.[6]

It is interesting that Newton makes a point of Farrand's insistence upon describ-ing herself as a landscape gardener — the older term, growing surely more old-fashioned as the century progressed, tied to the old traditions of the garden and home. Could it have represented for her, in spite of the enviable commissions she was receiving, some ratification of her woman's involvement in a man's profes-sional world? After all, no less a person than Frederic Law Olmsted had referred upon one occasion to his eminent fellow practitioner as a person who was "supposed to be in some way inclined to dabble in Landscape Architecture."[7]

Early Opportunities for Women

It is undeniable that the pioneering women who entered the profession of landscape architecture in the early decades of the twentieth century encountered discrimination in a variety of forms. For one thing, the initial promise of equal educational opportunity through academic programs in the land-grant colleges of the Midwest was seriously compromised by later developments. Harvard University had established the first full-fledged school of landscape architecture in 1900 and had absorbed MIT's program, locking women out in that region. But the energy and determination of the women seeking avenues to professional status in landscape architecture seem to have been indomitable. Two outstanding schools devoted to the separate but equal education of women in landscape architecture were founded in Massachusetts: the Lowthorpe School of Landscape Architecture, Gardening and Horticulture for Women in Groton, Massachusetts, which by the 1930s was one of only thirteen accredited programs in the country; and the Cambridge School of Architecture and Landscape Architecture in Cambridge, until Harvard University finally opened its doors to women in 1942. Professor Henry Frost, one of the founders of the Cambridge school, later reflected on the climate of those early years:

> A study of the period will show that there was a certain unrest among women, a desire to broaden their horizons and their activities. This had been developing gradually . . . but in 1915–16 the plight of the average girl who aspired to what were considered men's careers was not enviable . . . We were too young to have a mature judgment of the educational and social changes that were going on quietly. . . . We had had no training that helped us to understand that we had quite by chance been caught up in a small eddy of a greater movement in which women were beginning to demand equal educational rights with their brothers.[8]

Long before there were schools of landscape architecture, apprenticeship with an established practitioner had been a necessary initiation to practice, and even with the advent of formal academic programs the need still existed — as it does even today — for the novice to gain experience after school in a professional office. This area is one in which a number of the early women practitioners encountered problems; graduates of the Cambridge school recollected that the major objections to their hiring argued by prospective employers had to do with the fear that women in drafting rooms would disrupt office "morale" (read "morals") and that women were not suited to fieldwork, to superintending construction and other on-site responsibilities. It is hardly surprising, therefore, that residential design work still offered the most opportunities, for in this kind of practice women could take advantage of the lingering connotations of landscape gardening as an area in which they might naturally excel.

Fortuitously, opportunities for women to find lucrative and important commissions doing this kind of work were greatly enhanced by the historic phenomenon now described as the Country Place Era. Large numbers of Americans had amassed considerable fortunes, and a primary expression of status was afforded by the development of a fine estate, house and grounds being planned at a genuinely lavish scale, frequently in imitation of European architectural and landscape styles. The collapse of the economy in the 1929 crash and the subsequent overhaul of federal tax policies brought about an abrupt end to this gilded era. But it was an expansive and prosperous one for most architects, although many saw the identification of the profession with services to a wealthy clientele as ultimately damaging to a proper understanding on the part of the public of the real scope of landscape architecture and its potential for public service. Nevertheless, the period in which large-scale residential commissions constituted the major focus of the profession had worked particularly to the advantage of women practitioners, a number of whom achieved national celebrity as designers.[9] It might be fair to say, in the language of contemporary social psychology, that landscape architecture in this period was less "gender typed" as a male profession. However, when the market for such services virtually collapsed, the professional offices run by men moved away from residential design, finding it no longer profitable, and concentrated instead on public and commercial work. Women were less competitive in these areas because such work requires larger offices and, more importantly, a recognition by prospective employers and clients that women are as competent as men to handle such projects.

Losing Ground

The depression years of the 1930s and the war years of the 1940s were difficult ones for landscape architecture generally but for women practitioners in particular. Feminine visibility in the profession declined radically. Ironically, women had been more of a presence in the field in the days before university programs were opened to them; when they had had to develop and staff their own schools, more women were involved in education and conspicuously successful in their practices. The world of landscape architecture had changed; all of the ties with the landscape gardening tradition that initially had favored women were no longer operative in any way. A number of women continued to elect to do the residential design work that most offices rejected, and there was an unspoken agreement in the male-dominated profession that that was where women would be tolerated — "doing the backyards." There were exceptions, of course; a few women did manage to find work in good offices, in government practice, or by establishing their own offices. But the fact remains that after the generation of Beatrix Farrand, Annette Hoyt Flanders, and Marion Coffin, all of whom made their reputations during the Country Place Era, no women have achieved their level of national recognition.

In 1972 the American Society of Landscape Architects, presumably in response to the concerns expressed at that time for equal opportunity in work, established a special task force to investigate the current status of women within the profession. The official report published the following year offered the following summary of their research.

> Although 50% of the population and 40% of the work force in this country is comprised [*sic*] of women, less than 5% of the American Society of Landscape Architects are women, there are no women landscape architects teaching on a fulltime basis, and there is a very small percentage of women employed in male-headed offices.
>
> Over two-thirds of both groups of women responding members and nonmembers of the ASLA had experienced discrimination in a variety of ways — from lower salaries and unfair hiring and advancement policies to the assumption that they should do clerical work as well, but were not suited to field work or supervision.[10]

What made these figures even more shocking was the fact that the great environmental thrust of the 1960s had resulted in substantial increases in the number of students seeking professional degrees in landscape architecture, with an exceptionally high percentage of these new students being women. By 1977, women fully constituted 25 percent of the undergraduate students in landscape architecture and 30 percent of the graduate students, with some graduate departments having a component as high as 60 percent. In the same year, only fifteen women were teaching full-time in a department of landscape architecture, and over 50 percent of the programs had no women teaching in any capacity on their staffs.[11] Most of the women students entering the profession at the present time are not even aware of the fact that women in the past have played a more significant part in shaping the public image of the profession than they do today. How could they know, when the standard text in the history of landscape architecture, Newton's *Design on the Land*, published in 1971, mentions only three women practitioners in all of its 700-plus pages? Newton fails to mention Gertrude Jekyll, although the work of William Robinson, arguably less famous than Jekyll's, is discussed; he gives not one word about the founding of the Cambridge school, although the establishment of Harvard's department of landscape architecture in 1900, open only to men, is treated at some length. Women students in landscape architecture departments today find themselves in male-dominated departments struggling to prepare themselves for a male-dominated profession in which a number of required skills — particularly in construction, engineering, and fieldwork — are looked upon as having masculine associations. It is undeniably true that the life-experience of men students has provided them with much better preparation in these areas and that their secondary school education consistently has included more of the science and math that are important prerequisites for such programs. In the same way, after graduation women interested in trying to organize their own firms have more than their public image as competent professionals to worry about. Too often, their educational background once again may have short-changed them, because men are more likely to have picked up training along the way in financial management and planning, tax accounting, personnel management, and real estate law.

Strategies for Change

Women students perform very well in departments of landscape architecture and seem for the most part hardly aware of any handicaps shadowing their chances for future success. Many are proud, as a consequence of the women's movement, of having chosen a nontraditional occupation. A recent study suggests that women students generally place a higher value than do their male counterparts on intrinsic job satisfaction as opposed to financial security and may still, in fact, be operating unconsciously out of the traditional assumption that women are not obliged to prepare themselves to act as breadwinners within the family structure.[12] It would be hard to gainsay the fact that a small percentage of women students may have chosen landscape architecture as a more flexible career option, conducive, as nursing and teaching are, to part-time involvement during a period of child rearing, even to a kind of acceptable dilettantism. This essay is not the place to rehearse the mental attitudes and behavior patterns adapted by women historically in response to cultural stereotyping; what *does* concern us here are the positive approaches available within the university community that will result in equalizing the opportunities that man and women students can anticipate when they become active in the profession.

The profession itself, through the activities of the Committee for Women in Landscape Architecture of the American Society of Landscape Architects, officially has demonstrated its awareness of the special problems facing women who choose landscape architecture as a career. The committee has established a number of relatively modest but practical goals, among which are the organization of short courses in such subjects as business and financial management for women professionals, promoting the increased involvement of women in committees and offices of the ASLA at the national and local levels, and sponsoring workshops and other occasions that will bring small groups of women professionals together informally to discuss issues of common concern.

Within the schools and universities, a single goal has received priority to the exclusion of any other; women professionals and women students, not to mention the affirmative action administration of the various campuses, have pressed for the recruitment of more women into teaching positions in departments of landscape architecture, to redress the reprehensible imbalances that exist at the present time. One hardly needs to argue the right of exposure to women teachers as role models. Elizabeth Douvan has spoken to this critical question of the role of models in women's professional development.[13]

Parenthetically, women in landscape architecture run the risk of being doubly deprived of female models and mentors, because the chances of serving an apprenticeship with a successful woman practitioner are statistically slim. I have referred above to the profession's long tradition of apprenticeship, an institutionalized equivalent of the protégé(e) system that determines advancement in a number of professions. The system has a propensity for inhibiting the progress of women because many professional men are wary of accepting a woman as protégée in preference to a male candidate — for reasons that range from fear that marriage and children will deflect her career, to ambiguous feelings about the propriety of initiating a loyalty/dependence relationship with a younger woman.[14] If more women were well established and successful practitioners, they would be more likely to accommodate this necessary role of protégée for women just entering the profession.

But perhaps the most critical qualification to be born in mind in any discussion of the problem of providing feminine models for women students in landscape architecture programs is that as a solution mere tokenism will not produce the systemic, lasting changes that a decent humanism demands. Women in landscape architecture are correct in thinking that the schools should be able to help in overcoming the disadvantaged position to which women have been reduced in the profession, but the strategies for change must go beyond a more committed recruitment of women teachers. Women and men educators must be challenged to examine the structure and content of curriculum in order to discover the ways in which it may be biased against the needs and rights of women students. At the most obvious level, we need a revisionist history that deliberately seeks out evidence of ways in which women denied access to the mainstream of practice have contributed to the shaping of the human landscape. Courses at any level ought not to presume experience where none may exist for women; a course requiring model building, for example, ought to offer supplementary instruction for students working with power tools for the first time. But most importantly, courses in professional practice — a required part of any curriculum in landscape architecture — need to be exploited for the opportunity they present to bring the whole issue of women's place in the profession out into the open. Such courses could be used to encourage an understanding of historic patterns of discrimination and their causes, the extent to which those patterns are still operative, and what changes in attitude and behavior will remedy them. Here is a unique opportunity to stimulate men and women students to reflect candidly together upon these issues, laying the groundwork for improved professional relationships in the future.

If it is true that high school and college counselors need to be made aware of the career potential in landscape architecture and should encourage women students to consider taking more science and math than they might otherwise, it is also true that the discipline of landscape architecture is not helped by the prevailing academic emphasis upon its scientific aspects. Men and women both would be better served by a reevaluation of priorities that the male-dominated profession has not pursued. Women ought not to be made to feel, in choosing a career in landscape architecture, that they must learn to "think like a man," much less to design like one. Rather, the full participation of women in the profession ought to be seen as opening the door to an inrush of new design energies, new insights and skills. We have lived long enough with the dream of the "White City" — and what a sterile and impoverished vision that has proved to be! It was the image of the garden — the place of refreshment and delight, of nurturance and beauty — that in an earlier time became identified with the landscape making of women; one could do worse than hope that landscape architecture might recover for its own place making the power of that ancient symbol.

Chapter 14

Does Equality Mean Sameness?

A Historical Perspective on the

College Curriculum for Women

with Reflections on the Current Situation

DEBRA HERMAN

Colleges for women first developed in the United States because the nation's existing colleges were essentially colleges for men, admitting few or no women students.[1] As a matter of educational equity, women's colleges sought to provide women students with opportunities equivalent to those already offered to men at existing institutions.[2] Perhaps because of this heritage, sameness in education — that is, offering women a course of study identical to that given to men — often has been viewed as the simplest and best means of validating women's intellectual capabilities and the most promising method of furthering their access to areas of endeavor commonly barred to their sex. Yet such training at times has seemed foolish in its apparent disregard for existing differences between women's and men's life experiences. Historically, institutions that chose to educate women in the same manner as men stood vulnerable to the charge that they educated women as if they were men and thereby ignored the needs of the large numbers of women who would spend most of their lives within their sex's traditional domain, the home.

But if the ideal of equality as sameness was imperfect, the most obvious alternative — offering women a course of study directly attuned to their eventual domestic responsibilities — also left much to be desired. Advocates of women's rights, in particular, understandably feared that any concessions to directing women's higher education toward preparation for home life might undermine the potentially liberating aspects of a college education for women. Such inclusions, they said, would reinforce cultural pressures that already pushed young women toward a primarily domestic existence after graduation; and no less importantly, such a sex-linked curriculum would fail to provide them with preparation necessary for entry into certain career fields.

These arguments, then, defined the dilemma facing feminist educators at least through the first decades of this century. It seemed that one either ignored the fact of sex entirely, insisting that there was a single curriculum appropriate for men and women, or risked directing women's education toward reinforcing the conservative notion that women occupy themselves within the home as wives and mothers upon graduation.

In the United States in the mid-nineteenth century, the institution most strongly associated with the idea of equality as sameness was Vassar College.[3] Founded in 1861, when a higher education was all but unobtainable if one happened to be female, Vassar not only sought to augment the educational opportunities available to the female sex but also challenged the widely held belief that women were unable, both mentally and physically, to master the rigors of the course of study commonly provided to college men. The issue in 1861 was, in large part, could women do it?[4] Until that question was put to rest, until women's basic abilities were established, the college of necessity would focus its efforts on providing a rigorous test of women's intellectual capabilities. This evaluation was to be accomplished, and not surprisingly so, through the simple device of modeling the college's curriculum on that of the era's most prestigious colleges for men. Vassar strove to make its educational offering equivalent to those of Harvard or Yale and thereby to establish its students as the intellectual equals of men.[5]

This approach was maintained despite the efforts of those who questioned less the ability of Vassar women to do college-level work than the appropriateness of a curriculum designed for men as the basis for a woman's education. Most prominent among these critics was Sara Josepha Hale, the editor of *Godey's Lady's Book,* who, though enthusiastic about the Vassar experiment, charged that the college's curriculum was defective because it failed to prepare women for their domestic responsibilities. Hale warned that the man who comes down with a limp collar to an ill-cooked breakfast will find no great satisfaction when matters go wrong in the laundry and the kitchen in the knowledge that "the directress of these departments is fully qualified, in case of necessity, to navigate a vessel or survey a township."[6] Hale's arguments, however, were brushed aside by the college's planners, who countered that college was an inappropriate setting for the attainment of domestic skills. In this manner, Vassar evaded the issue. It avoided directly challenging women's traditional responsibilities to the home by placing elsewhere the burden of preparing women for these tasks.[7]

Vassar's success in making only minimal concessions to the sex of its student body in formulating its curriculum established the college as a unique educational experiment dedicated to establishing women's intellectual capacities. But the success of this experiment did not mean that the concerns expressed by Hale and others were either silenced or satisfied. Just the opposite proved to be the case. Ironically, the college's successful operation over time demonstrated not simply that women were capable of enduring the rigors of a higher education but also that the lives of women, college educated or not, remained strikingly different from those of men.[8] Given this fact, the pressure to take into account the divergent life prospects of men and women persisted. For a number of reasons, this pressure became more intense in the first decade of this century.

In part, concern with the content of women's higher education grew with the success of that part of the Vassar experiment dedicated to establishing women's ability to do college-level work. Institutions like Vassar demonstrated that women had minds worthy of nurturance through the device of training them *as if* they were men. Once women's capabilities were established beyond question, many contended that the time had come to give women an education specifically fitted to the needs of their own sex. Men's education, critics like the *Outlook* argued in 1899, must no longer serve as the standard with women's education "made to conform to it." The "next step forward" in the higher education of women, the magazine claimed, would be the insistence on a curriculum adjusted not "to masculine standards" but to women's own needs and preferences.[9] Now that women no longer suffered from the stigma of intellectual inferiority, the argument continued, they might be released from the limitations of the experiment that had proven their abilities. With equality of mind a fact, sameness in education would become a relic of the past, a necessary stage in the evolution of women's education, but only a stage, not the goal itself.

Of course, many who advocated an adjustment in the college curriculum for women were motivated less by concern for the well-being of college alumnae than by the fear that sameness in education might lead to disturbing changes in women's role outside the college. Significantly, the *Outlook* discussion of curriculum reform assumed that trouble inevitably followed an education that assumed "in the schoolroom that woman is to be prepared to serve in the world in competition with men in breadwinning employment outside the home," and assumed "in society that marriage is not to be foreseen and prepared for, but to be fallen into by chance that may be happy or otherwise as an inscrutable fate may direct."[10] Another observer, in this case a Vassar graduate, charged that "the general atmosphere of college and the attitude of many of the instructors, all goes, consciously or unconsciously, toward the discrediting, or at least putting in the background, the very things which should be emphasized in the training of girls."[11] The prominent psychologist and notorious anti-feminist G. Stanley Hall also allied himself with the curriculum reformers when he warned against the pernicious influence of those who argued that it was " 'not desirable' that women students should study motherhood, because they do not know whether they will marry; who encourage them to elect 'no special subjects because they are women,' and who think infant psychology 'foolish.' "[12]

Arguments such as these had a strong appeal for those fearful of changes in women's roles, but curriculum reformers were able to draw upon more than just the fear that college-educated women would be prone to leap from their properly assigned spheres. One indication that this support existed is the broad appeal the cause had among college alumnae. By the first decade of this century, calls for the creation of a college curriculum designed to meet the distinctive needs of women as women held sufficient sway with alumnae to alarm those pioneers who had struggled to establish women's right to a higher education in the first place. M. Carey Thomas, president of Bryn Mawr, warned in 1908: "Women are rapidly coming to control women's college education. It rests with us to decide whether we shall barter for a mess of pottage the inheritance of girls of this generation which the girls of my generation agonized to obtain for themselves and for other girls."[13]

The "mess of pottage" Thomas referred to generally amounted to what we would today term home economics. Thomas herself noted a demand for such courses as "infant psychology," "chemistry with special reference to cooking, and food values, and domestic science generally," and "physiology with special reference to motherhood and wifehood."[14] Most often such offerings were expected to supplement the existing curriculum rather than to supplant it. Yet however limited their place in the course of study, they represented a prod to students lest they forget their responsibilities to the home and a recognition of the reality that most, with or without such special training, were bound for "careers" as housewives.[15]

Why then did college women give their support to such a narrowing of their education and presumably their future options as well? There is no simple answer to this question, but the central cause of dissatisfaction may stem from the contrast between a curriculum that presumed no essential differences between the educational needs of men and women and a society that dictated divergent roles and responsibilities for the sexes. But the explanation can be made more specific. Not coincidentally, the demand for a new curriculum for women coincided with the appearance on campus of a new type of college woman. By 1900, the decision to attend college was no longer the anomalous act of a pioneer but the increasingly fashionable course of action for bright girls of the upper middle class.[16] Few such women came to college with the intention of setting themselves apart from others of their sex. But in college, particularly colleges like Vassar, these women acquired ideas and aspirations hard to reconcile with a traditional woman's life. Trained in the same manner as their brothers, their postgraduate futures still were expected to be those of traditional women, college-educated or not.

This discontinuity proved disturbing to both the graduate and her family. One Vassar father complained that college had unfitted his daughters "for the place in life that they were designed to fill."[17] Margaret Miner, Vassar class of 1920, wrote of the "College Blight," a vague but nevertheless quite real affliction that led the college woman to stick out like a sore thumb in her home community.

Critics like Miner saw "a charming, clever, popular eighteen-year-old enter college" only to come out "changed." "She is," in Miner's words, "not only four years older but four years more serious, a good supply of a sense of humor having been left behind somewhere. She is four years more confident in herself and four years less cooperative. She went in full of fun and came out full of opinions."[18] Or as Charles F. Thwing of Northwestern University noted in 1894, four years of college life tended to leave a woman "strangely out of sympathy with the world in which she must henceforth move."[19]

In 1901, the editor of the *Vassar Miscellany* advised her fellow students to accept whatever life offered them "cheerfully and gracefully" so that they might provide "strong and irrefutable" evidence that college did not unfit women for their proper role in life.[20] But adhering to such advice could prove difficult for women whose entire college training pointed in a different direction. College tended to give women a taste for activities other than domestic. The college woman was taught to think, in one alumna's words, "from the point of view of a man, or a woman who is doing man's work." Under the circumstances, could it be surprising that the college alumna was frequently "dissatisfied with her home"?[21]

Logically, such dissatisfaction need not have dictated the need for *educational* reforms. As one graduate noted, there was "a serious fault somewhere," but whether it was in the "college system" or "the larger system of our Society" remained to be established.[22] As this statement indicates, the dissatisfied graduate unable to find contentment within woman's traditional role might have asked for some readjustment with that role itself rather than finding fault with the education that presumably fueled her discontent. Evidence indicates, however, that students were far more likely to question college-bred ambitions than societal norms. Why then did so many college alumnae turn on an alma mater that offered a vision of possibilities desired but perhaps not immediately obtainable rather than a society that systematically denied those possibilities?

Part of the problem stems from the fictions assumed by those who were party to the Vassar experiment and other experiments like it. Conservative and feminist educators both created myths that attempted to reconcile sameness in education with a world characterized by divergent life prospects for the sexes. The conservative educators who presided over Vassar College claimed that women could receive an education as challenging and rigorous as that given to men and still return contently to their homes after graduation. For the feminist educators at Vassar and elsewhere, a higher education for women was promoted as paving the way toward expanded career options for women. In both cases, the presumptions proved at least partly mistaken.

The conservative claim that women could be educated like men and still remain women — that is, traditional women — formed a crucial bulwark of the Vassar experiment as officially defined. A Vassar education was sold to the public on the presumption that it would not seriously alter the status quo. More simply put, Vassar College, like most institutions of higher learning open to the female sex, was in no way intended to be a feminist institution. At Vassar, from an official perspective at least, higher education for women was not supported as a means of facilitating women's efforts to go beyond what was commonly assumed to be their sex's province. [23]

Such a view helped make higher education for women more widely acceptable, but it also produced a phenomenon aptly summed up by the cliché, "all dressed up with no place to go." Armed with an education as stimulating and rigorous as that given to men, the female graduate was to take it nowhere other than back into the home. And back into the home most went, though not without the stresses and strains many came to attribute to a misguided education. In the eyes of many graduates the fact that their college curriculum failed to "bear so definite and satisfactory relation to the after lives of women as it does to those of men" lessened the likelihood that the woman who married and remained a housewife would find happiness within her home. [24] This failure represented a serious concern for the housewife/alumna.

These concerns are echoed in a 1950 survey of the alumnae of Vassar College that revealed that a significant number of early twentieth century graduates regretted the fact that their Vassar education did not offer formal training in the care of children and the running of a home. In their minds, domestic education was preferable to the traditional classical curriculum Vassar had long offered as well as the career-oriented program others advocated. Indeed, their central claim was that marriage represented *the* woman's career while a Vassar education, as then constituted, failed to adequately prepare its graduates for home life or to inspire them to tackle such responsibilities in what one graduate termed a "creative" manner. [25]

Obviously, not all Vassar graduates shared these complaints, but summed up they amounted to the charge that the college failed to take into account the future responsibilities of a significant part of its constituency — those who married and cared for families. And if college offered no practical training, no specific preparation to aid these women in the tasks that daily occupied their minds and bodies, it also seemed to suggest that fulfillment and prestige lay elsewhere, in the world outside the home.

But what of those graduates who actively sought careers outside the home? Were not they staunch supporters of the view that equality meant sameness as the justification for the system of education by which they obtained the training necessary to launch their careers? The answer is: not always. Here the complicating factor was the presumption that properly prepared women would without great difficulty enter into occupations previously barred to their sex. This presumption proved problematical. In many cases, preparation alone did not allow women to enter into or succeed in male-dominated professions. In practice, Vassar alumnae found that they might freely use their talents and training only in what were commonly recognized women's occupations, most notably teaching. Although they studied the same curriculum as college men, their employment experience was divergent. Mastery of Latin grammar and higher mathematics might establish a woman's intellectual abilities but it did not pave the way to equal employment opportunity.[26]

Those Vassar graduates who did venture into male-dominated career fields found that a thick skin, willingness to engage in long struggle, and financial independence could be helpful, even essential, attributes. Women lawyers, "an expert" warned, "must be willing to be pioneers." Alice L. Carson advised the woman journalist that she would have to "steel herself to the difficulties." The same could be said in numerous other professions potentially attractive to the college-educated woman. Nowhere could she get by with the same energy, determination, or courage that would suffice for a man in the same field. Everywhere she would need to be better.[27]

Compounding external barriers were internal uncertainties. Frequently, graduates found that conflicts between womanhood and professionalism went beyond considerations of chivalry and struck at the heart of the "feminine" personality. Thus attorney Ella Halburd Young noted that assertiveness constituted an asset for a lawyer but was not a virtue in a woman.[28] Even more disturbing could be the seeming incompatibility of marriage and career. Those who hoped not for a choice between the two but for a combination of a "profession and marriage with justice and profit to all concerned" faced what to many must have seemed to be insurmountable difficulties.[29] No wonder Ida Tarbell, a critic of sameness in education for the sexes, could remark in 1929 that attaining equality for women seemed as easy a task to early feminists as it still did to newcomers: "Pass a few laws, open a few doors," and all would be well.[30] The struggle, as Tarbell and others who attempted to pioneer new occupational paths for women knew well, was far more complex than some had at first imagined.

From the perspective of the early twentieth-century college woman, then, the essential pitfall of the equality-as-sameness model of women's higher education was not that it attempted to challenge the view that the sexes had divergent talents but that it failed to address adequately the complexities of women's situation. Equalizing educational opportunity without looking beyond the college's gates was to attempt a piecemeal reform effort that left the beneficiaries of such training to cope, as best they might, with the ensuing personal and social problems.

Today, it seems fair to conclude, we have gone beyond the simple dichotomy between equality as sameness and difference as a defense of women's socially prescribed role. Certainly few now encourage young women to direct their college training toward preparation for marriage and motherhood. The model of equality as sameness, however, has retained, even gained, appeal, with the passage of time. For example, the wave of coeducation that swept many of the nation's most prestigious colleges only a decade or so ago gave women more complete access to educational opportunities while at least initially reinforcing the notion that men and women have essentially similar educational needs capable of being met in similar or, in this case, the same institutions. In most instances, coeducation proceeded on the theory that access alone was sufficient, that all that needed to be done was to plug women into institutions and programs of study once open to men only. This approach was adopted by my own alma mater, Yale University, which orginally conceived of coeducation as requiring few more substantial changes than new lettering on some bathroom doors and some minor concessions to what were deemed feminine aesthetic sensibilities — that is, new furniture for women's dormitory rooms.[31]

In the face of expanded opportunities for women at what were once all-male colleges some, for a time at least, came to see the women's colleges as obsolete, atavistic survivals of an age when women could not attend Harvard, Princeton, or Yale. And for a time, many thought their days numbered. Though their future may be uncertain still, more sober reflection has revealed a potentially important role for women's colleges as feminist institutions, as nurturers of female talent and alternatives to the male-dominated universities so many women attend.[32]

Women's studies programs also have faced criticisms from the adherents of the equality-as-sameness ideal who fear they will distract the liberated woman from her true agenda. As one critic of the University of Georgia women's studies program remarked: "It is not the best use of time for women to study women. The mastering of the professions is the key to emancipation."[33] Yet to such critics, I wish to suggest that access to male-defined and dominated institutions alone will not bring about the good of women's liberation, and furthermore that access alone will not build or sustain a feminist movement among college-educated women. The weight of historical experience suggests that educators concerned with both the future of feminism and of college women pay close attention to what earlier critics of the equality-as-sameness model termed "women's peculiar needs as women." These requirements need not be interpreted in the most conservative light as education for women's traditional place but rather as an attempt to recognize the strictures of women's existing situations even while promoting change.

Here women's studies programs can play a vital role in providing women with the historical perspectives and feminist awareness that can give meaning to the long, uphill struggle most will face. Here too, the women's college, once the product of a society that excluded women from signficant educational opportunities, must take on a new role. It must take care neither to mirror the college for men nor to cater in a reactionary manner to women's presumed special nature, but must dedicate itself openly and wholeheartedly to equipping women for an ongoing struggle for full and true equality. With anything less than such a commitment, today's women's colleges will run the risk so many colleges for women faced in the early years of this century—choosing between ignoring women's real life situation or pandering to current sexist notions of what should be a woman's life.

Finally, I wish to suggest that the debate over whether equality means sameness also touches on the questions of what is to be the standard. If women seek access alone, then the standard will continue to be male defined. In seeking to address women's needs in a time of transition, it seems vital to pay close attention to women's self-perceived needs as women and particularly the problems and dissatisfactions expressed by those embarking upon paths once reserved for men only. The difficulties or hesitations women experience in such efforts must be seen not simply as weakness or the unfortunate results of sexist upbringings that failed to adequately prepare young women for competition with men but as clues to what might be lacking in the male-dominated institutions, career paths, and lifestyles that so many young women are now seeking to emulate.

Chapter 15

Sex Differences in the Brain:

Implications for Curriculum Change

INA JANE WUNDRAM

That males and females are different is knowledge as old as the human race. In all populations there are noticeable average differences between men and women for height, muscle mass, fat distribution, hormones, amount of body hair, and a host of other anatomical and physiological qualities. However, the question of sex differences in the brain has created some controversy among students of human behavior and has inspired considerable research efforts in recent years. Is it nature or nurture that is responsible for the differences in males and females? Is there something in a little boy's brain that makes him more rambunctious than his sister? Are little girls really more verbal than their male classmates, or does our culture expect them to be that way? These questions hold significant interest for a number of scientific disciplines and educators interested in the developing child but are a long way from being answered.

Sexual Dimorphism

The problem of sex differences in the brain is part of a phenomenon known as sexual dimorphism. This term refers to the condition in a species whereby the males and females are different from one another in size or shape, and usually these structural differences correlate with behavioral differences. Human beings are members of the order of primates and, like many other members of this order, are sexually dimorphic for a number of characteristics.

It often helps in understanding the human situation to place it in perspective with that of other primates. For example, the savanna baboon is a very sexually dimorphic species. The males are twice the size of the females and have powerful bodies equipped with long canines. The smaller females are virtually defenseless against the tyranny of their mates, who collect as many females as they can into closely guarded harems. However, baboons are monkeys and not very closely related to human beings. Much nearer our own kind in an evolutionary sense are the great apes, who also exhibit sexual dimorphism. Male chimpanzees, gorillas, and orangutans are larger and more powerful than their female counterparts, but male-female relationships among these three species are quite different. The male gorilla is a benevolent soul who rules his family with quiet looks and serene dominance, while the male orangutan is viciously hostile to most females and prefers his solitude. By comparison, the chimps are quite gregarious, and male and female enjoy mutual respect. Chimpanzees are the least sexually dimorphic of the great apes and show the greatest similarity in male-female behavior. There is one group of primates, the lesser apes, that has very little sexual dimorphism and is the only group besides humans that is monogamous, choosing one mate for life. The males and females in this group are so similar in size, appearance, and behavior that only a specialist in primatology can tell the sexes apart and then only at close observation.[1]

Human beings are primates with slight sexual dimorphism (figure 15.1). In the population as a whole, the males average slightly higher than females in height and body weight, but it is well known that there are many females who are much larger than many males. Thus the differences are statistical ones. There is some evidence to indicate that in our evolutionary past this narrow margin was not the case, but instead the males were significantly larger than females long ago. These early hominids exhibited much greater sexual dimorphism than humans do today.[2] Why this difference should be so is under investigation by paleontologists, but the fact remains that in the present form of the human species the differences between males and females are much less than in any other higher primate except the lesser apes. However, while biology makes small distinctions between males and females, human culture greatly exaggerates these.

Sex, Roles, and Gender

Human beings are animals unique in the possession of culture. While it is difficult to define precisely the word "culture," most anthropologists agree that it is a learned system of belief and categories that structures experience or external reality and that is passed on from one generation to the next. The process whereby culture is transmitted is known as enculturation, and in the Western world this process is accomplished primarily through the educational system. To what extent does our culturally determined learned behavior affect males and females differently?

All cultures assign different roles to the two sexes.[3] Males and females are expected to dress, walk, act, and, in some cultures, speak differently. These distinctions are not biological but cultural, and what is masculine in one culture may be considered effeminate in another. Gender differences in roles and behavior are arbitrary and not necessarily based on innate abilities of either sex.

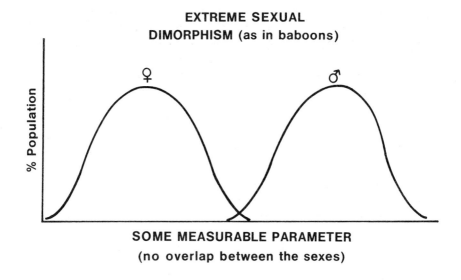

EXTREME SEXUAL DIMORPHISM (as in baboons)

% Population

♀　　　　　　♂

SOME MEASURABLE PARAMETER
(no overlap between the sexes)

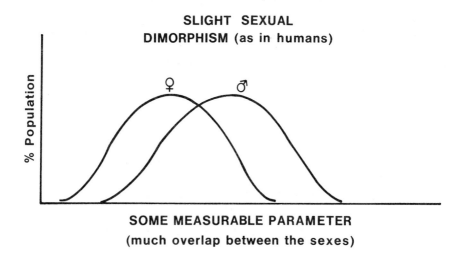

SLIGHT SEXUAL DIMORPHISM (as in humans)

% Population

♀　　♂

SOME MEASURABLE PARAMETER
(much overlap between the sexes)

Figure 15.1. Types of Sexual Dimorphism

For example, weaving is a male task among the Hopi, and every little boy wants to grow up to be considered a real "man" and be allowed to weave with the other men of his village. By contrast, their neighbors the Navaho assign the task of weaving to the females, and traditionally every girl child wants to learn to weave the beautiful blankets that her mother and aunts and grandmothers do. There are cultures where women must tend the garden and others where gardening is the role of men. In some parts of the world men gather the firewood, a task that elsewhere belongs to women. Do these various cultural expectations for boys and girls affect their developing minds in a differential manner? In other words, is the effect of upbringing powerful enough to influence the growth of the human brain?

Cerebral Lateralization

The human brain is unusual in the animal kingdom because it is functionally asymmetrical: the right and left hemispheres of the cerebrum do not perform in an identical fashion. Each hemisphere is specialized for different cognitive, motor, and perceptual tasks. While individual variation does exist, the consensus is that in the majority of right-handed people the left hemisphere governs the right side of the body and performs tasks related to language, mathematics, logic, and time. The right hemisphere controls the left side of the body, handles spatial information, and is considered more holistic and creative than the linear-minded left hemisphere.

Recently it has come to the attention of anthropologists and psychologists alike that a number of culturally determined beliefs and attitudes can be associated with functions ascribed to one or the other cerebral hemispheres. Robert E. Ornstein, for example, has argued that the Oriental (or Eastern) way of life is a "right-hemisphere" culture, as contrasted with our Western lifestyle, which he labels "left-hemisphere."[4] Thus, Orientals value such modes of thought as holistic perception and intuitiveness, while the Westerners value logic and rationality. Ornstein also points out the association of maleness and femaleness with the two hemispheres' functions. Thus we have a list of familiar opposites:

left hemisphere	right hemisphere
right hand	left hand
male	female
sky	earth
sun	moon
time	space
rational thought	intuitive thought

In many cultures around the world there are similar associations that distinguish between male and female and that relate to cerebral lateralization. Almost invariably, the right hand is associated with maleness and all things culturally proper, while the left hand is associated with femaleness and all things improper, even evil. In some cultures, such as in the Netherlands Indies in the last century, the left arm was bound in children to render it completely inactive. The sign of a well-brought-up child for these people was one whose left hand was incapable of any independent action. Among the Maori, all objects in the universe are either male or female. The male side is the right side and is sacred, powerful, and just. The female side is the left side and is profane, feeble, suspicious. It probably could be said that every culture on earth distinguishes between maleness and femaleness and associates these distinctions, rightly or wrongly, with the functional asymmetry of the brain.[5] But these are matters of folk belief and tradition. What scientific evidence is there for sex differences in the brain?

Sex Differences in the Brain

The actual research dealing with male and female brains is less than a decade old, and virtually all of it focuses on differences in cerebral lateralization. The techniques for studying functional asymmetry still are being developed and have depended on the results of certain sophisticated neurosurgical procedures that by separating the two halves of the brain have demonstrated previously unknown functions of the right (nonlinguistic or "silent") hemisphere.[6]

Prior to 1970, researchers interested in sex differences had to rely on "whole-brain" studies, which often produced conflicting results. For example, it could be shown by various tests that males excel in spatial abilities and mathematics and females excel in reading and writing, but the reasons for this specialization were a mystery. The role of cultural upbringing could not be ignored, and with the advent of feminist ideology it was assumed that differential treatment of the sexes was responsible for the differences in test scores. An excellent review of past research in this area is Eleanor E. Maccoby's and Carol N. Jacklin's *The Psychology of Sex Differences*.[7] The authors concluded that most studies were either ambiguous or downright invalid and that much of the outcome was no better than myth, strongly biased by the sex roles and gender expectations of society. However, they barely mentioned the brain as a possible source of sex differences, and this lack occurs because at that time virtually no one had ever studied the brain in that light.

Now that scientific interest has focused on the phenomenon of cerebral lateralization, it seems as if this aspect of our neural makeup may provide the key to unraveling the tangle of confusion surrounding male-female differences. In other words, it is highly probable, in the light of recent evidence, that the male

Figure 15.2. Sex Differences in Cognition

	"Left-hemisphere" skills	"Right-hemisphere" skills
Males excel in:	Mathematical skills, especially geometry, trigonometry (More language difficulties: stammering, dyslexia)	Visuospatial skills, such as copying designs, following mazes, mental rotation of objects in space
Females excel in:	Language skills: articulation, comprehension, use of verbal information in learning (More math difficulties; math anxiety)	Nonverbal communication: gesture, recognition of faces

SOURCE: M. A. Wittig and A. C. Petersen, eds., *Sex-Related Differences in Cognitive Functioning: Developmental Issues* (New York: Academic Press, 1979).

right hemisphere differs from the female right hemisphere, and the same differences hold for the left.

How exactly do they differ? The evidence is new, still accumulating, and far from conclusive, so, rather than presenting this evidence in its entirety, a general summary of results is given below and tabulated in figure 15.2. Males tend to excel in tasks that involve visual and spatial processing, such as copying complex designs, solving mazes, and mentally rotating objects in space. They also tend to be superior in mathematical abilities, particularly those involving spatial concepts, such as geometry and trigonometry. Females tend to excel in various language skills, such as articulation and comprehension, and appear to be excellent in nonverbal communication with the use of the gesture and recognition of faces. Notice that neither sex is "left" or "right" dominant. Mathematics and language are both left-hemisphere processes, while visuospatial skills and nonverbal communication are located in the right hemisphere. It is also important to recall that these sexually dimorphic characteristics are overlapping, such that many females surpass many males in mathematical skills, and many males have better language abilities than many females. The differences are statistical only and do not predict the cognitive functioning of any given individual. But are these differences biologically innate, or are they the result of socialization and environment?

Effects of Culture

Very few investigators have studied the sex differences in the brain from a cross-cultural perspective. Jerre Levy, a prominent researcher in the field of cerebral lateralization, believes that the differences in the brain are innate but may be influenced by culture in their expression.[8] In other words, there is no way a parent or teacher could force a child to become lateralized in a fashion contrary to the brain's natural predisposition, but it is possible that selectively rewarding the sexes for different behavior patterns might promote more rapid maturation of certain hemispherically localized functions. For example, if a little boy is given erector sets, building blocks, and other such toys requiring visuospatial skills, then this experience will stimulate and thus develop this aspect of his right hemisphere more rapidly than that of his female peers, who are given dolls and thus develop their right hemisphere's social skills at the expense of the visuospatial skills. So it is possible that culturally determined gender expectation could influence the rate of maturation of inborn neural patterns.

Some rather startling results on the effects of culture on the lateralization of the brain have come from Japan. A specialist in hearing disorders, Tadanobu Tsunoda, has shown that Japanese raised in America differ considerably from those raised in Japan in how language is lateralized in the brain.[9] These people are genetically quite similar but culturally very different, and presumably it is these cultural distinctions that are responsible for the differences in cerebral lateralization. However, Tsunoda makes no mention of sex differences in the two groups.

Thus we may say that culture shapes differences in male-female behavior, and culture can affect the patterns of cerebral lateralization, but can culture be responsible for affecting sex differences in the brain? A study of the development of spatial processing in school children from different urban subcultures suggests that it can.

Sexual Dimorphism in Spatial Processing

A procedure for testing spatial processing ability, the dichhaptic stimulation test, was devised by S. F. Witelson.[10] The procedure is similar to dichotic listening tests in that two spatial stimuli are presented to the brain simultaneously, but the one actually perceived by the individual is the one received by the hemisphere dominant for handling spatial information. Witelson found that male and female children differ in the manner in which they process spatial information in that the boys in her study seemed to be lateralized in the right hemisphere for this function by age six, but the girls remained bilateral up to age thirteen. She does not mention the cultural background(s) of her subjects.

To test the hypothesis that culture is a variable in the development of sexual dimorphism in spatial processing, I repeated the Witelson procedure, using subjects from different populations: upper-middle-class suburban blacks, upper-middle-class suburban whites, lower-class inner-city blacks, and lower-class inner-city whites.[11] These populations were chosen because of their size and availability as well as the cultural differences among them. The term "culture" is used here to include all human-made environmental conditions that a developing child encounters, including socioeconomic class and urban/suburban lifestyle. Race, while having biological implications, is also a cultural factor here, because children who are sociologically defined as "black" are as genetically diverse as children labeled "white." Thus each of these genetically heterogeneous populations is unified by cultural factors that include race and socioeconomic status.

Each child was administered the dichhaptic stimulation test as described by Witelson.[12] The test requires the subject to feel with the first two fingers of each hand two different meaningless shapes that are hidden from view. The subject then tries to identify which two shapes were felt by pointing to a visual display of six such shapes, only two of which are correct. The scores are the number of correctly identified shapes for each hand in ten trials. A higher left-hand score indicates right-hemisphere specialization for spatial processing, equal left and right accuracy implies bilateral representation, while high right-hand scores indicate left-hemisphere dominance for this function.

The results of this study are consistent with the findings of others that there is sexual dimorphism in spatial processing ability. Close scrutiny of the combined means of all males and all females (figure 15.3) reveals some differences in the results from Witelson's findings, in that instead of being right-lateralized by age six, the young males of this study appear to be bilateral (equal right and left accuracy) by age twelve. The females begin with a slight accuracy lead that is lost by age twelve, but the degree of right-lateralization has increased. These discrepancies can be explained by breaking down the data into the four subcultural groups, as shown in figure 15.4. Here it can be seen that the male and female patterns differ from one population to the next. A multivariate analysis of variance performed on the data shows a correlation between culture and sex differences in spatial processing. Of course, much more work needs to be done on these and other populations to determine which aspects of culture are critical in shaping these differences, but the study suggests that male and female brains do differ and that culture may be partly responsible.

Implications for Curriculum Change

If we are to accept the accumulating evidence that boys and girls have different sorts of brains, what is implied for our educational system? Should boys and girls

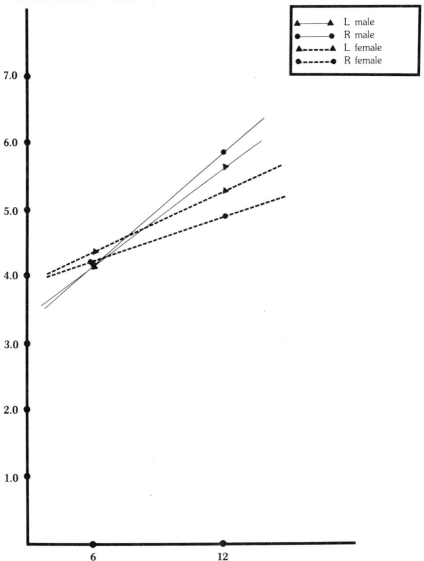

Combined Means: All Males & All Females

▲———▲	L male
●———●	R male
▲-----▲	L female
●-----●	R female

Figure 15.3. Results for Dichhaptic Stimulation Scores

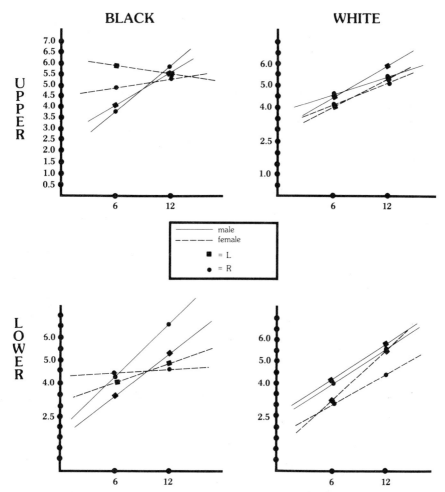

Figure 15.4. Sex and Race Differences in Dichhaptic Stimulation Scores

be taught differently? The answer seems to be an emphatic No. It cannot be emphasized often enough that the differences being uncovered by researchers are statistical ones and cannot predict the neural makeup of any given child. Many boys will be superior to many girls in such "female" skills as verbal processing, just as many females make excellent mathematicians and architects. The sexual dimorphism in the population for any cognitive ability is overlapping.

However, I am not suggesting that current educational philosophy should go unchallenged. Both males and females are discriminated against at various times during their childhood years by a system that ignores some very real differences in the ways the sexes develop. Diane McGuinness has pointed out this discrimination in an elegant essay in which she observes that in Western classrooms six-year-old children are expected to act like girls.[13] They must sit still in one place for a relatively long period of time, remain attentive to a single task, and process verbal information by listening, reading, and writing. Female children on the whole have less difficulty than male children satisfying their teachers in this regard. In fact, boys who cannot meet these demands are often labeled hyperactive, or learning disabled, stigmas that are difficult to erase in later years. Males are more likely to learn through action than communication, by manipulating objects rather than by listening or reading. Later on in school, the situation is reversed. Higher mathematics like geometry and sciences like physics, which require visuospatial processing, become emphasized, and it is the girls who face the greater difficulties.

It is unfortunate that schools have not recognized these sex-related problems and implemented programs to minimize them. One of the reasons for this failure is the belief that all children should be given an identical education because all normal brains are similar in development. When more information is gathered on the diversity of cerebral potential in a population, this situation could change. As McGuinness says, "The sexes do not differ in overall intelligence, but in the ability to select appropriate information, in their choice of an efficient strategy, and in the motor efficiency that first programs the brain and later governs execution. Putting the pressure of time on children makes it less likely that they will overcome their respective difficulties.[14]

Boys and girls should not be taught differently. Both sexes should be given a greater variety of learning opportunities with more individual choice. Thus, girls who learn best by doing and manipulating will benefit, as will the boys who learn by listening. They may be in the minority in many classroom situations but they will not feel like oddballs because both sexes are given the freedom to learn in a variety of ways.

Using "right-hemisphere" techniques to teach "left-hemisphere" skills is being experimented with in a number of disciplines, and the results of these attempts are quite promising.[15] For example, use of visuospatial devices for teaching reading to children with dyslexia may be applied to the normal classroom situation to enrich the development of reading skills in all students. A single concept can be taught in a number of ways, using as many cognitive abilities as we are aware of: singing, dancing, painting, writing, reading, listening, miming, acting, film viewing, and so on. Not every child's brain will respond equally to all approaches, but both sexes will have an opportunity to develop cerebral potential according to individual need. Rather than turning out a few graduates with great ability in a few areas, we should strive to create a system that turns out many graduates who have developed their potential to the fullest and are thus quite diverse in their skills. This diversity will not be divisible into two camps, labeled "male" and "female," because the sex differences in the population are slight. Recognition of individual potential is vastly more important than assigning a child to one of the two categories.

In conclusion, then, biology is *not* destiny. The brain is a highly flexible, adaptable organ. Whatever innate differences exist between the sexes in a statistical sense do not condemn a person to one way of being. The variation seen in either sex's abilities is much greater than the variation between the sexes. Individual variation and population diversity should be recognized and developed to the fullest. This challenge is one that our education system must meet if we are to provide all our children with an equal opportunity to grow.

Chapter 16

Human Sexuality:

New Insights from Women's History

ANNE L. HARPER

The contemporary women's movement has stressed women's need to know their history and to know their bodies. What has yet to receive adequate emphasis is the history of our bodies. In particular, human sexuality and reproduction must be understood as social as well as biological phenomena. Few people have thought of sexuality as a socially created phenomenon because most of us experience our own sexuality as completely "natural" and immutable. Thus sexuality seems in a commonsense way to be primarily an aspect of nature rather than of culture. But research into women's history, which has moved steadily away from the study of "great women" and toward the study of the social organization of daily life, is beginning to demonstrate not only that activities such as work and child rearing have a history but that human sexuality itself may have a history, too. The research now under way on the history of homosexuality and of lesbianism in particular is beginning to show that even something that appears to be as natural, as universal, and as timeless as our bodies and our sexuality may have a malleability, a history, a meaning that changes.

Clearly this new research and the new conception of sexuality that may emerge from it raise questions about what we are now doing in the area of sex education. John H. Gagnon and William Simon have pointed out that there is greater resistance to systematic research in the sexual area than there is to sex education in the schools. This resistance seems to occur because sex education is still often regarded as "a community's insurance policy against venereal disease or pre-marital pregnancy."[1] When the goal of sex education is not regarded as imparting constraint, it is often regarded as imparting competence. Part of the 1960s' liberal politics of joy was the notion of the joy of sex, if performed with skill, enlightenment, and the appropriate emotional balance. Courses in sex education thus have tended to focus on reproductive biology, anatomy of the genital organs, dating practices, and ethical standards, largely ignoring the human motivations and the social institutions involved in sexuality and reproduction. Whether the goal of sex education is constraint and contraception or competence and performance, the assumption underlying these courses is that we already know what sex is. We focus on genital heterosexuality without ever asking the prior question: What is sexuality?

This question is not easy to answer. In looking for a definition (as I have), one is apt to find instead an enumeration of the spheres in which sexuality operates: reproduction, the family, gender socialization, intercourse, and love. As Robert A. Padgug has pointed out, sexuality is almost perfectly congruent with what is viewed as the "private sphere" of life, that which pertains to the individual, as opposed to the "public" sphere of work, production and politics. There are analogous dualities that establish our current understanding. We view the sexual sphere as part of nature and we study it in the disciplines of psychology and biology, while we view the public sphere as an aspect of culture that we can study through history, economics, and political science. The private, sexual sphere is thought to be the realm of consumption and of use value, while the public sphere is the realm of production and of exchange value. The sexual sphere often is associated with the female and the homosexual, while the public sphere is often associated with the male and the heterosexual. Above all, we think of the sexual sphere as concerned with the individual and the public sphere as concerned with the community. Despite the dualities that tend to define and enclose it, sexuality in the twentieth century appears both "as narrow and limited and as universal and ubiquitous. Its role is both overestimated as the very core of being and underestimated as a merely private reality."[2]

Individuals today are encouraged to see themselves as sexual selves, to think of their identity as most authentic in their private lives, apart from work and politics. The "real me" is detached from socioeconomic characteristics, which appear by contrast as external and imposed. Sexuality thus seems to be located in some inner space. "Sexuality we imagine to define a territory of who we are and what we feel. . . . Whatever we experience must in some way touch our sexuality, but sexuality *is*. We uncover it, we discover it, we come to terms with it, but we do not master it."[3] Sexuality seems to be experienced today as an "expressive state" rather than an "expressive act."[4] It is something we are, not something we do. "It appears as a *thing,* a fixed essence which we possess as part of our very being; it simply *is*. And because sexuality is itself seen as a thing, it can be identified, for certain purposes at least, as inherent in particular objects, such as the sex organs, which are then seen as, in some sense, sexuality itself."[5] While most modern sexual theorists posit sexuality as a universally shared human essence, they also posit subcategories of the essence that are appropriate to the male, the female, the child, the homosexual, the rapist, and so on. This categorization has led to the understanding of sexuality as the dominant aspect of personality.

> In sum, the most commonly held twentieth-century assumptions about sexuality imply that it is a separate category of existence (like "the economy," or "the state,"

other supposedly independent spheres of reality), almost identical with the sphere of private life. Such a view necessitates the location of sexuality within the individual as a fixed essence, leading to a classic division of individual and society and to a variety of psychological determinisms, and, often enough, to a full-blown biological determinism as well. These in turn involve the enshrinement of contemporary sexual categories as universal, static, and permanent, suitable for the analysis of all human beings and all societies.[6]

Our sexuality is, of course, grounded in our bodies, in nature, and the biological potential for certain physiological responses would seem to be universal. But we cannot avoid observing the wide variety of sexual behaviors among people of different cultures, not to mention the richness of human sexual behavior when compared to that of animals. Why then have we come to see sexuality as so much more a part of nature than a part of culture?

French social theorist Michel Foucault postulates that the historical emergence of the very concept of sexuality was an aspect of new ways of organizing knowledge, which, in turn, affected the organization of social and sexual relations. In the provocative introduction to his projected six-volume series on the history of sexuality, Foucault argues that there has been a growing, explicit commentary on sexuality, beginning in the seventeenth century. Far from suffering a repression of discourse on sexuality, we have witnessed an explosion of discourse on sexuality. Foucault points out, "What is peculiar to modern societies, in fact, is not that they consigned sex to a shadowy existence, but that they dedicated themselves to speaking of it *ad infinitum,* while exploiting it as *the* secret."[7]

Originating in the Christian confession, the will to knowledge about sex came to be administered by the medical profession, which scrutinized and codified sexual behavior, producing a *scientia sexualis* that served "to strengthen the disparate forms of sexuality." Whether Christian or psychiatric, obligatory confession was used to produce the true discourse on sex. Foucault contrasts what he calls this "knowledge-power," produced within relations of domination and coercion, to the *ars erotica* of some other societies where truth and sex are joined in the spontaneous transmission of an esoteric knowledge from a master to an initiate. Despite "the guise of its decent positivism," the science of sexuality has functioned as a kind of erotic art by inventing a different kind of pleasure, "the specific pleasure of the true discourse on pleasure. . . the 'pleasure of analysis' (in the widest sense of the latter term) which the West has cleverly been fostering for several centuries." Thus Foucault rejects the prevailing "repression hypothesis" (Victorianism) in favor of a social control hypothesis that focuses on "the operation of a subtle network of discourses, special knowledges, pleasures, and powers."[8]

Foucault expects a new theory or "analytics" of power to develop out of his studies of the history of sexuality. Power, he suggests, is "not an institution, and not a structure; neither is it a certain strength we are endowed with; it is the name that one attributes to a complex strategical situation in a particular society." Foucault views sexuality as instrumental and amenable to the most varied strategies, rather than as an autonomous agency that produces effects in the nonsexual realm. "On the contrary," he says, "sex is the most speculative, most ideal, and most internal element in a deployment of sexuality organized by power in its grip on bodies and their materiality, their forces, energies, sensations, and pleasures."[9] Foucault emphasizes the malleability of sexuality in the service of nonsexual ends, accordingly seeing that much of the variety of sexual conduct is due to subtle mechanisms of social control.

The medical profession produced most of the discourse about sexuality in the nineteenth century by observing every kind of person and providing exhaustive accounts of the variety of sexual experience — "the clinical eye" of which Foucault spoke in *The Birth of a Clinic* "extends its gaze and its determining presence into the very bed of pleasure, whether marriage bed, hotel 'quickie,' or haystack."[10] This discourse provided four great strategies of power in the nineteenth century: "the sexualization of children, the hysterization of women, the specification of the perverted, and the regulation of populations."[11] Foucault does not give extensive evidence of these processes — the five volumes to follow presumably will — but he does offer the observation that sexuality first was made problematic in the bourgeois rather than the proletarian family. It was there that the sexuality of schoolboys was prescribed and the sexuality of idle women was medicalized. The organization and supervision of sexuality did not become a mechanism for the social control of the proletariat until the 1830s.[12]

While the particulars of Foucault's theory remain to be substantiated with more empirical data, there does seem to be enough evidence to show that sexuality was not always understood as an intrinsic personal characteristic. It came to be so understood in the late nineteenth century as changes in the mode of production created the notions of work and family as separate spheres of human relations within the bourgeoisie. "The very creation of work as 'work' — that is the transformation of role-defined useful work into valueproducing wage labor" — is central to the creation of sexuality as "sexuality" — that is, the transformation of disparate sexual acts and relations into personality-defining instincts or drives. Thus we must analyze "in a unified and interconnected way, both the political economy of sex and the sexual economy of work."[13]

Clearly we must reject the concept of sexuality as a natural instinct akin to hunger and begin to see it as a socially constructed phenomenon akin to taste or appetite. "What Marx suggests for hunger is equally true of the social forms of sexuality: 'Hunger is hunger, but the hunger gratified by cooked meat eaten with a knife and fork is a different hunger from that which bolts down raw meat with the aid of hand, nail and tooth.' "[14] The innate component of sex is merely the capacity for sexual arousal and orgasm. While the physiological mechanism of orgasm may be largely involuntary, the mechanism of sexual arousal is extraordinarily changeable and conditionable.

> Through conditioning, the arousal which stimulation of the genitals brings can be evoked by touching other parts of the body and above all by imagination and other thought-processes. The context in which sexual stimulation occurs will determine the other emotional responses that become associated with it. It is worth mentioning that Albert Bandura and Richard Walters (in their study, *Adolescent Aggression)* found that youths who had a history of conflict with their parents, associated sexual arousal with aggressive feelings. Among other youths, sexual arousal was coupled with tender feelings.[15]

In adolescence (if not earlier) one usually discovers that when arousal reaches a certain pitch it triggers a second, orgasmic mechanism. As this link becomes firmly established, one begins to expect orgasm as the outcome of arousal and may no longer experience arousal as pleasurable in and of itself, due to frustration when it does not lead to orgasm. Sexual appetite may thus be at least partially understood as a habit by which one has learned to associate pleasurable arousal and orgasm in certain situations. Derek Wright observes, "Sex is sustained and directed much more by stimuli the individual has learned to perceive as arousing, and by his own self-directed imagining, than by physiology."[16]

Thus there cannot be any abstract or universal category of "the erotic" or "the sexual" that would apply to all societies in all times.

> The content and meaning of the eroticism of Christian mysticism is by no means reducible to that of Henry Miller, nor is the asceticism of the monk identical to that of the Irish peasants who delay their marriages to a relatively late age.
>
> The forms, content, and context of sexuality always differ. . . . Any view which suggests otherwise is hopelessly mired in one or another form of biologism, and biologism is easily put forth as the basis of normative attitudes toward sexuality, which if deviated from, may be seen as rendering the deviant behavior "unhealthy" and "abnormal." Such views are as unenlightening when dealing with Christian celibacy as when discussing Greek homosexual behavior.[17]

Sexuality is socially constructed in the relationships between individuals in a particular society. It is created as individuals interact with one another in specific relationships. Sexual categories may be developed to understand the relationships of members of entire groups (e.g., wives to husbands) but these categories change as these relationships change over time.

We can understand this process by examining categories such as homosexuals and heterosexuals. The difficulty Alfred Kinsey and his coworkers experienced in trying to define individuals as in one category or the other makes it clear that homosexual and heterosexual are not sexual essences but groupings of closely related behaviors that have been converted into case studies of persons and ultimately into subcultures. Prior to the fourteenth century, for example, homosexuality was not regarded as "a unified set of acts, much less a set of qualities defining particular persons."[18] The word "homosexual" was not even coined until the late nineteenth century and was a category that had no meaning, for example, in ancient Athens.[19] I do not mean to suggest that there are no similarities in the forms of human sexual behavior but rather to point to the very different meanings of sexual relations between two men, for example, when they are citizens of ancient Athens, or Western Plains Indians participating in *berdache,* or twentieth-century residents of San Francisco.

> "Homosexual" and "heterosexual" *behavior* may be universal; homosexual and heterosexual *identity and consciousness* are modern realities. These identities are not inherent in the individual. In order to be gay, for example, more than individual inclinations (however we might conceive of those) or homosexual activity is required; entire ranges of social attitudes and the construction of particular cultures, subcultures, and social relations are first necessary. To "commit" a homosexual act is one thing; to *be* a homosexual is something entirely different.[20]

Sexuality does not merely consist of acts; it is relational. Of course, the sexual relations that are possible for individuals at any point in time are conditioned and limited to some extent by the existent social relations. Hence, sexuality must always be studied and discussed within the context of social relations. It cannot be ripped out of context and examined as an autonomous aspect of human life.

Because the categories of homosexual and heterosexual are peculiar to modern society, they provide a compelling example of the social construction of sexuality. It may be more difficult for us to grasp the categories of "male" and "female" this way. While Nancy Chodorow has speculated on what she calls the "social construction of gender," her work is curiously ahistorical and lacks adequate attention to class differences.[21] Although all societies divide their members into "male" and "female," these categories can have different meanings from society to society or even by class within one society. Another category that appears as universal is kinship, and yet not only the peculiar institutions of kinship differ in various societies but the conception of kinship itself differs.[22]

The categories created in any society by the interactions of its members tend to become normative and ideological, defining how individuals ought to act. They must be recognized and studied as such. In particular we must study the relationship between sexual activity and its categories and nonsexual activities and their categories. The connections between sexuality and the economy, for example, are so numerous that the idea of sexual relations and economic relations as constituting separate spheres is evidently ideological. A colleague and I experienced this notion several years ago when he was trying to teach a course on the history and politics of work and I was trying to teach one on the history and politics of the family. We both concluded that one had to teach about "work *and* family" or about "economy *and* sexuality."

We also need to develop a more adequate psychology to explain the experience of individuals as they encounter the sexual categories that form part of the context in which they live. Clearly the Freudian emphasis on inborn drives that infants must gradually repress in the process of their development is inadequate to the task. This orientation pits an essentially ahistorical desiring individual against a social reality that must win if civilization is to continue. This polarization of the individual and society replicates the dominant way in which our society currently conceives of the relations among its members. But this explanation can in no way adequately account for the interactions among community members. We create and are created by the specific relationships we experience as individuals. We are both subjects and objects in this process. Society is the expression of this complex activity. It is not an entity, a thing, outside of and beyond the people who create it.

Freud's "emphasis on the role of biological drives in the development of personality" characterizes "human beings as mechanistic systems whose aim is to maximize instinctual gratification."[23] In Freud's view infants establish human relationships for the purpose of instinctual gratification. This view of human nature as self-centered and isolated, seeking human relations only as a means to an end, requires the development of a control apparatus (ego/superego) that will repress or modify these selfish tendencies that might otherwise make human interaction impossible.

One psychological theory that may have the potential for overcoming this idea of the bifurcation of the individual from society is a British offshoot of psychoanalysis called "object relations theory."

> Object relations theorists reject the mechanistic conceptions and instinctual constructs of both the Freudian and ego psychologists, and place primary emphasis on the importance of personal relationships in the formation of personality . . . it is the child's earliest interpersonal experience, rather than instinctual needs, which is considered to be the major determinant of personality. Social relationships, not biological drives, motivate human development.[24]

Rather than seeing isolation and self-centeredness as fundamental to human existence, it is interaction with other people that determines personality.

> People are viewed as seeking interaction with other people as an end in itself, rather than as a means toward the end of tension reduction . . . By describing the social construction of personality through such relationships, object relations theory takes human connection and sociality (rather than isolation and self-centeredness) as

integral aspects of human nature. Development is then viewed as the process by which human connection and sociality are nurtured and their expression facilitated by the young child's social environment, rather than as a process by which a control apparatus develops to restrict instinctual needs so that civilized interaction between persons is possible.[25]

This essay is not the place to go into the details of object relations theory or into the possible pitfalls to which it is subject. (Like most psychological theories it tends to be ahistorical.) Suffice it to say that its contribution to our understanding of human interaction is its "focus on people's lives in terms of their relationships to other people, not . . . in terms of their physiological functioning."[26] It is a psychological theory that reduces us neither to biology nor to economics. As such it may have the potential to provide a greater understanding of sexuality as it is created and experienced by individuals in particular societies.

My speculations on the social construction of sexuality have a particular bearing on the question of the relationship between sex and gender. Although "sex" formally refers to the two divisions of organic beings defined as male and female as distinguished by their reproductive organs, it is commonly used to refer both to a biological or personality characteristic and to erotic behavior. Gender can be used to refer to the nonerotic and nonbiological aspects of males and females. Although various aspects of our lives are difficult to separate, we need to consider how the differences in men's and women's social, political, and economic relations affect their sexual relations, and vice versa. The recent studies by social historians of women's productive and reproductive activities need to be integrated with studies of human sexuality in order to reveal the changes in both areas over time.

If human sexuality is clearly understood as historically and socially constructed, the orientation of research in this area should change as should the content of sex education courses. Most major universities are now offering courses called "Human Sexuality" or "Human Sexual Development." Judging from the few textbooks I have seen that are intended for use in such courses, the predominant perspective is a supposedly value-free behaviorism that is ahistorical and that focuses on sexuality as a personality attribute relatively unconnected to the rest of one's life. William Masters's and Virginia Johnson's pioneering work on the physiology of orgasm has become the foundation for these courses of study as well as for the sex therapy that is now widely available in our society. While knowledge of the physiology of orgasm has been particularly important to understanding some aspects of female sexuality, and perhaps that of older people, it has led to an even greater emphasis on human sexuality as heterosexual genital intercourse and how to produce it. Sexuality once again appears as universally, biologically determined. Performance problems are treated behaviorally and the cultural, political, and economic aspects of sexual relations are largely ignored.

A recent lecture that I heard in a "Human Sexual Development" course at a large state university illustrates this kind of approach to sex education. The topic for the day was "Sexuality and the Elderly," and the guest speaker was affiliated with that university's Center for Gerontology, located in the College of Home Economics. The lecturer began by saying that "the elderly" were, unfortunately, victims of society's attitude about appropriate sexual behavior for "the elderly" and victims of their own attitudes or stereotypes about appropriate sexual behavior at their age. She then moved on to more specific considerations of sexual functioning, describing in detail the hormonal changes that occur to men and women as they get older — decreasing levels of testosterone (which begins at seventeen years of age) and of estrogen, and so on. She proceeded to describe how these hormonal changes affect human sexual response, using the "four-phase" analysis of Masters and Johnson.[27] She described the slower production of erections and lubrications in the excitement phase, the lessened intensity and duration of female orgasm, the reduction in force and amount of seminal fluid expelled, the increased rapidity of female "resolution," and so on.

Following this exclusively genital account of human sexuality in the elderly, she offered possible explanations for sexual difficulties that these people experience. First, there are general medical problems and the medication for those problems, which may produce side effects on the sexual organs. But far more important, she said, were psychological problems that inhibit sexual satisfaction. Among these, she said, were society's association of sexual conduct with reproduction or with youth and beauty, the negative attitudes of adult children toward their parents' sexuality, environmental factors such as chemical hazards and office pressures that men [sic] experience in their occupations, lack of sexual partners (particularly among women, who tend to live longer than their husbands), boredom with one's spouse, and lack of privacy for those living in nursing homes.

To help the elderly cope with these sexual difficulties, there are a variety of medical and behavioral forms of therapy. These remedies range from estrogen replacement therapy to instruction in sexual technique and in improving communications. The latter two therapies almost exclusively are oriented toward couples, a fact that the speaker hoped would change with the realization that there are far more single women among the elderly than there are married couples. The speaker described some aspects of sex therapy in detail. She said that one goal is to teach the elderly men not to be so "performance bound" regarding their own erections. Thus they are urged to "spend more time on the female" and both are urged to enjoy the lengthened excitement and plateau phases. The couple is taught techniques that are supposed to make them feel more excited about one another, in order to overcome boredom that may have developed through many years of marriage. The professionals who do this kind of therapy do not accept people with "marital problems," only those with "sexual problems," whose goal or need is to improve their sexual expression.

This speaker concluded by emphasizing that sexual satisfaction has "lots of beneficial effects." For instance, it can help relieve some physical problems like arthritis. Furthermore, there are many psychological benefits. The speaker maintained that sexual satisfaction is a "right" of the elderly. Finally she reiterated a point that she had made earlier: sexual activity is especially important for elderly men because if they don't "have sex" for six months to a year they will lose the ability to ever have it again. "They just lose it and that's it."

I watched the college students get up and head toward the door. The young men in particular looked stricken: they were shaking their heads and mumbling to one another. I sat in my chair, stricken too. My mind was filled with the images of the older people in my family. I pictured my mother-in-law (age sixty-three), impeccably dressed in her business suit, traveling to Houston and Denver in her work for a corporate regional office. I saw my father-in-law (age seventy-six) sitting at home with his cats and the television, retired from employment for fifteen years now. I pictured my grandparents, braving the midwestern cold in their snug apartment, worrying that each new illness or broken bone will spell the end of their ability to care for themselves. All four of these older people write or call us often, requesting news and visits from us. Above all it is our four-year-old daughter whom they want to hear, see, and touch.

But what about their sexuality? What is it? Where is it?

The problem with the kind of sex education that this speaker had offered is that it isolates human sexuality from the rest of human relations. At no point did this speaker say anything about the place of older people in our society today — about their de facto segregation and isolation, cut off from employment and coworkers at an arbitrary age, distant from their children and grandchildren due to our housing patterns and geographical mobility, impoverished due to the effect of inflation on their fixed incomes and savings. Nor did she mention the retirement communities of Florida and Arizona, the active church life of many older persons, or political organizations like the Gray Panthers.

She barely seemed aware that she was talking about persons. The images she conjured up were of drying vaginas and limp penises, ready to be revived by therapists. These sexual organs seemed only tenuously attached to bodies and those bodies only tenuously related to one another as human beings. In addition to the lack of any social context, the speaker employed only a crude understanding of human psychology and of the relationship between sexual conduct and a whole range of other feelings and behavior, from gender identity to sensuous experience. This bifurcation between the sexual and the sensual was nowhere more evident than in her claim (no data were offered) that some sex relationships among the elderly were largely for the purpose of "touching" but were not "sexual." Her discussion of sex therapy for the elderly showed no critical awareness of the problems with these procedures and with the prevalent conception in all such therapy of sex as work or as performance. She conveyed the information that some couples had experienced severe depression after learning all these techniques, but she responded to this revelation by simply recommending that we had better "watch out for these side effects." The lack of psychological sophistication was also evident in her uncritical comment that sex therapists for the elderly only take clients with sexual problems, not marital problems.

One comment this speaker made about sexual difficulties that did relate them to the rest of people's environment was that sexual performance could be affected by men's occupational hazards and stress. But the sex and class bias of this remark, in addition to its narrow historical applicability, vitiated its value. Finally, the speaker characterized the sexual values held by elderly people as "stereotypes" and as formulated in the "Victorian era, 1910 to 1930." The patronizing attitude, not to mention the historical inaccuracy, was unfortunate indeed.

What are we to make of such a presentation? How could a person who works with older people and who was obviously well meaning give such a lecture? Unfortunately the orientation in what little research is done on sexuality has been primarily physiological or genital in nature. While we may applaud some of the goals and results of this research — which has shown us the physiological properties of female orgasm, the continuing sexual response of some people aged fifty-five to sixty-five, and the physical harmlessness of masturbation — it has unfortunately led to an emphasis on achieving female orgasm, on achieving orgasm after age sixty-five, and on masturbating in order to achieve complete sexual satisfaction. In short, the emphasis has been on genital sex and on the achievement of orgasm. While some of this information is useful and important to both health professionals and lay people, much of it is not. This perspective tends to emphasize the most narrowly physiological aspects of sexuality and to deal with them in terms of abstract sociological categories. The likely outcome is a presentation on "Orgasm and the Elderly."

The previous example may have been something of an aberration, so I would like to take another, where the problem is more subtle and the lecturer more familiar. In the early 1970s I was a member of the speakers' bureau of a planned parenthood organization for which I often gave presentations to high school and junior college family life classes on contraceptive methods and the services of our organization and clinic. Several universities I know provide similar kinds of programs through their student health services. My lectures (and those I have observed elsewhere) usually began with a brief overview (I hope a review) of reproductive physiology. I usually had some charts with diagrams of the male and female reproductive organs, and quite often a plastic model of the female (never the male) reproductive apparatus. After reminding the audience of how conception occurs — the sperm meets the egg in the fallopian tubes and they travel down to the uterus together where, if it is hospitable, they embed — I would move on to the next set of visual aids, my kit of contraceptive devices containing prophylactics, spermicidal foam, diaphragms, oral contraceptive pills, and intrauterine devices (notably, and regrettably, the Dalkon shield). After discussing and usually minimalizing some of the possible side effects or medical complications with each of these methods, I presented some data on the "effectiveness" of each one by drawing a chart showing their "theoretical" failure rates and the "actual" failure rates. But I offered no explanation of these data. Recent contraceptive lectures that I have attended have addressed the "effectiveness" data by discussing the motivation for using or not using contraception and have raised the question of one's willingness and ability to accept responsibility for one's sexual behavior. But in discussing the reasons people give themselves and others for not using contraception — embarrassment, confusion, inconvenience, desire for romance or spontaneity, and fear of displeasure or rejection — the larger question of the social inequality between the partners in a heterosexual relationship rarely has been mentioned. In other words, the social context of sexuality, and especially the relationship of sex and gender, usually does not come up.

When I gave these kinds of lectures myself I thought they were very informative and important. I still think that, but I am beginning to see that they may have little impact on how the students who hear them live their lives because the information provided does not offer much help in understanding sexual conduct. Linda Gordon has pointed out that there are many complex prerequisites for women if they are to be able to use and benefit from contraception.

One prerequisite is motivation, which must stem from aspirations other than motherhood, aspirations which appear realizable. Another prerequisite appears to be a somewhat active attitude, a sense of mastery . . . over one's sexual life. Closely related is the need for a sense of entitlement to sex without any "consequences." Also needed is societal respect for women, sources of recognition, love, and pride from other than one's children. . . . Most women of the world do not have the prerequisites that would allow them to use contraception as their own tool, nor to see it as such. Most women do not have vocational or even avocational opportunities that can compete with mothering. Women's sexual freedom is limited, and violence against women continues to pressure all of us into cautiousness at venturing out of our few safe spaces. Many birth control methods are so clumsy or dangerous that it is hard to see them as trusted tools. The attack on abortion attacks the very morality of reproductive control, even as, ironically, the difficulty many women experience in using contraception increases their reliance on abortion.[28]

These kinds of things need to be discussed in a lecture on contraception. The social relations that affect sexual relations cannot be swept under the rug by vague references to theoretical versus actual failure rates (my former approach) nor can they be subsumed under some psychological rubric that purports to explain motivation, rationalization, passion, guilt, and so on, as merely the psychological desiderata of some individuals. Those women and men who do not use contraception even when conception is clearly undesirable are not merely irresponsible individuals but participants in a broader network of social and sexual relations. Once again we return to the observation made when discussing the elderly: particular aspects of sexuality cannot be fully understood if separated from social, economic, and political context.

In the particular case of contraception, we must shift our teaching focus from an exclusive concern with currently available methods to the history and politics of birth control. I would now begin any contraceptive education in the classroom by discussing the long history of women's attempt to control their fertility, the formation of the birth control movement in the nineteenth century as a political movement on the part of radicals and feminists, alongside the formation of the population control movement as a political movement to promote social and economic stability. Our students (and women especially) need to know this history of the struggle to legalize and disseminate birth control methods. Ideally, every women who uses a diaphragm should know who Margaret Sanger was. If women today had even a glimmering of the political struggle over birth control they might begin to use it as an aspect of their reproductive freedom rather than as merely a technique of avoiding pregnancy that may in fact make them more vulnerable to male sexual demands. Not only the history but the current politics of contraception need to be addressed, including such topics as the medical profession's control over most methods, the role of the drug corporations, the use and abuse of sterilization to control the fertility of poor, minority, and mentally handicapped women, and so on. We must also remember that contraception would be only a minor concern in our society if it were not for the overemphasis on heterosexual intercourse as the most acceptable form of sexual interaction.

There are many other topics I would add to current courses on human sexuality and changes I would make in how some current topics tend to be taught. For example, cross-cultural data gathered by anthropologists have been used to demonstrate that there are no sexual norms, but the varieties of sexual behavior often are merely cataloged for students and not analyzed in conjunction with other aspects of particular societies. Sex education texts cite a number of societies that encourage or tolerate childhood masturbation, coitus before marriage, extramarital coitus, and so on, but they give very little else about gender identity, work patterns, and kinship systems that would allow a fuller understanding of the social context and meaning of these behaviors in various societies. The examination in detail of one non-Western, nonindustrial society would be preferable to this hodge-podge. A topic that needs to be added to the curriculum is race relations and their effect on sexual relations. Another is maternal sexuality and other midlife changes in sexuality. Above all, the perspective needs to be social and historical. We must begin to think of sex education not only as education about the sex organs but as education about the relations between the sexes.

Notes

Chapter 1: The Genesis of Feminist Visions (Diane L. Fowlkes and Charlotte S. McClure)

1. See especially Florence Howe and Carol Ahlum, "Women's Studies and Social Change," in *Academic Women on the Move,* ed. Alice S. Rossi and Ann Calderwood (New York: Russell Sage Foundation, 1973).

2. See Donna Jean Wood, "Women's Studies Programs in American Colleges and Universities: A Case of Organizational Innovation" (Ph.D. diss., Vanderbilt University, 1979).

3. See *Forum for Liberal Education* 4 (October 1981), whole issue, including a valuable annotated resource bibliography for those wishing to pursue feminist curriculum reform.

4. Howe and Ahlum, "Women's Studies and Social Change."

5. See also Wood, "Women's Studies Programs"; and Diane L. Fowlkes, "Environmental, Organizational and Attitudinal Correlates of Gender-Balancing the Curriculum in Higher Education" (Paper presented at the Annual Meeting of the American Political Science Association, New York, September 3–6, 1981).

6. Diane L. Fowlkes and Charlotte S. McClure, Codirectors, "A Model for Gender-Balancing the General Curriculum in Higher Education," Project #565AH90049, grant no. G007901140, U.S. Department of Education. The activity that is the subject of this book was produced under a grant from the U.S. Department of Education under the auspices of the Women's Educational Equity Act. Opinions expressed herein do not necessarily reflect the position or policy of the department, and no official endorsement should be inferred.

7. See the issue of *Forum for Liberal Education* cited in note 3.

8. For the fullest expression of the idea of a feminist transformation of the curriculum, refer to the conferences and institutes directed by Beth Reed, Women's Studies Program, Great Lakes Colleges Association, 220 Collingwood, Suite 240, Ann Arbor, MI 48103. These include "Toward a Feminist Transformation of the Academy" (1980) and "Toward a Feminist Transformation of the Academy, II" (1981) and "The Structure of Knowledge: A Feminist Perspective" (1979).

9. See Peggy McIntosh, "The Study of Women: Implications for Reconstructing the Liberal Arts Disciplines," *Forum for Liberal Education* 4 (October 1981): 1–3, on reconstructing the disciplines. On reconstructing the theoretical underpinnings of the knowledge on which the disciplines are based, see, for the natural sciences, Thomas S. Kuhn, *The Structure of Scientific Revolutions,* 2d ed. (Chicago: University of Chicago

Press, 1970), and for the social sciences, Richard J. Bernstein, *The Restructuring of Social and Political Theory* (Philadelphia: University of Pennsylvania Press, 1978).

10. Suzanne K. Langer, *Philosophical Sketches* (Baltimore: Johns Hopkins University Press, 1962), p. 147.

11. John C. Bollens and Henry J. Schmandt, *The Metropolis: Its People, Politics, and Economic Life,* 3d ed. (New York: Harper and Row, 1975).

12. The conference was held March 4–7, 1981, at Georgia State University as part of the project cited in note 6.

Chapter 2: Women as Knowers (Catharine R. Stimpson)

1. This essay expands upon and refines an earlier essay of the author's, "The New Scholarship About Women: The State of the Art," *Annals of Scholarship* 1 (Spring 1980): 2–14.

2. Natalie J. Sokoloff, *Bibliography on the Sociology of Women and Work: 1970s,* offprint from *Resources for Feminist Research,* 8 (1979), p. 4. Available from RFR/DRF. Department of Sociology, OISE, 252 Bloor Street, W., Toronto, Canada M5S 1V6.

3. Joan Kelly, "The Doubled Vision of Feminist Theory: A Postscript to the Women and Power Conference," *Feminist Studies* 5 (Spring 1979): 225.

4. Nancy Chodorow, *The Reproduction of Mothering: Psychoanalysis and the Sociology of Gender* (Berkeley: University of California Press, 1978), p. vii.

5. See, for example, the conclusion of Millicent Bell, "The Education of Clover Adams," review of *Clover,* by Otto Friedrich, *New York Review of Books* 26 (January 24, 1980): 20.

6. For one bold, strong example of reperiodization, see Gerda Lerner, ed., *The Female Experience: An American Documentary* (Indianapolis: Bobbs-Merrill, 1977).

7. See Lenore Davidoff, "Class and Gender in Victorian England: The Diaries of Arthur J. Munby and Hannah Cullwisk," *Feminist Studies* 5 (Spring 1979): 86–141.

8. For example, see Linda Gordon, "What Should Women's Historians Do: Politics, Social Theory, and Women's History," *Marxist Perspectives* 1 (Fall 1978): 131.

9. For example, see Jean McCrindle and Sheila Rowbotham, eds., *Dutiful Daughters: Women Talk About Their Lives* (Austin: University of Texas Press, 1977), dedication page.

10. Michelle Z. Rosaldo, "The Use and Abuse of Anthropology: Reflections on Feminism and Cross-Cultural Understanding," *Signs: Journal of Women in Culture and Society* 5 (Spring 1980): 389–417.

11. See *Ford Foundation Letter* (October 1, 1980), p. 2, for a report of an award of $128,000 to several Latin American institutes, in Latin America itself, to study women.

12. Alice S. Rossi, "A Biosocial Perspective on Parenting," *Daedalus* 106 (Spring 1977): 1–31. For comments on that article, and Rossi's comments on the comments, see *Signs: Journal of Women in Culture and Society* 4 (Summer 1979): 695–717.

13. For good introductions to contemporary French Feminist theory, see Elaine Marks and Isabelle deCourtivron, *New French Feminists* (Amherst: University of Massachusetts Press, 1980), and the relevant essays in Hester Eisenstein and Alice Jardine, eds., *The Future of Difference* (Boston: G. K. Hall, 1980).

14. For a devastating critique of a recent sociobiological escapade that made much of sex differences, see Clifford Geertz, "Sex and Sociobiology," review of *The Evolution of Human Sexuality* by Donald Symons, *New York Review of Books* 26 (January 24, 1980): 3–4.

15. Midge Decter, "On Affirmative Action and Lost Self-Respect," *New York Times,* Sunday, July 6, 1980, p. E-17.

16. Adrienne Rich, "Planetarium" in Rich, *Poems Selected and New, 1950–1974* (New York: W. W. Norton, 1975), p. 148.

Chapter 3: Women Knowing (Charlotte S. McClure and Diane L. Fowlkes)

1. Sheila Tobias, "Foreword," in Sheila Ruth, *Issues in Feminism: A First Course in Women's Studies* (Boston: Houghton Mifflin, 1980), p. ix.

2. Joan I. Roberts, ed., *Beyond Intellectual Sexism: A New Woman, A New Reality* (New York: David McKay, 1976), p. 23.

Chapter 4: Research on Women's Communication (Julia T. Wood, Eva M. McMahan, and Don W. Stacks)

1. M. H. Landis and H. E. Burtt, "A Study of Conversations," *Journal of Comparative Psychology* 4 (1924): 81–89.

2. Reports in academic journals include: Lewis M. Termin and Catherine C. Miles, *Sex and Personality: Studies in Masculinity and Femininity* (New York: McGraw-Hill, 1936); Fred Strodtbeck, "Husband-Wife Interaction Over Revealed Differences," *American Sociological Review* 16 (1951): 141–45; G. A. Milton, "The Effects of Sex-Role Identification Upon Problem-Solving Skill," *Journal of Abnormal and Social Psychology* 55 (1957): 208–12; Edward M. Bennett and Larry R. Cohen, "Men and Women: Personality Patterns and Contrasts," *Genetic Psychology Monographs* 59 (1959): 101–55; Gloria L. Carey, "Sex Differences in Problem-Solving Performance as a Function of Attitude Differences," *Journal of Abnormal and Social Psychology* 56 (1958): 256–60; Edwin I. Megaree, "Influence of Sex Roles on Manifestation of Leadership," *Journal of Applied Psychology* 53 (October 1969): 377–82.

Popular forums include: Betty Friedan, *The Feminine Mystique* (New York: W. W. Norton, 1963); Germaine Greer, *The Female Eunuch* (New York: McGraw-Hill, 1971); Margaret Adams, "The Compassion Trap," in *Women in Sexist Society,* ed. Vivian Gornick and Barbara Moran (New York: Basic, 1972), pp. 555–75; Nancy Henley, *Body Politics: Power, Sex, and Nonverbal Communication* (Englewood Cliffs, N.J.: Prentice-Hall, 1977).

3. Lawrence B. Rosenfeld and Gene D. Fowler, "Personality, Sex and Leadership Style," *Communication Monographs* 43 (1976): 320–24. See also Janet Yerby, "Attitude, Task and Sex Composition as Variables Affecting Female Leadership in Small Problem-Solving Groups," *Speech Monographs* 42 (1975): 164–68.

4. Cheris Kramer, "Women's Speech: Separate But Unequal?" *Quarterly Journal of Speech* 60 (1974): 14–24.

5. Linda Putnam, "In Search of Gender: A Critique of Communication and Sex-Roles Research," *Women's Studies in Communication* 5 (Spring 1982): 1–9.

6. M. Gerrard, J. Oliver, and M. Williams, eds., *Women in Management* (Austin, Texas: Center for Social Work Research, 1976); Ernest G. Bormann, Jerie Pratt, and Linda Putnam, "Power, Authority and Sex: Male Response to Female Leadership," *Communication Monographs* 45 (1978): 119–55; John E. Baird and Patricia H. Bradley, "Styles of Management and Communication: A Comparative Study of Men and Women," *Communication Monographs* 46 (1979): 101–11.

7. Baird and Bradley, "Styles of Management"; Margaret Hennig and Anne Jardim, *The Managerial Woman* (Garden City: Doubleday, 1977).

8. Gaeda W. Bowman, Beatrice Worthy, and Stephen A. Greyser, "Are Women Executives People?" *Harvard Business Review* 43 (July–August 1965): 14–28, 164–78; Bernard M. Bass, J. Krusell, and R. A. Alexander, "Male Managers' Attitudes Toward Working Women," *American Behavioral Scientist* 15 (1971): 221–36; Charles D. Orth III and Frederick Jacobs, "Women in Management: Pattern for Change," *Harvard Business Review* 49 (July–August 1971): 139–47; Dennis R. Day and Ralph M. Stogdill, "Leader Behavior of Male and Female Supervisors: A Comparative Study," *Personnel Psychology* 25 (1972): 353–60; Bormann, Pratt, and Putnam, "Power, Authority and Sex"; Yerby, "Attitude, Task and Sex Composition."

9. Bowman, Worthy, and Greyser, "Are Women Executives People?"

10. Rosabeth M. Kanter, *Men and Women of the Corporation* (New York: Basic, 1977).

11. Benson Rosen and Thomas Jerdee, "Effects of Employee's Sex and Threatening Versus Pleading Appeals on Managerial Evaluations of Grievances," *Journal of Applied Psychology* 60 (August 1975): 442–45.

12. Stephen L. Cohen and Sally Leavengood, "The Utility of the WAMS: Shouldn't It Relate to Discriminatory Behavior?" *Academy of Management Journal* 21 (1978): 742–48.

13. Bormann, Pratt, and Putnam, "Power, Authority and Sex"; Virginia E. Schein, "Sex Role Stereotyping, Ability and Performance: Prior Research and New Directions," *Personnel Psychology* 31 (1978): 259–67.

14. Putnam, "In Search of Gender."

15. Eleanor E. Maccoby and Carol N. Jacklin, *The Psychology of Sex Differences* (Stanford, Calif.: Stanford University Press, 1974); Barbara Eakins and Gene Eakins, *Sex Differences in Human Communication* (Boston: Houghton Mifflin, 1978).

16. Putnam, "In Search of Gender."

17. Julia T. Wood and Gerald M. Phillips, "Metaphysical Metaphors and Pedagogical Practice," *Communication Education* 29 (1980): 146–57.

18. Linda Keller Brown, *The Woman Manager in the United States: A Research Analysis and Bibliography.* Washington, D.C.: Business and Professional Women's Foundation, 1981.

19. Susan Brownmiller, "The Enemy Within," in *Women's Liberation: Blueprint for the Future,* ed. Sookie Stambler (New York: Ace, 1970), pp. 17–22.

20. See Betty L. Harragan, *Games Mother Never Taught You* (New York: Warner, 1977).

21. Putnam, "In Search of Gender."

22. Wood and Phillips, "Metaphysical Metaphors."

23. Adrienne Rich, "Taking Women Students Seriously," in Rich, *On Lies, Secrets, and Silences: Selected Prose 1966–1978* (New York: W. W. Norton, 1979), p. 240.

24. Beverly Hyman, "Responsive Leadership: The Woman Manager's Asset or Liability," *Supervisory Management* 25 (August 1980): 40–43.

25. Rich, "Taking Women Students Seriously," p. 244; Henley, *Body Politics,* p. 207.

26. Elizabeth Janeway, *Man's World, Woman's Place: A Study in Social Mythology* (New York: Dell, Delta, 1971), p. 305.

27. Henley, *Body Politics,* p. 205.

28. Brownmiller, "Enemy Within"; Rich, "Taking Women Students Seriously," p. 244.

29. Arlene K. Daniels, "Feminist Perspectives in Sociological Research," in *Another Voice: Feminist Perspectives on Social Life and Social Science,* ed. Marcia Millman and Rosabeth M. Kanter (Garden City: Doubleday, Anchor Press, 1975), pp. 340–80; Henley, *Body Politics*.

30. Brownmiller, "Enemy Within"; Kate Millett, *Sexual Politics* (New York: Avon, 1969).

31. Daniels, "Feminist Perspectives," p. 349.

32. Millman and Kanter, *Another Voice*.

33. Millett, *Sexual Politics*.

34. Daniels, "Feminist Perspectives," p. 346.

35. Ibid., p. 368.

36. Women's Studies Group, ed., *Women Take Issue: Aspects of Women's Subordination* (London: Hutchinson, 1978), p. 7.

37. Daniels, "Feminist Perspectives," p. 370.

Chapter 5: Darwin and Sexism (Sue V. Rosser and A. Charlotte Hogsett)

1. Hilary Rose and Steven Rose, "The Myth of the Neutrality of Science," in *Science and Liberation,* ed. Rita Arditti, Pat Brennan, and Steve Cavrak (Boston: South End Press, 1980), p. 17.

2. Rita Arditti, "Feminism and Science," in Arditti, Brennan, and Cavrak, *Science and Liberation*.

3. Douglas Webster and Molly Webster, *Comparative Vertebrate Morphology* (New York: Academic Press, 1974).

4. Thomas S. Kuhn, *The Structure of Scientific Revolutions,* 2d ed. (Chicago: University of Chicago Press, 1970).

5. Charles Darwin, *On the Origin of Species: A Facsimile of the First Edition* (1859; reprint ed., New York: Atheneum, 1967).

6. Rose and Rose, "Myth of Neutrality," p. 28.

7. Compare Michael Rose, *The Darwinian Revolution* (Chicago: University of Chicago Press, 1979).

8. Charles Darwin, *The Descent of Man, and Selection in Relation to Sex* (London: John Murray, 1871), p. 618.

9. *Origin of Species,* p. 89.

10. *Descent of Man,* p. 564.

11. Antoinette L. B. Blackwell, *The Sexes Throughout Nature* (1875; reprint ed., Putnam, New York: Hyperion Press, 1976).

12. *Origin of Species,* p. 40.

13. Ibid., pp. 310–11.

14. Ibid., p. 40.

15. Ibid., p. 61.

16. Ibid., p. 62.

17. Ibid., p. 63.

18. Ibid., pp. 62, 322, 412, 116, 108.

19. Ibid., p. 424.

20. *Descent of Man,* p. 565.

21. Shulamith Firestone, *The Dialectic of Sex* (New York: William Morrow, 1970), p. 122.

22. *Origin of Species,* p. 425.

23. Marian Lowe and Ruth Hubbard, "Sociobiology and Biosociology: Can Science Prove the Biological Basis of Sex Differences in Behavior?" in *Genes and Gender II,* ed. Ruth Hubbard and Marian Lowe (New York: Gordian Press, 1979), p. 94.

24. E. O. Wilson, *Sociobiology: The New Synthesis* (Cambridge: Harvard University Press, 1975).

Chapter 6: A Feminist Challenge to Darwinism (Marie Tedesco)

1. Rosalind Rosenberg, "The Dissent From Darwin, 1890–1930: The New View of Woman Among American Social Scientists" (Ph.d. diss., Stanford University, 1974), pp. 6–7. On nineteenth-century conceptions of woman's nature see idem, "In Search of Woman's Nature, 1850–1920," *Feminist Studies* 1 (Fall 1975): 141–54.

Recently many works have been written on woman's nature as it was perceived by medical authorities who thought woman's reproductive functions dominated her entire being. See, for example: Carroll Smith-Rosenberg and Charles Rosenberg, "The Female Animal: Medical and Biological Views of Woman and Her Role in Nineteenth-Century America," *Journal of American History* 60 (September 1973): 332–56; John S. Haller and Robin M. Haller, *The Physician and Sexuality in Victorian America* (Urbana: University of Illinois Press, 1974); G. J. Barker-Benfield, *The Horrors of the Half-Known Life: Male Attitudes Toward Women and Sexuality in Nineteenth-Century America* (New York: Harper and Row, 1976); and Barbara Ehrenreich and Deidre English, *For Her Own Good. 150 Years of the Experts' Advice to Women* (Garden City, N.Y.: Doubleday, Anchor Press, 1978), chap. 4.

2. Edward T. James, Janet Wilson James, and Paul S. Boyer, eds., *Notable American Women (NAW),* 3 vols. (Cambridge, Mass.: Harvard University Press, Belknap Press, 1971), 1:158. Frances A. Willard and Mary A. Livermore, eds., *American Women,* 2 vols. (Detroit: Gale, 1973), 1:90. See also Blanche Hersh, *The Slavery of Sex: Feminist-*

Abolitionists in America (Urbana: University of Illinois Press, 1978), p. 120, for a group portrait of antebellum feminists such as Blackwell.

3. *NAW,* 1:158–59; Elinor Rice Hays, *Those Extraordinary Blackwells* (New York: Harcourt, Brace, 1967), pp. 116–18. On antebellum education for women see Thomas Woody, *A History of Women's Education in the United States,* 2 vols. (New York: Science Press, 1929); Eleanor Wolf Thompson, *Education for Ladies, 1830–1860. Ideas on Education in Magazines for Women* (New York: King Crown's Press, 1947); Keith Melder, "Mask of Oppression: The Female Seminary Movement in the United States," *New York History* 55 (July 1974): 261–79; Anne Firor Scott, "Ever Widening Circle: The Diffusion of Feminist Values From the Troy Female Seminary, 1822–72," *History of Education Quarterly* 19 (Spring 1979): 3–25; Katharine Kish Sklar, "The Founding of Mount Holyoke College," in *Women of America, A History,* ed. Carol Ruth Berkin and Mary Beth Norton (Boston: Houghton Mifflin, 1979), pp. 178–98. Gerda Lerner comments on professionalization in teaching and the effects of education on middle-class feminists in "The Lady and the Mill Girl: Changes in the Status of Women in the Age of Jackson," in Lerner, *The Majority Finds Its Past. Placing Women in History* (New York: Oxford University Press, 1979), pp. 15–30. For changes in education from the 1840s to the present in the United States and England see Sara Delamont, "The Contradictions in Ladies Education," in *The Nineteenth-Century Woman. Her Cultural and Physical World,* ed. Delamont and Lorna Duffin (New York: Barnes and Noble, 1978), pp. 134–64. Delamont's essay "The Domestic Ideology and Women's Education," ibid., pp. 164–87, discusses the influence of the domestic ideology on mass education and curriculum changes in the United States and England in the years from 1840 to the present. Literature on antebellum reform is voluminous. Some representative works are: Alice Felt Tyler, *Freedom's Ferment: Phases of American Social History from the Colonial Period to the Outbreak of the Civil War* (Minneapolis: University of Minnesota Press, 1947); Ronald G. Walters, *American Reformers, 1815–60* (New York: Hill and Wang, 1978); David Brion Davis, ed., *Ante-Bellum Reform* (New York: Harper and Row, 1967); Timothy L. Smith, *Revivalism and Social Reform in Mid-Nineteenth Century America* (New York: Harper and Row, 1965); Louis Filler, *The Crusade Against Slavery, 1830–1860* (New York: Harper and Row, 1963); Aileen Kraditor, *Means and Ends in American Abolitionism* (New York: Pantheon, 1969); James B. Stewart, *Holy Warriors: The Abolitionists and American Slavery* (New York: Hill and Wang, 1976); John Allen Krout, *The Origins of Prohibition* (New York: Alfred A. Knopf, 1925); and Joseph R. Gusfield, *Symbolic Crusade: Status Politics and the American Temperance Movement* (Urbana: University of Illinois Press, 1966). For the relationship between abolitionism and feminism the following are useful: Gerda Lerner, *The Grimke Sisters from South Carolina* (New York: Schocken, 1971); Keith Melder, *The Beginnings of Sisterhood: The American Women's Rights Movement, 1800–50* (New York: Schocken, 1973), chap. 7; Hersh, *Slavery of Sex;* Lois Banner, *Elizabeth Cady Stanton. A Radical for Woman's Rights* (Boston: Little, Brown, 1980), chap. 2; Ellen Carol DuBois, *Feminism and Suffrage: The Emergence of an Independent Women's Movement in America, 1848–69* (Ithaca: Cornell University Press, 1978), chap. 1

4. The introduction and chap. 6 of Hersh's book, *Slavery of Sex,* contains discussions of antebellum feminists' views on the "spheres question." For briefer discussions of this problem consult DuBois, *Feminism and Suffrage,* pp. 36–38; Melder, *Beginnings of*

Sisterhood, chap. 1; and Walters, *American Reformers,* pp. 101–12. On the Grimke sisters' feminism see Lerner, *Grimke Sisters,* and DuBois, "Struggling into Existence: The Feminism of Sarah and Angelina Grimke," *Women: A Journal of Liberation* 1 (1970): 4–11. Carroll Smith-Rosenberg, "Beauty, the Beast and the Militant Woman: A Case Study in Sex Roles and Social Stress in Jacksonian America," *American Quarterly* 23 (October 1971): 562–84, focuses on sex roles. For a "domestic feminist" interpretation of women's spheres, see Nancy F. Cott, *The Bonds of Womanhood: "Woman's Sphere" in New England, 1780–1835* (New Haven: Yale University Press, 1977).

5. *NAW,* 1:159; Hersh, *Slavery of Sex,* pp. 52–54.

6. Herbert Spencer's *Quarterly Review* essays were published in three volumes as *Essays: Scientific, Political and Speculative* (London: Longman, Brown, Green, Longman and Roberts, 1858–74); and in one volume under the same title (New York: D. Appleton, 1864). Spencer's works became very popular in the United States, especially beginning in the 1860s. His influence and popularity are discussed in Richard Hofstadter, *Social Darwinism in American Thought* (Boston: Beacon Press, 1955), chap. 2, and in Cynthia E. Russett, *Darwin in America, The Intellectual Response, 1865–1912* (San Francisco: W. H. Freeman, 1976), chap. 4.

On the first American edition of the *Origin* see Francis Darwin, ed., *The Life and Letters of Charles Darwin,* 2 vols. (New York: D. Appleton, 1896), 2:51.

In "Dissent from Darwin," p. 42, Rosalind Rosenberg quotes Blackwell as saying that she began to read the early essays of Spencer and Darwin in 1853. In the 1850s Darwin did not publish any essays as such. The 1842 and 1844 essays on natural selection did not appear in print until 1909 *(The Foundations of the Origin of Species: Two Essays Written in 1842 and 1844 by Charles Darwin,* ed. Francis Darwin [Cambridge: Cambridge University Press]). Through English scientific societies he did publish, however, some rather technical zoological monographs. It is unlikely that Blackwell could have obtained these monographs. Moreover, even if she read them, it is difficult to understand how, as Blackwell later recalled, they contributed to a crisis in faith. The monographs, largely descriptive, did not focus, for example, on natural selection. Blackwell, eighty-four years old at the time she recited the autobiography to Claude U. Gibson, probably suffered a slip of memory. The autobiography is located at Radcliffe College, Blackwell Family Papers. Examples of Charles Darwin's 1850s' works are: *A Monograph on the Sub-class Cirripedia* (London: Ray Society, 1851–54) and *A Monograph on the Fossil Lepadidae, or Pedunculated Cirripedes of Great Britain* (London: Paleontological Society, 1851).

7. *STN* (New York: G. P. Putnam's Sons, 1875) was a collection of five essays. The opening essay, "Sex and Evolution" ("SaE"), and the closing essay, "The Trial by Science" ("TbS"), Blackwell composed especially for this volume. The other three essays previously had appeared in print. "The Alleged Antagonism Between Growth and Reproduction" ("AABGR") appeared in *Popular Science Monthly* 5 (September 1874): 606–10. "Sex and Work" ("SaW"), *Woman's Journal* 5 (March–June 1874), and "The Building of a Brain" ("BoB"), ibid., 5 (December 12, 1874): 345, were revised and expanded for *STN.*

For example, works published before 1875 that used evolution to prove women's mental and physical inferiority to men include: the German naturalist Carl Vogt's *Lectures on Man, His Place in Creation, and in the History of the Earth,* ed. James Hunt (London: Longman, Green, Longman and Roberts, 1864); German anthropologist Alexander

Ecker's article, "On a Characteristic Peculiarity in the Form of the Female Skull, and Its Significance for Comparative Anthropology," *Anthropological Review* 6 (1868): 350–56; American physician Edward H. Clarke's *Sex in Education* (1873; reprint ed., New York: Arno Press, 1972); English anthropologist J. McGrigor Allen's article, "On the Real Differences in the Minds of Man and Woman," *Journal of the Anthropological Society* 7 (1869): 196–215; and an article by another English anthropologist, Luke Owen Pike, "On the Claims of Women to Political Power," ibid., pp. 47–55. Herbert Spencer dealt with women in *The Principles of Biology,* 2 vols. (New York: D. Appleton, 1869–73) and *The Principles of Psychology,* 2 vols. (New York: D. Appleton, 1864–67).

Articles in mass-consumption journals include: E. G. Anderson, "Sex in Education," *Fortnightly Review* 22 (April 1874): 582–85; Henry Maudsley, "Sex in Mind and Education," ibid., pp. 466–81; J. S. Patterson, "Women and Science, A Chapter on the Enfranchisement and Education of Women," *Radical* 7 (March 1870): 169–84; Frances Emily White, "Woman's Place in Nature," *Popular Science Monthly* 6 (January 1875): 292–301; and Herbert Spencer, "The Psychology of the Sexes," ibid., 4 (November 1873): 30–38.

Well-known and influential works on the origins of civilization that examine woman's role and status include the following written by English anthropologists: Sir Henry Maine, *Ancient Law: Its Connection with the Early History of Society, and Its Relations to Modern Ideas,* 4th ed. (London: John Murray, 1870); and Sir John Lubbock, *The Origin of Civilization and the Primitive Condition of Man* (London: Longmans, Green, 1879). Scotsman John F. McLennan's *Primitive Marriage. An Inquiry into the Origin of the Form of Capture in Marriage Ceremonies* (Edinburgh: A. and C. Black, 1865), and American Lewis Henry Morgan's *Systems of Consanguinity and Affinity of the Human Family* (Washington, D.C.: Smithsonian Institution, 1871) were also quite influential.

Susan Sleeth Mosedale, "Science Corrupted: Victorian Biologists Consider 'The Woman Question,'" *Journal of the History of Biology* 11 (Spring 1978): 1–48; Elizabeth Fee, "The Sexual Politics of Victorian Social Anthropology," in *Clio's Consciousness Raised: New Perspectives on the History of Women,* ed. Mary S. Hartman and Lois Banner (New York: Harper and Row, 1974), pp. 86–102; and Fee, "Nineteenth-Century Craniology: The Study of the Female Skull," *Bulletin of the History of Medicine* 53 (Fall 1979): 415–33, discuss scientists' treatment of the "woman question."

8. On pre-Darwinian evolution consult, for example: Milton Millhauser, *Just Before Darwin: Robert Chambers and Vestiges* (Middletown, Conn.: Wesleyan University Press, 1959); and Richard Burkhardt, Jr., *The Spirit of System. Lamarck and Evolutionary Biology* (Cambridge: Harvard University Press, 1977). Chaps. 1–6 of Michael Ruse's *The Darwinian Revolution* (Chicago: University of Chicago Press, 1979) examine pre-*Origin* scientific thought, mainly in England.

For the impact of Darwin's theory in the United States see: Edward Pfeifer's essay, "United States," in *The Comparative Reception of Darwinism,* ed. Thomas Glick (Austin: University of Texas Press, 1974), pp. 168–206; Russett, *Darwin in America;* and Bert Loewenberg, "Darwinism Comes to America, 1859–1900," *Mississippi Valley Historical Review* 28 (December 1941): 339–68.

For the British press's reception of Darwin's theory see Alvar Ellegard, *Darwin and the General Reader. The Reception of Darwin's Theory of Evolution in the British Periodical Press, 1859–1872* (Goteborg: Goteborgs Universitets Arsskrift, 1958). David L. Hull, ed., *Darwin and His Critics. Reception of Darwin's Theory of Evolution by the Scientific Community* (Cambridge: Harvard University Press, 1973), contains British, Continental, and American reviews of the *Origin*.

Popular American and English journals include *Popular Science Monthly, North American Review, Independent, Forum,* and *Fortnightly Review*. In the United States in the years from 1865 to 1885, for example, the number of mass periodicals increased significantly. According to Frank Luther Mott, in 1865 there were 700 periodicals and in 1885 there were 3,300. Science, in particular, was a very popular topic. See Mott, *A History of American Magazines,* vol. 3, *1865 – 1885* (Cambridge: Harvard University Press, 1938), pp. 5 – 9, 103 – 09.

9. Some representative 1870s' pro-feminist works that use science and evolution theory are: "The Weaker Sex," *Revolution* 5 (February 10, 1870): 91; "Woman's Power," ibid., 8 (August 3, 1871); "Woman's Wits," ibid., 7 (July 27, 1871); Henry B. Blackwell, "The Physiological Argument," *Woman's Journal* 7 (February 12, 1876): 52; Thomas Higginson, "Sex in Mind," ibid., 5 (December 12, 1874); and Julia Ward Howe, ed., *Sex in Education: A Reply to Dr. E. H. Clarke's Sex in Education* (Boston: Roberts Brothers, 1874). John Stuart Mill's classic work, *On the Subjection of Women* (London: Longmans, Green, Reader and Dyer, 1869), briefly discusses the "woman question" in relation to science.

10. *STN,* "TbS," p. 231.

11. *STN,* preface, pp. 7, 6.

12. Herbert Spencer, *Social Statics* (New York: D. Appleton, 1865); idem, *Principles of Biology.*

13. *STN,* "SaE," pp. 13 – 16.

14. Ibid., pp. 14, 16.

15. Ibid., p. 11.

16. Ibid., p. 42. Italics in original.

17. For definitions of force and energy see, *The Encyclopedia of Philosophy,* "Force," 3:209 – 12; and "Energy," 2:511 – 17. For Spencer's discussions of force see *Principles of Biology* and *Principles of Psychology.* Darwin's view can be found in *Descent of Man,* p. 581. Max Jammer, *Concepts of Force: A Study in the Foundation of Dynamics* (New York: Harper, 1962), covers major theories on force from the ancient period to the twentieth century. D. W. Theobald, *The Concept of Energy* (London: E. & F. N. Spon, 1966), discusses different types of energy (e.g., mechanical, thermal). Helmholtz's essay was "On the Conservation of Force" (Berlin: G. Reimer, 1847). Subsequently, in the 1850s William Thomson (Lord Kelvin) refined Helmholtz's work.

18. Charles Darwin, *On the Origin of Species, A Facsimile of the First Edition* (1859; reprint ed., Cambridge: Harvard University Press, 1964), p. 63.

19. Ibid., pp. 80 – 81.

20. Peter J. Vorzimmer, *Charles Darwin: Years of Controversy. The Origin of Species and Its Critics, 1859 – 1882* (Philadelphia: Temple University Press, 1970), pp. 188 – 89.

21. Charles Darwin, *The Descent of Man, and Selection in Relation to Sex* (1871; reprint ed., New York: Modern Library, 1959), p. 567.

22. *STN,* "SaE," p. 38.

23. Ibid., pp. 33 – 34.

24. Ibid., p. 29.

25. Ibid. For other examples of equivalent functions see pp. 37–41, 63–64, 74–75, 84–85, and 94–95.

26. Ibid., pp. 29–30.

27. Ibid., pp. 24–30, 113; "AABGR," p. 143.

28. *STN*, "SaE," pp. 113, 115–16.

29. Ibid., p. 31. Italics in original.

30. *Descent of Man*, p. 570. Darwin's fellow scientist and the codiscoverer of natural selection theory, Alfred Russel Wallace, especially objected to the notion of animals exerting will and choice in sexual selection. For the controversy between Darwin and Wallace on the derivation of differences in coloration and the roles played by choice and protective needs, see Vorzimmer, *Years of Controversy,* pp. 191–97.

31. *Descent of Man*, pp. 584, 586. Darwin explained further that there was a tendency to inherit traits at corresponding ages. Thus a character appearing early in life, or one appearing late, would be inherited by offspring at a corresponding age. Darwin also recognized the existence of sex-related traits. Tortoiseshell cats, for example, tended to be female, and crops in pouter pigeons were well developed in males (p. 586).

32. *STN*, "SaE," pp. 20–21.

33. Ibid., pp. 119–21.

34. Ibid., p. 124.

35. Ibid., p. 128.

36. *STN*, "SaW," p. 177.

37. Ibid., pp. 205–06.

38. *STN*, "SaE." For Spencer's views see "Psychology of the Sexes," pp. 30–38.

39. *STN*, "SaE," p. 62. Italics mine.

For a definition of vitalism see *The Encyclopedia of Philosophy,* "Vitalism," 8:253–56. On nineteenth-century vitalism consult: Thomas S. Hall, *Ideas of Life and Matter,* 2 vols. (Chicago: University of Chicago Press, 1969), vol. 2, chaps. 36–46; William Coleman, *Biology in the Nineteenth Century. Problems of Form, Function and Transformation* (New York: Wiley, 1971), especially chap. 6; Timothy O. Lipman, "The Response to Liebig's Vitalism," *Bulletin of the History of Medicine* 40 (1966): 511–24, and "Vitalism and Reductionism in Liebig's Physiological Thought," *Isis* 58 (Summer 1967): 167–85.

On physicalism see: Oswei Temkin, "Materialism in French and German Physiology in the Early Nineteenth Century," *Bulletin of the History of Medicine* 20 (1946): 322–27; and Everett Mendelsohn, "Physical Models and Physiological Concepts of Explanation in Nineteenth-Century Biology," *British Journal of the History of Science* 2 (June 1965): 201–19.

William Carpenter's combination of vitalism and conservation of energy was "On the Mutual Relations of the Vital and Physical Forces," *Philosophical Transactions of the Royal Society, London,* pt. 2, 140 (1850): 727–57.

40. *Descent of Man*, pp. 867, 873.

41. Ibid., p. 873.

42. *STN*, "SaE," p. 122.

43. Ibid., pp. 117–18.

44. *STN*, "BoB," pp. 221, 223, 225.

45. *STN*, "SaW," pp. 149, 152–53, 175–76.

46. Ibid., pp. 166–67, 191–94, 218.

47. *STN,* "SaE," p. 135; "AABGR," p. 147; "TbS," p. 239.

48. *STN,* "AABGR," p. 147.

49. R. Rosenberg, "Dissent From Darwin," p. 45.

50. *STN,* "SaE," pp. 119, 122, 132–34.

51. For example, such antebellum feminists as Maria Weston Chapman and Elizabeth Chandler defended the idea that woman's moral superiority was based on her greater selfishness. Elizabeth Cady Stanton and Susan B. Anthony perhaps were more skeptical than most on this issue, yet still they thought women had "special qualities" that made them superior to men. For further explanation of antebellum feminists' views see Hersh, *Slavery of Sex,* introduction and chap. 6. The six volumes of the *History of Woman Suffrage* (ed. Elizabeth Cady Stanton et al. [1881–1922; reprint ed., New York: Arno Press, 1969]) contain numerous references to female superiority, as do the issues of the 1870s' feminist journal, *Revolution.* In addition, for the years 1870 to 1900, *Woman's Journal* provides an apt source for views on women's superiority. Aileen Kraditor, *The Ideas of the Woman Suffrage Movement, 1890–1920* (New York: Doubleday, 1971), discusses women's superiority in relation to suffrage and other reforms and also to anti-suffragism. See chaps. 2, 3, and 5.

Charlotte Perkins Gilman, in *Women and Economics* (1898; reprint ed., New York: Harper and Row, 1966), discusses the origin of altruism (pp. 60–64). *Forerunner* (1909–16), edited by Gilman, served as a forum for her views and contains numerous articles that express her scientific/feminist theories. On Gilman see Carol Ruth Berkin, "Private Woman, Public Woman: The Contradictions of Charlotte Perkins Gilman," in Berkin and Norton, *Women of America,* pp. 151–73; and Mary A. Hill, *Charlotte Perkins Gilman: The Making of A Radical Feminist* (Philadelphia: Temple University Press, 1980).

One of the best expressions of the idea that suffrage should be granted because of sex differences produced by evolution is Carrie Chapman Catt's 1893 speech, "Evolution and Woman's Suffrage." A manuscript of the speech is located in the Catt Collection, New York Public Library.

Gerda Lerner contends that women were like most groups who fought status oppression in that they formulated a compensatory ideology of female superiority. She disagrees with Norton Mazinsky's contention, expressed in "An Idea of Female Superiority," *Midcontinent American Studies Journal* 2 (Spring 1961): 17–26, that female superiority was defined clearly beginning only in 1874. See Lerner, notes to "The Lady and the Mill Girl," in *Majority Finds Its Past,* pp. 185–86.

52. R. Rosenberg, "Dissent From Darwin," p. 46. A recent article by Estelle Freedman investigates the public organizing aspects of what she refers to as the "strategy of separatism." See Freedman, "Separatism as Strategy: Female Institution Building, and American Feminism, 1870–1930," *Feminist Studies* 5 (Fall 1979): 512–29. Carroll Smith-Rosenberg, "The Female World of Love and Ritual: Relations Between Women in Nineteenth-Century America," *Signs: Journal of Women in Culture and Society* 1 (Fall 1975): 1–29, focuses on the private side of separatism.

53. On providential evolution and nomothetic creation as they developed in the Anglo-American scientific community consult Neal C. Gillespie, *Charles Darwin and the Problem of Creation* (Chicago: University of Chicago Press, 1979), especially chap. 5.

54. *STN,* "SaE," p. 135.

55. Lorna Duffin, "Prisoners of Progress: Women and Evolution," in Delamont and Duffin, *Nineteenth-Century Woman,* pp. 57–91, discusses American and English scientists' use of evolution as a static theory that justified the nineteenth-century status quo of sex-role divisions.

56. In her essay, "Placing Women in History: Definitions and Challenges," in *Majority Finds Its Past,* pp. 145–59, Lerner theorizes on "woman-defined" history.

57. For example, Catt's previously mentioned speech, "Evolution and Woman's Suffrage," Gilman's *Women and Economics,* and Eliza Burth Gamble's *The Evolution of Woman. An Inquiry into the Dogma of Her Inferiority to Man* (New York: G. P. Putnam's Sons, 1894) express views similar to those expressed by Blackwell.

58. Hamilton Cravens, *The Triumph of Evolution. American Scientists and the Heredity-Environment Controversy, 1900–1941* (Philadelphia: University of Pennsylvania Press, 1978), analyzes trends, beginning in 1890, in biology, psychology, sociology, and eugenics. Franz Boas's most influential book was *The Mind of Primitive Man* (New York: Macmillan, 1911). R. Rosenberg, "Dissent From Darwin," discusses changing trends among social scientists. Garland Allen, *Life Science in the Twentieth Century* (New York: Wiley, 1975), begins with discussion of the influence of Darwinian thought in the late nineteenth century, then traces subsequent developments in genetics, physiology, chemistry, and molecular biology. L. C. Dunn, *A Short History of Genetics* (New York: McGraw-Hill, 1965), treats the post-1900 period. Mark H. Haller, *Eugenics: Hereditarian Attitudes in American Thought* (New Brunswick, N.J.: Rutgers University Press, 1963), analyzes the eugenics movement in the United States. In addition to Cravens on psychology, see Allen Buss, ed., *Psychology in Social Context* (New York: Halstead, 1979). The essay by Franz Samelson, "Putting Psychology on the Map: Ideology and Intelligence Testing" (pp. 103–68), deals with World War I mental testing.

59. Some recent works on sex differences include: Allen Buss and Wayne Poley, eds., *Individual Differences: Traits and Factors* (New York: Garden Press, 1976); Eleanor E. Maccoby and Carol N. Jacklin, *The Psychology of Sex Differences* (Stanford, Calif.: Stanford University Press, 1974); Diana L. Hall, "Biology, Sex Hormones, and Sexism," *Philosophical Forum* 5 (1973–74): 81–86; and Estelle Ramey, "Sex Hormones and Executive Ability," *Annals of the New York Academy of Sciences* 208 (March 1973): 237–45.

Chapter 7: The Contest between Androgyny and Patriarchy (Judith Ochshorn)

1. See, for example, *The Two Gentlemen of Verona; The Merchant of Venice; As You Like It; Twelfth Night, Or, What You Will; Cymbeline.*

2. Sarah B. Pomeroy, *Goddesses, Whores, Wives, and Slaves* (New York: Schocken, 1976), pp. 185–89.

3. See, for example, Mary Wollstonecraft, *A Vindication of the Rights of Woman* (1792; reprint ed., New York: W. W. Norton, 1967); idem, *Letters on the Equality of the Sexes and the Condition of Woman* (1838; reprint ed., New York: Burt Franklin, 1970); Elizabeth Cady Stanton, "The Solitude of Self," speech delivered before a U.S. Senate

committee in favor of the women's suffrage amendment, 1894, reprinted in Gerda Lerner, ed., *The Female Experience: An American Documentary* (Indianapolis: Bobbs-Merrill, 1977), p. 490, and Stanton, *The Woman's Bible* (1898; reprint ed., New York: Arno Press, 1972); Charlotte Perkins Gilman, *Women and Economics* (1898; reprint ed., New York: Harper and Row, 1966); Virginia Woolf, *A Room of One's Own* (1929; reprint ed., New York: Harcourt, Brace, 1957); Mary Beard, *Woman as Force in History: A Study in Traditions and Realities* (New York: Macmillan, 1947); Simone de Beauvoir, *The Second Sex*, trans. and ed. H. M. Parshley (1949; reprint ed., New York: Bantam, 1970).

4. See President's Commission on the Status of Women, *American Women* (Washington, D.C.: Government Printing Office, 1963).

5. Joan Kelly-Gadol, "The Social Relations of the Sexes: Methodological Implications of Women's History," *Signs: Journal of Women in Culture and Society* 1 (Summer, 1976): 809.

6. See, for example, Lerner, *Female Experience*; Eve Merriam, *Growing Up Female in America: Ten Lives* (New York: Dell, 1971); Carroll Smith-Rosenberg, "The Female World of Love and Ritual: Relations Between Women in Nineteenth-Century America," *Signs: Journal of Women in Culture and Society* 1 (Fall, 1975): 1–29.

7. See, for example, Nancy F. Cott, "Eighteenth-Century Family and Social Life Revealed in Massachusetts Divorce Records," *Journal of Social History* 10 (1976): 20–43.

8. See, for example, G. J. Barker-Benfield, *The Horrors of the Half-Known Life: Male Attitudes Toward Women and Sexuality in Nineteenth-Century America* (New York: Harper Colophon, 1977); Ronald G. Walters, *Primers for Prudery: Sexual Advice to Victorian America* (Englewood Cliffs, N.J.: Prentice-Hall, 1974).

9. Lerner, *Female Experience*.

10. Ibid., p. xxvii; Smith-Rosenberg, "Female World of Love"; idem, "Beauty, the Beast, and the Militant Woman: A Case Study in Sex Roles and Social Stress in Jacksonian America," *American Quarterly* 23 (October 1971): 562–84.

11. Nancy F. Cott, "Passionlessness: An Interpretation of Victorian Sexual Ideology, 1790–1850," *Signs: Journal of Women in Culture and Society* 4 (Winter, 1978): 219–36.

12. Nancy F. Cott and Elizabeth H. Pleck, eds., *A Heritage of Her Own: Toward a New Social History of American Women* (New York: Simon and Schuster, 1979).

13. See, for example, Joan Kelly-Gadol, "Did Women Have A Renaissance?" in *Becoming Visible: Women in European History,* ed. Renate Bridenthal and Claudia Koonz (Boston: Houghton Mifflin, 1977), pp. 137–64.

14. See, for example, Bernard Frank Batto, *Women at Mari* (Baltimore: Johns Hopkins University Press, 1974); Georges Dossin and Andre Finet, *Archives Royales de Mari: Correspondence Feminine* (Paris: Librairie Orientaliste Paul Geuthner, 1978); Jo Ann McNamara and Suzanne F. Wemple, "The Power of Women Through the Family in Medieval Europe: 500–1100," in *Clio's Consciousness Raised: New Perspectives on the History of Women,* ed. Mary S. Hartman and Lois Banner (New York: Harper Colophon, 1974), pp. 103–18.

15. See, for example, Juliet Mitchell, *Woman's Estate* (New York: Vintage, 1973).

16. See, for example, Berenice Carroll, ed., *Liberating Women's History: Theoretical and Critical Essays* (Urbana: University of Illinois Press, 1976), pts. 1 and 4.

17. Friedrich Engels, *The Origin of the Family, Private Property, and the State* (1884; reprint ed., New York: International Publishers, 1942); Kathleen Casey, "The Cheshire Cat: Reconstructing the Experience of Medieval Women," in Carroll, *Liberating Women's History,* pp. 224–49; Ruby Rohrlich, "State Formation in Sumer and the Subjugation of Women," *Feminist Studies* 6 (Spring 1980): 76–102; Jo Ann McNamara and Suzanne F. Wemple, "Sanctity and Power: The Dual Pursuit of Medieval Women," in Bridenthal and Koonz, *Becoming Visible,* pp. 90–118; Michelle Z. Rosaldo, "The Use and Abuse of Anthropology: Reflections on Feminism and Cross-Cultural Understanding," *Signs: Journal of Women in Culture and Society* 5 (Spring 1980): 389–417.

18. See, for example, Elaine Cravitz and Elizabeth Buford, "Teresa of Avila," "Florence Nightingale," "Marie Curie," in Cravitz and Buford, *Courage Knows No Sex* (North Quincy, Mass.: Christopher Publishing House, 1978), pp. 25–45, 73–98, 153–74; Carol Ruth Berkin, "Private Woman, Public Woman: The Contradictions of Charlotte Perkins Gilman," in *Women of America: A History,* ed. Carol Ruth Berkin and Mary Beth Norton (Boston: Houghton Mifflin, 1979), pp. 150–76; Sylvia Plath, *The Bell Jar* (1st U.S. ed., New York: Harper and Row, 1971).

19. Kelly-Gadol, "Social Relations of the Sexes," pp. 817–22.

20. Judith Ochshorn, *The Female Experience and the Nature of the Divine* (Bloomington: Indiana University Press, 1981), chaps. 2–4.

21. Ibid., pp. 107–10.

22. See, for example, Kelly-Gadol, "Did Women Have a Renaissance?" and see Lawrence Stone, "The Rise of the Nuclear Family in Early Modern England: The Patriarchal Stage," in *The Family in History,* ed. Charles E. Rosenberg (Philadelphia: University of Pennsylvania Press, 1978), pp. 13–57.

23. Cyrus H. Gordon, *Ugarit and Minoan Crete* (New York: W. W. Norton, 1966), pp. 28, 151–53.

24. Sarah B. Pomeroy, "A Classical Scholar's Perspective on Matriarchy," in Carroll, *Liberating Women's History,* p. 220.

25. Euripides, *Medea,* trans. Frederic Prokosch, in Dudley Fitts, ed., *Greek Plays in Modern Translation* (New York: Dial Press, 1955), pp. 195–240.

26. Aeschylus, *Agamemnon,* trans. Richard Lattimore, in Fitts, *Greek Plays,* pp. 47–53.

27. Sophocles, *Antigone,* trans. Dudley Fitts and Robert Fitzgerald, in Fitts, *Greek Plays,* pp. 470–99.

28. See, for example, Elaine Pagels, *The Gnostic Gospels* (New York: Random House, 1979); Halldor Hermannson, *Old Icelandic Literature: A Bibliographical Essay* (1933; reprint ed., New York: Kraus Reprint, 1966); Hugo Bekker, *The Nibelungenlied: A Literary Analysis* (1945; reprint ed., Toronto: University of Toronto Press, 1971).

29. Katherine M. Rogers, *The Troublesome Helpmate: A History of Misogyny in Literature* (Seattle: University of Washington Press, 1966), pp. 56–99.

30. Geoffrey Chaucer, "The Wife of Bath's Prologue," in *Canterbury Tales,* trans. Nevill Coghill (Baltimore: Penguin, 1952), quoted in Susan G. Bell, ed., *Women: From the Greeks to the French Revolution* (Belmont, Calif.: Wadsworth, 1973), p. 149.

31. Philip Slater, *The Glory of Hera: Greek Mythology and the Greek Family* (Boston: Beacon Press, 1968).

32. Pomeroy, *Goddesses, Whores, Wives, and Slaves,* pp. 120–25; Evelyne Sullerot, *Woman, Society and Change,* trans. Margaret Scotford Archer (New York: McGraw-Hill, 1971), p. 33.

33. McNamara and Wemple, "Power of Women," p. 109.

34. McNamara and Wemple, "Sanctity and Power," pp. 108, 109.

35. Henrik Ibsen, *Collected Works,* ed. William Archer and C. H. Herford, 13 vols. (New York: Charles Scribner's Sons, 1916), 1:xxvii.

36. Ochshorn, *Female Experience,* chap. 4; Pagels, *Gnostic Gospels.*

37. Sullerot, *Woman, Society and Change,* p. 33.

38. Keith Thomas, "Women and the Civil War Sects," in *Crisis in Europe, 1560–1660,* ed. Trevor Aston (New York: Basic, 1965), pp. 317–40.

39. Lina Eckenstein, *Woman Under Monasticism* (Cambridge: Cambridge University Press, 1896).

40. Emily James Putnam, *The Lady: Studies of Certain Significant Phases of Her History* (1910; reprint ed., Chicago: University of Chicago Press, 1970), pp. 81–82.

41. Rosemary Radford Ruether, "Misogynism and Virginal Feminism in the Fathers of the Church," in *Religion and Sexism: Images of Women in the Jewish and Christian Traditions,* ed. Rosemary Radford Ruether (New York: Simon and Schuster, 1974), pp. 117–47.

42. Tacitus, *Germania,* 8, trans. H. Mattingly (Harmondsworth, England: Penguin, 1960), pp. 18, 115.

43. Casey, "Cheshire Cat," pp. 233–34.

44. Jakob Burckhardt, *The Civilization of the Renaissance in Italy: An Essay,* 2d rev. ed. (Oxford and London: Phaidon Press, 1945), p. 241.

45. Pomeroy, *Goddesses, Whores, Wives, and Slaves,* pp. 52–56.

46. See, for example, Eliza Burth Gamble, *The Sexes in Science and History* (1st printed in 1894 as *The Evolution of Woman;* reprint ed., New York: G. P. Putnam's Sons, 1916), pp. 330–45; Pomeroy, *Goddesses, Whores, Wives, and Slaves,* pp. 92, 141, 174–75; Juvenal, *The Sixteen Satires,* trans. Peter Green (Baltimore: Penguin Classics, 1967), Satire 6, ll. 434–56.

47. Burckhardt, *Civilization of the Renaissance,* pp. 242–43; Hannelore Sachs, *The Renaissance Woman,* trans. Marianne Herzfeld (New York: McGraw-Hill, 1971), p. 52.

48. Kelly-Gadol, "Did Women Have a Renaissance?" pp. 146–47.

49. Pomeroy, *Goddesses, Whores, Wives, and Slaves,* pp. 38, 162–63, 177.

50. *The Burgundian Code,* trans. Katherine Fischer Drew (Philadelphia: University of Pennsylvania Press, 1949), pp. 32, 59, 71–73, and cited in Julia O'Faolain and Lauro Martines, eds., *Not in God's Image: Women in History from the Greeks to the Victorians* (New York: Harper Colophon, 1973), pp. 99–100; *Leges Visigothorum,* p. 174, IV, 2, 1, also cited in O'Faolain and Martines, *Not in God's Image,* pp. 99–100.

51. See, for example, *Fuero Jusgo,* codified after 1241 (Madrid, 1815), IV, ii, 9, cited in O'Faolain and Martines, *Not in God's Image,* p. 148; *Die Kolner Schreinsbucher des 13. und 14. Jahrunderts,* H. Planitz and T. Buyken, eds., Weimar, 1937, in Gesellschaft fur Rheinische Geschichtskunde, XLVI, p. 197, cited in O'Faolain and Martines, *Not in God's Image,* p. 149.

52. A. Abram, "Women Traders in Medieval London," *Economic Journal* (London) 26 (1916): 276–85.

53. Diane Hughes, "Domestic Ideals and Social Behavior: Evidence From Medieval Genoa," in C. Rosenberg, *Family in History,* pp. 115 – 43.

54. Ochshorn, *Female Experience,* chaps. 3 and 4.

55. Drew, *Burgundian Code,* p. 68.

56. Mary Nelson, "Why Witches Were Women," in *Women: A Feminist Perspective,* ed. Jo Freeman (Palo Alto, Calif.: Mayfield, 1979), p. 454.

57. See, for example, Jules Michelet, *Satanism and Witchcraft: A Study in Medieval Superstition,* trans. A. R. Allinson (1939; reprint ed., New York: Citadel Press, 1946), pp. 98 – 118.

58. Nelson, "Why Witches Were Women," pp. 451 – 68; Stone, "Rise of the Nuclear Family," pp. 13 – 57.

59. Willystine Goodsell, *A History of the Family as a Social and Educational Institution* (New York: Macmillan, 1930), pp. 217, 261 – 62.

60. Burckhardt, *Civilization of the Renaissance,* pp. 12 – 13.

61. Mary Lynn McDougall, "Working-Class Women During the Industrial Revolution, 1780 – 1914," in Bridenthal and Koonz, *Becoming Visible,* pp. 270 – 72; Judith R. Walkowitz and Daniel J. Walkowitz, "'We Are Not Beasts of the Field': Prostitution and the Poor in Plymouth and Southampton Under the Contagious Diseases Acts," in Hartman and Banner, *Clio's Consciousness Raised,* pp. 192 – 225.

62. Pomeroy, *Goddesses, Whores, Wives, and Slaves,* pp. 37 – 40.

63. Ibid., pp. 166 – 68.

64. Nelson, "Why Witches Were Women," pp. 463 – 64.

Chapter 8: Against the Grain (Sandra L. Langer)

1. Pat Hills, "Art History Text Books: Hidden Persuaders," *Artforum* 14 (June 1976): 58 – 61; Gloria Orenstein, "Art History," *Signs: Journal of Women in Culture and Society* 1 (Winter 1975): 505 – 25.

2. Elizabeth Fries Lummis Ellet, *Women Artists in All Ages and Countries* (New York: Harper, 1859); Clara Erskine Clement, *Women in the Fine Arts* (Boston and New York: Houghton Mifflin, 1904); Walter Shaw Sparrow et al., *Women Painters of the World* (London: Hodder and Stoughton, 1905); Eleanor Tufts, *Our Hidden Heritage: Five Centuries of Women Artists* (New York and London: Paddington Press, 1974); Karen Petersen and J. J. Wilson, *Women Artists: Recognition and Reappraisal* (New York: Harper and Row, 1976); Ann Sutherland Harris and Linda Nochlin, *Women Artists: 1550 – 1950* (New York: Random House, 1976); Elsa Honig Fine, *Women and Art* (Montclair, N.J.: Abner Schram, 1978); Germaine Greer, *The Obstacle Race: The Fortunes of Women Painters and Their Work* (New York: Farrar, Straus and Giroux, 1979); Eleanor Munro, *Originals: American Women Artists* (New York: Simon and Schuster, 1979).

3. Sandra L. Langer, "Emerging Feminism and Art History," *Art Criticism* 1 (Winter 1979/80): 66 – 83.

4. Ibid., p. 81.

5. Mary Daly, *Gyn/Ecology* (Boston: Beacon Press, 1978).

6. Kate Chopin, *The Awakening: An Authoritative Text, Contexts, Criticism,* ed. Margaret Culley. The text of first edition, 1899 (New York: W. W. Norton, 1976), p. 114.

7. Evelyn Reed, *Woman's Evolution from matriarchal clan to patriarchal family* (New York: Pathfinder Press, 1975), p. 53. My thanks to Sarah Slavin for directing me to this resource.

8. Adrienne Rich, "Diving into the Wreck," in Rich, *Diving into the Wreck* (New York: W. W. Norton, 1973), p. 24.

9. See Langer, "Emerging Feminism."

10. Ibid., p. 68.

11. Ibid., pp. 69–70.

12. Bobbi Rothstein, "Book Review Digest," *Best Seller* 39 (December 1979): 501.

13. See Linda Nochlin, *New York Times Book Review* 84 (October 28, 1979): 3t, and Lucy Lippard, *Nation* 229 (November 17, 1979): 501–03.

14. In all fairness to Nochlin one certainly must cite her as a creative figure in feminist theory in the arts, but nowhere in her prose does one find the emergence of a new language.

15. *The Woman Question: Selections from the Writings of Karl Marx, Frederick Engels, V. I. Lenin and Joseph Stalin* (New York: International Publishers, 1979), p. 21.

16. Naomi Weisstein, " 'How can a little girl like you teach a great big class of men?' the Chairman Said, and Other Adventures of a Woman in Science," in *Working It Out,* ed. Sara Ruddick and Pamela Daniels (New York: Pantheon, 1977), p. 249.

17. Daly, *Gyn/Ecology,* pp. 20–21.

18. Carol Duncan, "Virility and Domination in Early 20th Century Vanguard Painting," *Artforum* 12 (December 1973): 30–39; idem, "The Esthetic of Power in Modern Erotic Art," *Heresies* 1 (January 1977): 46–50.

19. Alessandra Comini, "Titles Can Be Troublesome: Misinterpretations in Male Art Criticism," *Art Criticism* 1 (Winter 1979/80): 50–54.

20. Edward Lucie-Smith, *Eroticism in Western Art* (New York: Praeger, 1972), pp. 134–35.

21. Daly, *Gyn/Ecology,* p. 29.

22. Judy Chicago, *The Dinner Party* (New York: Doubleday, Anchor Press, 1979), pp. 57, 95–97.

23. Carol Duncan, "Happy Mothers and Other Ideas in French Painting," *Art Bulletin* 55 (December 1973): 570–83.

24. Adelyn Breeskin, *Mary Cassatt: A Catalogue Raisonne of Oils, Pastels, Watercolors, and Drawings* (Washington, D.C.: Smithsonian Institution Press, 1979).

25. Gillian Perry, *Paula Modersohn-Becker* (New York: Harper and Row, 1979), p. 57.

26. Martha Kearns, *Kathe Kollwitz: Woman and Artist* (New York: Feminist Press, 1976), p. 107.

27. Barbara Hepworth, *Carvings and Drawings* (London: Lund Humphries, 1952), pp. 135–36.

28. Fine, *Women and Art,* p. 212. I am indebted to Fine for this description and quotation.

Chapter 9: The Fallen Woman in Fiction (Jane Flanders)

1. A short list of novels focusing on the "fallen" woman, or in which a deviant woman appears as a subordinate character, is as follows: Daniel Defoe, *Moll Flanders* and

Roxana, or the Fortunate Mistress; Samuel Richardson, *Clarissa;* John Cleland, *Fanny Hill;* Mary Wollstonecraft, *Maria or the Wrongs of Woman;* Choderlos de la Clos, *Les Liaisons Dangereuses;* Susanna Rowson, *Charlotte Temple, A Tale of Truth;* Charles Brockden Brown, *Arthur Mervyn, or Memoirs of the Year 1793;* Nathaniel Hawthorne, *The Scarlet Letter;* Gustave Flaubert, *Madame Bovary;* George Eliot, *The Mill on the Floss* and *Adam Bede;* Leo Tolstoi, *Anna Karenina;* Thomas Hardy, *Tess of the d'Urbervilles;* Henry James, *Daisy Miller* and *The Ambassadors;* Stephen Crane, *Maggie, Girl of the Streets;* Kate Chopin, *The Awakening;* Bram Stoker, *Dracula;* Theodore Dreiser, *Sister Carrie* and *An American Tragedy;* Willa Cather, *A Lost Lady;* Anita Loos, *Gentlemen Prefer Blondes;* William Faulkner, *Sanctuary;* Jean Rhys, *Voyage in the Dark;* Sylvia Plath, *The Bell Jar.*

2. Georg Lukacs, *The Theory of the Novel,* trans. Anna Bostock (Cambridge, Mass.: MIT Press, 1971), pp. 85–88, and passim.

3. Virginia Woolf, *A Room of One's Own* (1929; reprint ed., New York: Harcourt, Brace, 1957), pp. 48–52.

4. Judith Rossner, *Looking for Mr. Goodbar* (New York: Simon and Schuster, 1975).

5. Annette Kolodny, "Dancing through the Minefield: Some Observations on the Theory, Practice and Politics of a Feminist Literary Criticism," *Feminist Studies* 6 (Spring 1980): 1–25.

6. See Sigmund Freud, *Civilization and Its Discontents* (New York: W. W. Norton, 1961); Lukacs, *Theory of the Novel;* Herbert Marcuse, *Eros and Civilization* (London: Sphere, 1969); Jan van den Berg, *The Changing Nature of Man: Introduction to a Historical Psychology,* trans. H. F. Croes (New York: Dell, 1975).

7. See Ian Watt, *The Rise of the Novel* (Berkeley: University of California Press, 1959).

8. Everett Knight, *A Theory of the Classical Novel* (New York: Barnes and Noble, 1970), p. 25.

9. See Fernand Braudel, *Capitalism and Material Life 1400–1800,* trans. Miriam Kochan (New York: Harper and Row, 1967); Lawrence Stone, *The Family, Sex and Marriage in England 1500–1800* (New York: Harper and Row, 1977); Peter Laslett, *The World We Have Lost* (New York: Charles Scribner, 1965).

10. For a discussion of the changing nature of marriage, see Eva Figes, *Patriarchal Attitudes* (Greenwich, Conn.: Fawcett, 1970); Simone de Beauvoir, *The Second Sex,* trans. and ed. H. M. Parshley (1949; reprint ed., New York: Alfred A. Knopf, 1962); Eli Zaretsky, *Capitalism, The Family and Personal Life* (New York: Harper and Row, 1976).

11. See L. L. Schucking, *The Puritan Family: A Social Study from the Literary Sources,* trans. Brian Battershaw (New York: Schocken, 1970).

12. For a classic statement of the argument, see Friedrich Engels, *The Origin of the Family, Private Property, and the State* (1884; reprint ed., New York: Pathfinder Press, 1972).

13. de Beauvoir, *Second Sex,* p. 75.

14. Schucking, *Puritan Family,* pp. 80–82.

15. Vern L. Bullough, *The Subordinate Sex; A History of Attitudes toward Women* (Baltimore: Penguin, 1974), p. 278.

16. See Figes, *Patriarchal Attitudes,* chap. 2; and Sherry Ortner, "Is Female to Male as Nature Is to Culture?" in *Woman, Culture and Society,* ed. Michelle Z. Rosaldo and Louise Lamphere (Stanford, Calif.: Stanford University Press, 1974).

17. de Beauvoir, *Second Sex,* p. 119.

18. This argument is central in L. C. Knights, *Drama and Society in the Age of Johnson* (1937; reprint ed., New York: W. W. Norton, 1968); see also R. H. Tawney, *Religion and the Rise of Capitalism* (1922; reprint ed., New York: New American Library, 1947).

19. Mary Wollstonecraft, *A Vindication of the Rights of Woman* (1792; reprint ed., New York: W. W. Norton, 1975), p. 71.

20. Kate Millett, *Sexual Politics* (New York: Avon, 1969), p. 46.

21. *The Harper's Bazaar Book of Decorum,* 1873, quoted in *The Genteel Female,* ed. Clifton Joseph Furness (New York: Alfred A. Knopf, 1931), pp. 138–39.

22. See Bullough, *Subordinate Sex,* pp. 278–88, and passim.

23. Figes, *Patriarchal Attitudes,* pp. 81–82.

24. Wollstonecraft, *Vindication,* p. 72.

25. Robert Bage, *Mount Henneth,* vol. 9 of Ballantyne's Novelist's Library (London: Ballantyne, 1824), p. 161.

26. Charles Brockden Brown, *Arthur Mervyn, or Memoirs of the Year 1793,* ed. Warner Berthoff (1798; reprint ed., New York: Holt Rinehart, and Winston, 1962), pp. 344–45; emphasis added.

27. R. F. Brissenden, *Virtue in Distress: Studies in the Novel of Sentiment from Richardson to Sade* (New York: Barnes and Noble, 1974), p. 183, observes that if one reads Clarissa's rape as an allegory it is "a violation not merely of Clarissa but also of the conventional values which she and her family represent." Her rape is the logical extension of her own rebellion against her family.

28. Wollstonecraft, *Vindication,* p. 73.

29. Woolf, *Room of One's Own,* p. 51.

30. Figes, *Patriarchal Attitudes,* pp. 35–36.

31. See Patricia Tobin, "The Third Term" (Paper written for the Department of English, Rutgers University).

32. For an excellent exposition of this idea, see Jan van den Berg, *Changing Nature of Man.*

33. Lukacs, *Theory of the Novel,* p. 112.

34. Ibid., p. 148.

Chapter 10: Redefining the Family (Mary Anglin)

1. Christopher Lasch, *Haven in a Heartless World* (New York: Basic, 1977).

2. Compare Juliet Mitchell, *Psychoanalysis and Feminism: Freud, Reich, Laing and Women* (New York: Pantheon, 1974); Dorothy Dinnerstein, *The Mermaid and The Minotaur, Sexual Arrangements and Human Malaise* (New York: Harper and Row, 1977); Gayle Rubin, "The Traffic in Women: Notes on the 'Political Economy' of Sex," in *Toward an Anthropology of Women,* ed. Rayna Reiter (New York: Monthly Review, 1975), pp. 157–210.

3. Ellen Ross, "Rethinking the 'Family,'" *Radical History Review* 20 (Spring/Summer, 1979): 76–84.

4. Carol Stack, *All Our Kin* (New York: Harper and Row, 1974); Eleanor B. Leacock, ed., *The Culture of Poverty: A Critique* (New York: Simon and Schuster, 1971).

5. Rayna Rapp, "Household and Family," *Feminist Studies* 5 (Spring 1979): 175–81.

6. Compare Jacques Donzelot, *The Policing of Families* (New York: Pantheon, 1979).

7. Southern Appalachian Center, unpublished data, n.d.

8. Compare Harriet Arnow, *The Dollmaker* (New York: Macmillan, 1954).

Chapter 11: Sexism and Racism (Mamie Locke)

1. H. J. Simons, *African Women: Their Legal Status in South Africa* (Evanston, Ill.: Northwestern University Press, 1968), p. 285.

2. Joy Zollner, "Women's Rights in Africa and the United States," *Africa Report* 22 (January–February 1977): 6.

3. "Women: The Neglected Human Resource for African Development," *Canadian Journal of African Studies* 6 (1972): 360.

4. Shelby Lewis, "African Women and National Development" in *Comparative Perspective of Third World Women: The Impact of Race, Sex, and Class,* ed. Beverly Lindsey (New York: Praeger, 1980), pp. 35–37.

5. Ibid., p. 37.

6. Clarice Stohl, ed., *Sexism: Scientific Debates* (London: Addison-Wesley, 1973), p. 1.

7. Hilda Bernstein, *For Their Triumphs and For Their Tears: Women in Apartheid South Africa* (London: International Defense Aid Fund, 1975), p. 9.

8. Elizabeth Landis, "Apartheid and the Disabilities of African Women in South Africa," *Freedomways* 15 (1975): 272.

9. Lewis, "African Women and National Development," p. 35.

10. Margarita Dobert and Nwaganga Shields, "Africa's Women: Security in Tradition, Challenge in Change," *African Report* 17 (July–August 1972): 14–17; Ivy Matsepe, "Underdevelopment and African Women," *Journal of Southern African Affairs* 2 (April 1977): 136.

11. Dobert and Shields, "Africa's Women," p. 14.

12. Ibid., p. 17; "Women: The Neglected Human Resource," p. 359.

13. Simons, *African Women,* pp. 187, 188.

14. Lewis, "African Women and National Development," p. 36.

15. Leith Mullings, "Women and Economic Change in Africa," in *Women in Africa: Studies in Social and Economic Change,* ed. Nancy J. Hafkin and Edna G. Bay (Stanford, Calif.: Stanford University Press, 1976), p. 247.

16. Dobert and Shields, "Africa's Women," p. 17.

17. Ibid., p. 18.

18. Lewis, "African Women and National Development," pp. 41, 43.

19. Dobert and Shields, "Africa's Women," p. 18; "Women: The Neglected Human Resource," p. 360.

20. Matsepe, "Underdevelopment," pp. 138–39.

21. Ester Boserup, *Woman's Role in Economic Development* (New York: St. Martin's Press, 1970), pp. 59–64, 91–99.

22. Walter Rodney, *How Europe Underdeveloped Africa* (Dar es Salaam: Tanzania Publishing House, 1972), p. 248.

23. Bernstein, *For Their Triumphs*, p. 8.

24. Audrey Wipper, "The Roles of African Women: Past, Present, and Future," *Canadian Journal of African Studies* 6 (1972): 145.

25. Bernstein, *For Their Triumphs*, pp. 8–9, 13.

26. Ibid., p. 18; Landis, "Apartheid," pp. 273–74.

27. Simons, *African Women*, pp. 263–65.

28. Ibid., pp. 281–82; Landis, "Apartheid," p. 275.

29. Landis, "Apartheid," p. 274.

30. Ibid., pp. 273–75; Simons, *African Women*, p. 271.

31. Simons, *African Women*, pp. 274–75.

32. Matsepe, "Underdevelopment," pp. 140–41.

33. Ibid., p. 141; Simons, *African Women*, p. 285.

34. Bonnie J. Schultz, "Women and African Liberation: Interview with Miriam Makeba," *Africa Report* 22 (January–February 1977): 13.

35. Matsepe, "Underdevelopment," p. 141.

36. Ibid.

37. Simons, *African Women*, p. 286.

38. Landis, "Apartheid," p. 276.

39. Martha Mueller, "Women and Men, Power and Powerlessness in Lesotho," *Signs: Journal of Women in Culture and Society* 3 (Fall 1977): 155.

40. Kenneth Little, *African Women in Towns: An Aspect of Africa's Social Revolution* (London: Cambridge University Press, 1973), p. 179.

41. See Bernstein, *For Their Triumphs*, pp. 69–71.

42. The Africa Research Group, *Race to Power: The Struggle for Southern Africa* (Garden City, N.Y.: Anchor Press, 1974), pp. 152–62.

43. Quoted in Mullings, "Women and Economic Change," p. 257.

44. Africa Research Group, *Race to Power*, pp. 215–16.

45. Schultz, "Miriam Makeba," p. 13.

46. Florence Mahoney, "Women of Africa," from course offered at Spelman College, Atlanta, Georgia, 1972, quoted in Ida Rousseau-Mukenge, "Conceptualizations of African Women's Role in Development: A Search for New Directions," *Journal of International Affairs* 30 (1976–1977): 261; Lewis, "African Women and National Development," p. 47.

47. "African Seminar on the Participation of Women in Economic Life," *International Labour Review* 105 (February 1972):176.

48. Lewis, "African Women and National Development," p. 42.

Chapter 12: Of Paradigm and Paradox (Elisabeth S. Muhlenfeld)

1. *A Diary from Dixie, as Written by Mary Boykin Chesnut, wife of James Chesnut, Jr., United States Senator from South Carolina, 1859–1861, and Afterward an Aide to*

Jefferson Davis and a Brigadier-General in the Confederate Army, ed. Isabella D. Martin and Myrta Lockett Avary (New York: D. Appleton, 1905; London: Heinemann, 1905). A second edition appeared in 1949: *A Diary From Dixie,* ed. Ben Ames Williams (Boston: Houghton Mifflin).

2. Ben Ames Williams based his central character, Cinda Dewain, on Mary Boykin Chesnut in *House Divided* (Boston: Houghton Mifflin, 1947); Mary Elizabeth Massey, *Bonnet Brigades* (New York: Alfred A. Knopf, 1966); Anne Firor Scott, *The Southern Lady: From Pedestal to Politics 1830–1930* (Chicago: University of Chicago Press, 1970); Carl N. Degler, *At Odds: Women and the Family in America from the Revolution to the Present* (New York: Oxford University Press, 1980); Edmund Wilson, *Patriotic Gore: Studies in the Literature of the American Civil War* (New York: Oxford University Press, 1962), pp. 279–80; Lyman Butterfield, quoted in Bell Irvin Wiley, *Confederate Women* (Westport, Conn.: Greenwood Press, 1975), p. 3.

3. Foreword by C. Vann Woodward in Elisabeth S. Muhlenfeld, *Mary Boykin Chesnut: A Biography* (Baton Rouge: Louisiana State University Press, 1981), p. xi. C. Vann Woodward's edition of the Chesnut journals is entitled *Mary Chesnut's Civil War* (New Haven: Yale University Press, 1981).

4. Mary Boykin Miller Chesnut (March 31, 1823–November 22, 1886), daughter of Mary Boykin Miller (1804–1885) and Stephen Decatur Miller (1788–1838). For a complete and fully documented study of Mary Boykin Chesnut's life, see Muhlenfeld, *Mary Boykin Chesnut;* the biographical information in this essay is, in the main, distilled from that source.

5. Mary Whitaker Boykin (d. 1833). Mary Boykin Chesnut (MBC) recorded her memories of her maternal grandmother in a manuscript memoir about Catherine Miller Williams, MBC's sister, written in 1876 (Williams-Chesnut-Manning Collection, South Caroliniana Library, Columbia, South Carolina). The memoir begins "We called her Kitty." MBC used much of the material in "We Called Her Kitty" in a largely autobiographical manuscript novel entitled "Two Years—or the Way We Lived Then," hereinafter cited as "Two Years." The manuscript of "Two Years" is in the Williams-Chesnut-Manning Collection. Quotations from "Two Years" are taken from the edited and annotated text of the novel that constitutes pt. 3 of Elisabeth S. Muhlenfeld, "Mary Boykin Chesnut: The Writer and her Work" (Ph.D diss., University of South Carolina, 1978).

6. See "Two Years," pp. 78–80 of edited text.

7. Ann Marson Talvande (born in Santo Domingo prior to 1800, died November 15, 1850). Chapters 9–12 of "Two Years" provide an excellent description of Madame Talvande's school.

8. "Two Years," pp. 57, 59 of edited text. Detailed descriptions of MBC's trips to Mississippi and of her courtship with James Chesnut, Jr. (January 18, 1815–February 1, 1885) may be found in Muhlenfeld, *Mary Boykin Chesnut.*

9. MBC's original Civil War journal, dated February 25, 1861, South Caroliniana Library, Columbia, hereinafter cited as Journal, followed by date of entry. A full transcript of the surviving portions of her original Civil War journal, edited by Elisabeth S. Muhlenfeld and Thomas E. Dasher, is available at South Caroliniana Library, the Library of Congress, and Yale University Library.

10. MBC's revised Civil War journal, written between 1881 and 1884, entry dated November 28, 1861, South Caroliniana Library, Columbia, hereinafter cited as Revised Journal, followed by date of entry.

11. Flyleaf, red volume of original Civil War journal.

12. Journal, April 4 and February 27, 1861.

13. Ibid., March 28 and September 1, 1861.

14. Ibid., April 27, August 12, and October 17, 1861.

15. Revised Journal, March 12 and February 26, 1865.

16. Ibid., April 19, 1865.

17. "Two Years of My Life," the title of MBC's first draft, was changed in subsequent drafts to "Two Years — or the Way We Lived Then" (see note 5 above). "The Captain and the Colonel," manuscript in Williams-Chesnut-Manning Collection; an edited and annotated text of this novel constitutes pt. 2 of Muhlenfeld, "Mary Boykin Chesnut."

18. Journal, March 18, 1861.

19. Revised Journal, November 27, 1861.

20. Ibid., December 10, 1863.

21. Ibid., August 27, 1861.

Chapter 13: Careers in Landscape Architecture (Catherine M. Howett)

1. Katherine L. Jacobs, "Celia Thaxter and Her Island Garden," *Landscape* 24 (1893): 12–17.

2. Mrs. Schuyler Van Rennselaer, *Art Out-Of-Doors* (New York: Charles Scribner's Sons, 1893), pp. 3, 353–58.

3. Ibid., pp. 7–8.

4. Ibid., p. 358.

5. George Arthur Yarwood, "History of Women in Landscaping Architecture," in *Report of the Task Force on Women in Landscape Architecture,* American Society of Landscape Artists Bulletin, July 1973.

6. Norman T. Newton, *Design on the Land: The Development of Landscape Architecture* (Cambridge: Harvard University Press, Belknap Press, 1971), pp. 387–88.

7. Dorothy May Anderson, "Women's Breakthrough Via the Cambridge School," *Landscape Architecture* 68 (March 1978): 148.

8. Ibid., p. 147.

9. Newton, *Design on the Land,* pp. 427–46.

10. "Introduction," *Report of Task Force on Women in Landscape Architecture.*

11. Miriam Easton-Rutz, "The Missing Sex in L. A. Classrooms," letter in *Landscape Architecture* 68 (March 1978): 102–03.

12. Jayne Elley Stake, "Motives for Occupational Goal Setting Among Male and Female College Students," *Journal of Applied Psychology* 63 (October 1978): 617–23.

13. Elizabeth Douvan, "The Role of Models in Women's Professional Development," reprinted in *The Psychology of Women: Selected Readings,* ed. Juanita H. Williams (New York: W. W. Norton, 1979), pp. 392–95.

14. Cynthia Fuchs Epstein, *Woman's Place: Options and Limits in Professional Careers* (Berkeley: University of California Press, 1970), pp. 168–70.

Chapter 14: Does Equality Mean Sameness? (Debra Herman)

1. Many of the ideas expressed in this chapter were first developed in Debra Herman, "College and After: The Vassar Experiment in Women's Education, 1861–1924" (Ph.D.

diss., Stanford University, 1979). Readers requiring more extensive bibliographical information or further documentation may consult that work.

2. Thomas Woody, *A History of Women's Higher Education in the United States,* 2 vols. (New York: Science Press, 1929), is still the most comprehensive account of the early history of women's higher education. More recent accounts include Roberta Frankfort, *Collegiate Women: Domesticity and Career in Turn-of-the Century America* (New York: New York University Press, 1977); Elaine Kendall, *"Peculiar Institutions": An Informal History of the Seven Sister Colleges* (New York: G. P. Putnam's Sons, 1975, 1976); and Mabel Newcomer, *A Century of Higher Education for American Women* (New York: Harper and Brothers, 1959). Some useful studies of individual institutions include Arthur C. Cole, *A Hundred Years of Mount Holyoke College: The Evolution of an Educational Ideal* (New Haven: Yale University Press, 1940); Ronald W. Hogeland, "Coeducation of the Sexes at Oberlin College: A Study of Social Ideas in Mid-Nineteenth Century America," *Journal of Social History* 2 (Winter 1972 – 73): 160 – 76; Helen R. Olin, *The Women of a State University: An Illustration of the Working of Coeducation in the Middle West* (New York: G. P. Putnam's Sons, 1909); and Kathryn Kish Sklar, "The Founding of Mount Holyoke College," in *Women of America, A History*, ed. Carol Ruth Berkin and Mary Beth Norton (Boston: Houghton Mifflin, 1979).

3. Vassar was not the first institution to call itself a college for women nor was it the first college to admit woman students. The school's claims of primacy rest with the fact that it was the first institution of higher education for women widely credited as being of collegiate rank and the first to offer a demonstrably collegiate level of education to significant numbers of women. See Herman, "College and After," p. 12.

4. Doubts about women's physical stamina and intellectual ability are evident in writings pertaining to the original formulation of the Vassar experiment. The most influential nineteenth-century attack on women's higher education as injurious to their health is Edward H. Clarke, *Sex in Education* (Boston: James R. Osgood, 1873). Clarke's book drew numerous responses from women who objected to his claims. Among the most important are Julia Ward Howe, ed., *Sex and Education: A Reply to Dr. E. H. Clarke's Sex in Education* (1874; reprint ed., New York: Arno Press, 1972).

5. Vassar's sole concession to the sex of its students was pragmatic recognition of the dismal state of women's college preparatory training. Largely for this reason, the college did not require Greek as a prerequisite for admission. A further recognition of this problem came with the establishment of a precollegiate preparatory program within the college itself, a device whereby the college in effect created its own constituency. See Herman, "College and After," chap. 3, on Vassar's entrance requirements and the preparatory program.

6. [Sara Josepha Hale], "Domestic Science for Young Ladies," *Godey's Lady's Book* 70 (January 1865): 95.

7. This argument held a great deal of weight in an age when higher education was avowed nonvocational for men as well as for women. On changing views of the purposes of higher education see: Frederick Rudolph, *The American College and University: A History* (New York: Alfred A. Knopf, 1962); idem, *Curriculum: A History of the American Undergraduate Course of Study Since 1636* (San Francisco: Jossey-Bass, 1978); and Laurence R. Veysey, *The Emergence of the American University* (Chicago: University of Chicago Press, 1965).

8. This conclusion is based in part on data available in the *Bulletin of Vassar College: Alumnae Biographical Register Issue* (Poughkeepsie, N.Y.: 1939), which contains data on the marital and career patterns and other activities of Vassar graduates.

9. "Concerning Women's Education," *Outlook* 61 (March 4, 1899): 582.

10. Ibid.

11. A Loyal Alumna, "The First Year Out of College, The College at Fault," *Vassar Alumnae Monthly* 2 (January 1911): 45.

12. G. Stanley Hall, *Adolescence, Its Psychology and Its Relation to Physiology, Anthropology, Sociology, Sex, Crime, Religion and Education* (New York: D. Appleton, 1904), p. 614.

13. M. Carey Thomas, "Present Tendencies in Women's Colleges and University Education," *Publications of the Association of Collegiate Alumnae,* series 3, no. 17 (February 1908), p. 54.

14. M. Carey Thomas, "Should the Higher Education of Women Differ from That of Men?" *Educational Review* 21 (January 1901): 1–10, reprinted in Barbara M. Cross, ed., *The Educated Woman in America, Selected Writings of Catherine Beecher, Margaret Fuller and M. Carey Thomas* (New York: Teachers College Press, 1965), p. 153. Other discussions of this same issue include: Kate Gordon, "Wherein Should the Education of a Woman Differ from that of a Man," *School Review* 13 (December 1905): 789–94; W. A. Neilsen, "Should Women Be Educated Like Men?" *Forum* 82 (February 1929): 102–05; C. S. Parrish, "Shall the Higher Education of Women Be the Same as That of Men?" *Educational Review* 22 (November 1901): 383–96; Charles F. Thwing, "Should Woman's Education Differ from Man's?" *Forum* 30 (February 1901): 728–36.

15. At Vassar home economics was termed "euthenics," a word coined by Ellen Swallow Richards, a member of the Vassar class of 1870 and a key figure in the home economics movement in the early part of this century. On the euthenics program at Vassar see Minnie Cummock Blodgett '84, "Euthenics: What Is It?" *Vassar Quarterly* 10 (November 1924): 7–12; H. N. MacCracken, "The Field of Euthenics," ibid., pp. 13–16; Annie Louise Macleod, "Euthenics in the Curriculum," ibid., pp. 17–20.

16. On the changing characteristics of college students see Herman, "College and After," chap. 6.

17. Helen Ekin Starett, *After College, What? For Girls* (New York: Thomas Y. Crowell, 1896), p. 5.

18. Margaret Miner, "The College 'Blight,'" *Vassar Quarterly* 14 (November 1929): 262.

19. Charles F. Thwing, *The College Woman* (New York: Baker and Taylor, 1894), p. 162.

20. "Editorial," *Vassar Miscellany* 30 (January 1901): 178.

21. A Loyal Alumna, "First Year Out of College," p. 45.

22. "The First Year Out of College," *Vassar Alumnae Magazine* 2 (November 1910): 10.

23. On the conservatism of the Vassar experiment see Herman, "College and After," chap. 1 and pp. 323–29.

24. Mary Roberts Smith, "Shall the College Curriculum Be Modified for Women?" *Publications of the Association of Collegiate Alumnae,* series 3, no. 1 (December 1898), p. 2.

25. Associate Alumnae of Vassar College, "Biographical Questionnaire" (1950).

26. The career patterns of Vassar classes are described in a number of sources, including Frances Bryan, "Occupations of Vassar Women," *Vassar Quarterly* 17 (February 1932): 26; Newcomer, *Century of Higher Education;* and Agnes Rogers, *Vassar Women: An Informal Study* (Poughkeepsie: Vassar College, 1940).

27. "Expert Advice," *Vassar Miscellany News* 3 (February 1916): 3–4; Alice L. Carson, "Opportunities for College Graduates in Journalism," *Vassar Alumnae Monthly* 2 (May 1911): 108. Additional accounts of the difficulties experienced by women pioneering in male-dominated career fields can be found in various Vassar College publications. For additional citations see Herman, "College and After," chap. 6. See also *Journal of the Association of Collegiate Alumnae* (1911–21). For an excellent account of the history of women in the medical profession see Mary Roth Walsh, *"Doctors Wanted: No Women Need Apply": Sexual Barriers in the Medical Profession, 1835–1975* (New Haven: Yale University Press, 1977). Also useful is Barbara J. Harris, *Beyond Her Sphere: Women and the Professions in American History* (Westport, Conn.: Greenwood Press, 1978).

28. Ella Hulburd Young, "The Law as a Profession for Women," *Journal of the Association of Collegiate Alumnae,* series 3, no. 5 (February 1902), p. 19.

29. Elizabeth Kemper Adams, *Women Professional Workers: A Study Made for the Woman's Educational and Industrial Union* (New York: Macmillan, 1921), p. 31.

30. Ida Tarbell, "A Rehearsal for Life; A Study of the Problems of Women's Colleges," *Good Housekeeping Magazine* 89 (November 1929): 20.

31. This conclusion is based largely on the author's personal experience as one of the first women undergraduates at Yale. For other student views see Barbara Deinhardt, "Mother of Men?"; Lisa Getman, "From Conestoga to Career"; and Katherine L. Jelly, "Coeducation: One Student's View," all in W. Todd Furniss and Patricia Albjerg Graham, *Women in Higher Education* (Washington, D.C.: American Council on Education, 1974).

32. See, for example, Susan Lydon, "The Case Against Coeducation, Or, I Guess Vassar Wasn't So Bad After All," *Ms.* 2 (September 1973): 52ff., and Mary J. Oates and Susan Williamson, "Women's Colleges and Women Achievers," *Signs: Journal of Women in Culture and Society* 3 (Summer 1978): 795–806. On the early history of coeducation see Rosalind Rosenberg, "The Academic Prism: The New View of American Women," in Berkin and Norton, *Women of America.*

33. University of Georgia Women's Studies Questionnaire, n.d. Other discussions consulted in preparing this essay include Jill Conway, "Coeducation and Women's Studies: Two Approaches to the Question of Woman's Place in the Contemporary University," *Daedelus* 103 (Fall 1974): 239–49; and Florence Howe, *Women and the Power to Change* (New York: McGraw-Hill, 1975).

Chapter 15: Sex Differences in the Brain (Ina Jane Wundram)

1. Alison Jolly, *The Evolution of Primate Behavior* (New York: Macmillan, 1972).

2. D. C. Johannsen and T. D. White, "A Systematic Assessment of Early African Hominids," *Science* 203 (1979): 321–30.

3. Ernestine Friedl, *Women and Men: An Anthropologist's View* (New York: Holt, Rinehart, and Winston, 1975).

4. Robert E. Ornstein, *The Psychology of Consciousness* (New York: Harcourt Brace Jovanovich, 1977).

5. Rodney Needham, ed., *Right and Left: Essays on Dual Symbolic Classification* (Chicago: University of Chicago Press, 1973).

6. R. W. Sperry, "Lateral Specialization in the Surgically Separated Hemispheres," in *The Neurosciences: Third Study Program,* ed. F. O. Schmitt and F. G. Worden (Cambridge, Mass.: MIT Press, 1974).

7. Eleanor E. Maccoby and Carol N. Jacklin, *The Psychology of Sex Differences* (Stanford, Calif.: Stanford University Press, 1974).

8. Jerre Levy, "The Mammalian Brain and the Adaptive Advantage of Cerebral Asymmetry," *Annals of the New York Academy of Sciences* 299 (September 1977): 264– 72.

9. Tadanobu Tsunoda, "Functional Differences Between Right- and Left-Cerebral Hemispheres Detected by Key-Tapping Method," *Brain and Language* 2 (1975): 152– 70.

10. S. F. Witelson, "Hemispheric Specialization for Linguistic and Non-Linguistic Tactual Perception Using a Dichotomous Stimulation Technique," *Cortex* 10 (1974): 1– 17.

11. Ina Jane Wundram, "Effects of Culture on Sexual Dimorphism in Cerebral Lateralization" (Paper presented to American Anthropological Association, Cincinnati, Ohio, 1979).

12. Witelson, "Hemispheric Specialization."

13. Diane McGuinness, "How Schools Discriminate Against Boys," *Human Nature* 2 (February 1979): 82– 88.

14. Ibid.

15. J. E. Bogen, "Some Educational Aspects of Hemispheric Specialization," *U.C.L.A. Educator* 17 (1975): 24– 32.

Chapter 16: Human Sexuality (Anne L. Harper)

1. American Medical Association, Committee on Human Sexuality, *Human Sexuality* (Chicago: American Medical Association, 1973), p. 153. Note that the AMA Committee on Human Sexuality opposes this attitude.

2. Robert A. Padgug, "Sexual Matters: On Conceptualizing Sexuality in History," *Radical History Review* 20 (Spring– Summer 1979): 7.

3. Richard Sennett, *The Fall of Public Man* (New York: Alfred A. Knopf, 1977), p. 7, as quoted in Robert Padgug, "Sexual Matters," p. 7.

4. Sennett, *Fall of Public Man,* p. 7.

5. Padgug, "Sexual Matters," pp. 7– 8.

6. Ibid., p. 8.

7. Michel Foucault, *The History of Sexuality, An Introduction,* trans. Robert Hurley, 1 vol. to date (New York: Random House, 1978), 1:35.

8. Ibid., p. 71.

9. Ibid., pp. 93, 155.

10. Elinor Shaffer, Review of *The History of Sexuality* by Michel Foucault, *Signs: Journal of Women in Culture and Society* 5 (Summer 1980): 813.

11. Foucault, *History of Sexuality,* p. 114.

12. Shaffer, Review, p. 819.

13. Joseph Interrante and Carol Lasser, "Victims of the Very Songs They Sing: A Critique of Recent Work on Patriarchal Culture and the Social Construction of Gender," *Radical History Review* 20 (Spring–Summer 1979): 84.

14. Karl Marx, *Grundrisse: Foundations of the Critique of Political Economy,* trans. Martin Nicolaus (Harmondsworth, England: Penguin Books, 1975), p. 92.

15. Derek Wright, "Sex: Instinct or Appetite?" in *Sex Education: Rationale and Reaction,* ed. Rex S. Rogers (London: Cambridge University Press, 1974), pp. 13–14.

16. Ibid., p. 14.

17. Padgug, "Sexual Matters," p. 11.

18. Ibid., p. 13. Also see William Simon and John H. Gagnon, "Femininity in the Lesbian Community," *Social Problems* 15 (Fall 1967): 212–21.

19. John Boswell, *Christianity, Social Tolerance, and Homosexuality: Gay People in Western Europe from the Beginning of the Christian Era to the Fourteenth Century* (Chicago: University of Chicago Press, 1980), p. 58. Also see Jeffrey Weeks, *Coming Out: Homosexual Politics in Britain from the 19th Century to the Present* (London: Quartet, 1977); and Bert Hansen, "The Historical Construction of Homosexuality," *Radical History Review* 20 (Spring–Summer 1979): 66–73.

20. Padgug, "Sexual Matters," p. 14.

21. Nancy Chodorow, *The Reproduction of Mothering: Psychoanalysis and the Sociology of Gender* (Berkeley and Los Angeles: University of California Press, 1978).

22. Foucault, *History of Sexuality,* pp. 106–08.

23. Carla Golden, "Psychology, Feminism, and Object Relations Theory" (Paper written for the Department of Psychology, Smith College, Northampton, Mass.).

24. Ibid.

25. Ibid., pp. 20–21.

26. Ibid., p. 33.

27. For a critique of the "four-phase" analysis see Paul Robinson, *The Modernization of Sex: Havelock Ellis, Alfred Kinsey, William Masters and Virginia Johnson* (New York: Harper and Row, 1976), pp. 126–33. Robinson also points out that Masters's and Johnson's research on "the elderly" actually involved clients aged fifty-one to sixty-five for the most part (p. 146).

28. Linda Gordon, Panel Discussion Proceedings, "From Voluntary Motherhood to Planned Parenthood: Perspectives on the Birth Control Movement in America," in the Papers from the Margaret Sanger Centennial Conference, Sophia Smith Collection, Women's History Archive, Northampton, Mass. (1981). Also see Linda Gordon, *Woman's Body, Woman's Right: A Social History of Birth Control in America* (New York: Grossman, 1976), pp. 403–18.

Selected Bibliography

The Process of Integrating Women's Studies into the Liberal Arts Curriculum

Dinnerstein, Myra, Sheryl R. O'Donnell, and Patricia MacCorquodale. "How to Integrate Women's Studies Into the Traditional Curriculum." Tucson: University of Arizona, Southwest Institute for Research on Women, 1981.

Dinnerstein, Myra, Sheryl R. O'Donnell, and Patricia MacCorquodale. "Integrating Women's Studies Into the Curriculum." Report to the Association of American Colleges on the Conference "Integrating Women's Studies into the Liberal Arts Curriculum." Tucson: University of Arizona, Southwest Institute for Research on Women, 1981.

Howe, Florence, and Paul Lauter. *The Impact of Women's Studies on the Campus and the Disciplines*. Washington, D.C.: National Institute of Education, 1980.

Reed, Beth, ed. "Toward a Feminist Transformation of the Academy, I, II." Ann Arbor: Women's Studies Program, Great Lakes Colleges Association, 1980, 1981.

"The Study of Women in the Liberal Arts Curriculum." *Forum for Liberal Education* 4 (October 1981): entire issue.

Woolf, Virginia. *Three Guineas*. London: Hogarth Press, 1938.

Feminist Perspectives on the Content to Be Integrated

Beck, Evelyn Torton, and Julia A. Sherman, eds. *The Prisms of Sex: Essays in the Sociology of Knowledge*. Madison: University of Wisconsin Press, 1979.

Bell, Roseann P., Bettye J. Parker, and Beverly Guy-Sheftal. *Sturdy Black Bridges: Visions of Black Women in Literature*. Garden City, N.Y.: Doubleday, Anchor Press, 1979.

Broude, Norma, and Mary D. Garrard, eds. *Feminism and Art History: Questioning the Litany*. New York: Harper and Row, 1982.

Cade, Toni. *The Black Woman*. New York: Mentor, 1970.

Cruikshank, Margaret. *Lesbian Studies: Present and Future*. Old Westbury, N.Y.: Feminist Press, 1982.

Davis, Angela Y. *Women, Race, and Class*. New York: Random House, 1982.

"Feminist Theory," *Signs: Journal of Women in Culture and Society* 7 (Spring 1982): entire issue.

Fetterley, Judith. *The Resisting Reader, A Feminist Approach to American Fiction*. Bloomington: Indiana University Press, 1978.

"French Feminist Theory," *Signs: Journal of Women in Culture and Society* 7 (Autumn 1981): entire issue.

Gilbert, Sandra M., and Susan Gubar. *The Madwoman in the Attic: The Woman Writer and the Nineteenth-Century Literary Imagination*. New Haven: Yale University Press, 1979.

Green, Rayna, comp. *Native American Women: A Bibliography*. Wichita Falls, Texas: OHOYO Resource Center, 1981.

Hooks, Bell. *Ain't I A Woman: Black Women and Feminism*. Boston: South End Press, 1982.

Hubbard, Ruth, Mary Sue Henifin, and Barbara Fried, eds. *Women Look at Biology Looking at Women: A Collection of Feminist Critiques*. Boston: G. K. Hall, 1979.

Hubbard, Ruth, and Marian Lowe, eds. *Genes and Gender II: Pitfalls in Research on Sex and Gender*. New York: Gordian Press, 1979.

Hull, Gloria T., Patricia Bell Scott, and Barbara Smith, eds. *All the Women Are White, All the Blacks Are Men, But Some of Us Are Brave: Black Women's Studies*. Old Westbury, N.Y.: Feminist Press, 1982.

Joseph, Gloria I., and Jill Lewis. *Common Differences: Conflicts in Black and White Feminist Perspectives*. New York: Doubleday, 1981.

Merchant, Carolyn. *The Death of Nature: Women, Ecology and the Scientific Revolution*. New York: Harper and Row, 1980.

Moraga, Cherrie, and Gloria Anzaldua, eds. *This Bridge Called My Back: Writings By Radical Women of Color*. Watertown, Mass.: Persephone Press, 1981.

Quest Staff. *Building Feminist Theory*. New York: Longman, 1981.

Rothschild, Joan, ed. *Machina Ex Dea*. Elmsford, N.Y.: Pergamon Press, 1983.

Spender, Dale, ed. *Feminist Theorists*. London: Women's Press, 1981.

————. *Men's Studies Modified: The Impact of Feminism on the Academic Disciplines*. Oxford: Pergamon Press, 1981.

"Women, Science and Society," *Signs: Journal of Women in Culture and Society* 4 (Autumn 1978): 1.

Journals in Women's Studies

Frontiers: A Journal of Women's Studies
FS: Feminist Studies
International Journal of Women's Studies
Quest: A Feminist Quarterly
Signs: Journal of Women in Culture and Society
Women's Studies
Women's Studies Abstracts
Women's Studies International Forum (formerly *Women's Studies International Quarterly*)
Women's Studies Quarterly (formerly *Women's Studies Newsletter*)

Contributors

MARY ANGLIN is a Ph.D. candidate at the New School for Social Research, New York City. She is currently writing a dissertation on the impact of economic development on women in southern Appalachia.

JANE FLANDERS teaches women's studies and American literature at the University of Pittsburgh and is an editor at the University of Pittsburgh Press. She has published articles on Katherine Anne Porter, William Styron, and problems in the teaching profession.

DIANE L. FOWLKES is a member of the Department of Political Science at Georgia State University. She has published articles on women in political parties and now chairs the American Political Science Association's Task Force on Women and American Government, the purpose of which is to integrate women into the American government curriculum. She is working on a study of women who are activists in political parties and social movement politics.

ANNE L. HARPER has taught at Smith College where she was a research associate and summer faculty fellow with the Project on Women and Social Change. Her article on teenage sexuality and public policy is included in *Families, Politics, and Public Policy*, edited by Irene Diamond (Longman, 1983). Currently Harper teaches at Virginia Polytechnic Institute and State University and pursues research on feminism and politics.

DEBRA HERMAN is a National Historical Preservation and Records Commission fellow working with the Samuel Gompers Papers project at the University of Maryland. She has taught American history at the University of Georgia where she also served as coordinator of the women's studies program. She now is completing a book tracing the interaction between the officially stated mission of Vassar College and the experiences of its early graduates.

A. CHARLOTTE HOGSETT is professor of French at Mary Baldwin College. She has published on literary theory and criticism in eighteenth-century France and has written papers on Prévost, Germaine de Stael, and others. In pursuit of her special interest in problems confronting women writers, Hogsett currently is working on a book about de Stael.

CATHERINE M. HOWETT, a landscape architect, historian, and critic of the American landscape, currently teaches in the School of Environmental Design at the University of Georgia. Her recent research interests have centered around the evolution of regional landscape forms in the Southeast and the interrelationship between landscape design and contemporary art.

SANDRA L. LANGER is a poet, critic, and historian of American art and is currently a member of the Department of Art at the University of South Carolina at its Columbia campus. Among her many publications are articles in *Art Criticism, Arts Magazine, Art Paper, International Journal of Women's Studies,* and *Women's Art Journal*. She is now writing a critical study on religious imagination in the life and art of John F. Kensett (1816–72).

MAMIE LOCKE is a member of the Department of Political Science at Hampton Institute and a Ph.D. candidate at Atlanta University. She is writing her dissertation on the impact of sex and race on the political and economic development of black women in Hinds and Sunflower counties, Mississippi.

CHARLOTTE S. McCLURE is a member of the Department of English and directs the Honors Program in the College of Arts and Sciences at Georgia State University. She has published a book and several articles on Gertrude Atherton, American realistic novelist, and articles on other women writers in the realistic period. McClure has served as chairwoman of the women's caucus on pedagogy and of the women's studies section of the South Atlantic Modern Language Association.

EVA M. McMAHAN is a member of the Department of Speech Communication at The University of Alabama. She has published articles on oral history interviewing and on nonverbal communication in scholarly journals that include the *International Journal of Oral History, Communication Monographs, Communication Education*, and *Communication Quarterly*.

ELISABETH S. MUHLENFELD is a member of the Department of English at Florida State University. She is a specialist in southern literature and William Faulkner and the author of a biography of Mary Boykin Chesnut. Currently she is at work with C. Vann Woodward on an edition of Chesnut's original diaries.

JUDITH OCHSHORN is director of the Women's Studies Program at the University of South Florida. She is the author of *The Female Experience and the Nature of the Divine* (Bloomington: Indiana University Press, 1981), an essay on mothers and daughters in the ancient Near East in *The Lost Tradition: Mothers and Daughters in Literature* (New York: Ungar, 1980), a chapter on Ishtar and her cult in a forthcoming book, *An Introduction to the Religion of the Goddess* (New York: Seabury, in press), and an essay on reclaiming woman's past in Mary Buckley and Janet Calven, eds., *Women's Spirit Bonding* (Pilgrim Press, in press). Currently she is working on an assessment of the historical and moral legacy of polytheism and its relevance to the present.

SUE V. ROSSER is an associate professor of biology and coordinator of women's studies at Mary Baldwin College. The focus of her research and teaching is making the information on the biology of women more accessible to the nonscientist. In that connection she has written articles such as "Genetic Androgyny and Sociobiology" and edited the textbook *The Biology of Women* (Ethel Sloane, John Wiley and Sons, 1980). She currently is the project director of a three-year LOCI grant from the National Science Foundation to make materials on biology of women more available.

DON W. STACKS is a member of the Department of Communication Arts at the University of South Alabama. His research and publication are concentrated in the area of social influence attempts and the study of nonverbal communication. He is now writing a book on nonverbal communication and is researching the area of decoding persuasive messages by brain hemispheres.

CATHARINE R. STIMPSON, a professor of English and director of the Institute for Research on Women at Rutgers University, is the author of fiction and nonfiction. Her most recent book was the novel *Class Notes*. A resident of New York City, she was the founding editor of *Signs: Journal of Women in Culture and Society*. She also serves as chairwoman of *Ms.* magazine's Board of Scholars.

MARIE TEDESCO is a member of the Department of History at North Dakota State University. Her research interests center on the relationship between nineteenth- and twentieth-century feminism and science.

JULIA T. WOOD is a member of the Department of Speech Communication at the University of North Carolina at Chapel Hill. She has published four books and numerous articles in the areas of leadership, group decision making, interpersonal communication, and women's communication. She served as editor of the spring 1982 issue of *Communication Quarterly*, which featured scholarly monographs on the theme "Women and Communication."

INA JANE WUNDRAM is a member of the Department of Anthropology at Georgia State University. She has published articles on nonreproductive sexual behavior, adaptations of urban wildlife, and the development of cerebral lateralization in children. She currently is studying the adaptive significance of functional asymmetry in hominid evolution.

Index

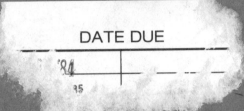